GW00502918

Managing Benefits

Optimizing the return from investments

London: TSO

Published by TSO (The Stationery Office) and available from:

Online
www.tsoshop.co.uk

Mail, Telephone, Fax & E-mail
TSO
PO Box 29, Norwich, NR3 1GN
Telephone orders/General enquiries: 0870 600 5522
Fax orders: 0870 600 5533
E-mail: customer.services@tso.co.uk
Textphone: 0870 240 3701

TSO@Blackwell and other Accredited Agents

First edition 2012
ISBN 9780117081109

Contents

List of Figures

List of Tables

List of Examples

Foreword

Welcome to this new guide to benefits management, a guide that some say is long overdue. Why do we carry out projects and programmes? Not for the benefit of those employed on them, as we used to think, but to achieve a return on the investment made by the owner or sponsor. This return is now thought of as the benefits that accrue from the investment: some financial, others perhaps harder to define, but nonetheless just as important in justifying the investment. Making sure that they are realized, and that unanticipated benefits are maximized, is as important as the initial justification, and without that many projects have earned a bad name for project management.

This Guide provides managers and practitioners from multiple disciplines, working in a wide variety of organizations, and in all sectors, with generally applicable guidance encompassing the principles, practices and techniques of benefits management. Specifically, this Guide provides:

- An overview of benefits management – what it is, the case for doing it, and some common misconceptions that can limit its effectiveness in practice.
- Descriptions of the seven principles upon which successful approaches to benefits management are built, and examples of how they can be/have been applied in practice.
- Details of the five practices in the Benefits Management Cycle and examples of how they can be/have been applied in practice.
- Guidance on how to apply benefits management at a portfolio level, as well as at an individual project or programme level.
- Advice on how to get started in implementing effective benefits management practices and how to sustain progress.

The Guide also provides the basis for accredited examinations from APMG-International, based on the Foundation and Practitioner formats used for much of the existing qualification portfolio (see http://www.apmg-international.com/). It adds value by:

- Consolidating existing good-practice guidance on benefits management in one place.
- Expanding on the existing guidance, by illustrating the theory with practical applications, examples and case studies from a variety of settings. This is important – the Guide emphasizes that benefits management should be based on an understanding of what works. Hence the importance of the research evidence quoted throughout the Guide and the examples and case studies from around the world.
- Representing an authoritative guide to effective benefits management reflecting the collective expertise and experience of a wide range of experienced practitioners, academics and thought leaders.
- Incorporating practices and lessons learned from a variety of disciplines – not only project and programme management (PPM) but also management accounting, economics, behavioural finance, change management, systems thinking, psychology and neuroscience.

There is also one other overriding factor behind the decision to produce this Guide. Benefits are not just another dimension of PPM – rather, they are the rationale for the investment of taxpayers' and shareholders' funds. As such, benefits should be the driver behind all change initiatives from initiation through to, and beyond, implementation. Yet the reality is that many organizations still struggle to demonstrate that the desired benefits are realized in practice. This Guide therefore represents a manifesto for change – change in relation to the management and successful realization of benefits from investments in change.

I sincerely hope this Guide enables you to deliver the full potential benefits from your project(s) and programme(s).

Alan Harpham

Alan Harpham
Chairman, APM Group

Acknowledgements

APMG-International is grateful to the following for their contributions to the planning, design, authoring and development of this Guide.

AUTHOR

Stephen Jenner FAPM, FCMA, MSt, MBA. Alongside writing this Guide (and being Chief Examiner for the accompanying examinations), Steve is co-author and Chief Examiner for 'Management of Portfolios' (MoP). He was previously Director of Criminal Justice IT, where the approach adopted to portfolio and benefits management won the 2007 Civil Service Financial Management Award. He is a regular speaker at international conferences, a trainer and writer on the subjects of portfolio and benefits management – he is the author of several books in the field – and is a professionally qualified management accountant and a Fellow of the APM. Steve also holds an MBA and Masters of Studies degree from Cambridge University.

PROJECT MANAGER

James Davies   APMG-International

DESIGN REFERENCE GROUP

The following advised on the scope of the Guide:

Rod Baker, Michael Dallas, Adrian Dooley, Peter Glynne, Alan Harpham and Craig Kilford.

REVIEWERS

The following reviewed and commented on the first and second drafts of this Guide:

APM Group

Rod Baker   APM Group Director

Best Management Practice

Michael Acaster	Cabinet Office, Efficiency Reform Group
Michael Dallas	MoV Lead author and Chief Examiner
Craig Kilford	MoP Co-author and P3O Lead Reviewer/Mentor
Keith Williams	P3M3 Specialist and 'Change Management' Chief Examiner

Benefits Management Practitioners

Peter Glynne	Co-Chair, APM Benefits Management Specific Interest Group (SIG)
Sarah Harries	Head of Business Improvement, BT
Steve Parker	(Interim) Value & Benefits Lead, TfL PMO Centre of Excellence
John Thorp	International Benefits Management Thought Leader

Accredited Training/Consulting Organizations and APM Group Assessor

Jeroen Geurtsen	European ATO representative, Zest Group BV
Mark Ives	Australian ACO representative, MetaPM
Paulo Keglevich	South American APM Group assessor
Patrick Mayfield	Part MSP author and UK ATO representative, pearcemayfield

Additionally, the following reviewed and commented on the second draft: Walter Dirix (Director, Lead Consultant and Trainer, GXO Change), Alan Ferguson (AFA), Melanie Franklin (Maven Training), Anne McGrath (Knowledge Xchange Ltd) and Svetlana Plotnikova (MetaPM).

PRACTITIONER CASE STUDIES AND EXAMPLES

The author and APMG-International would like to express their sincere gratitude to the following who provided many of the examples and case studies that illustrate the application of the benefits management principles, practices and techniques in this Guide.

Name	Position
Paul Arrigoni	Director Business Change and ICT, Bristol City Council
Matthew Briggs	Programme Manager, Tell Us Once
Robert Buttrick	Project Workout Limited
Richard Caton	London Borough of Hackney
Claire Dellar	Benefits Realization Manager, Norfolk and Suffolk NHS Foundation Trust
Tanya Durlen	Surface Transport Portfolio Benefits Manager, TfL
Charlotte Eales	Department for Education
David Elliott	Director, PBM Consulting
Alison Esse	The Storytellers
Jorgen Haglind	Senior Vice President Communications, Tetra Laval
Sarah Harries	Head of Business Improvement, BT
Mårten Janerud	Enterprise Ministry, Sweden
Craig Kilford	Co-author of MoP, practitioner and mentor, Cansoti
Kelly McJannett	Communications & Marketing Manager, Fair Business
Hugo Minney	The Social Return Co.
Rachel Naisbitt	Benefits Manager, Western Australia Police
Hirokazu Okumura	The University of Tokyo
Peter Röthig	WiBe-TEAM, Germany
Jim Runnacles	Openreach
Nick Wensley	Director, Farthing Consulting
Terry Wright	Victorian Department of Treasury and Finance

Members of the APM Benefits Management SIG who provided invaluable input to this Guide – in addition to those named above: Gerald Bradley, Trevor Howes, Lorraine Trenchard and David Waller.

The author would like to record his thanks, in particular, to Sarah Harries for her extensive and constructive input throughout the development of this Guide, and to James Davies for suggesting the concept in the first place – and then providing support beyond the call of duty throughout its development.

Chapter 1

Chapter 1 – Introduction

1.1 OVERVIEW OF THIS CHAPTER

This chapter summarizes: the purposes of the Guide; the main areas covered in the subsequent chapters; where the Guide fits with existing Cabinet Office *'Best Management Practice'*; and the target audience. It also provides an overview of the main themes of the Guide.

1.2 PURPOSES OF THIS GUIDE

The main purpose of this Guide is to provide managers and practitioners from multiple disciplines, working in a wide variety of organizations, with generally applicable guidance encompassing benefits management principles, practices and techniques. Specifically, this Guide provides these managers and practitioners with:

- An overview of benefits management – what it is, the case for doing it, and some common misconceptions that can limit its effectiveness in practice.
- Descriptions of the seven principles upon which successful benefits management practices are built, and examples of how they can be/have been applied in practice.
- Details of the five practices in the Benefits Management Cycle relating to individual change initiatives, and examples of how they can be/have been applied in practice.
- Guidance on how to apply benefits management at a collective or portfolio level encompassing all projects and programmes included in the change portfolio.
- Advice on how to get started in implementing effective benefits management practices and how to sustain progress.

The Guide also provides the basis for accredited examinations from APMG-International, based on the Foundation and Practitioner formats used for much of the existing qualification portfolio (see http://www.apmg-international.com/). These examinations enable candidates to demonstrate they possess and can apply the knowledge and understanding to work effectively in a range of benefits management roles.

Besides preparation for the accompanying examinations, the potential benefits from reading and, more importantly, applying this guidance include: enhanced professional competence, a sense of achievement, and improved returns on investment for the organizations in which these managers and practitioners work. It is also hoped that this will be an enjoyable read – and one which leads to further exploration of the subject, including the sources listed in Chapter 12.

But why develop this Guide when aspects of benefits management are addressed in existing Cabinet Office *'Best Management Practice'* guidance, including *'Managing Successful Projects with PRINCE2'* (PRINCE2®), *'Managing Successful Programmes'* (MSP®), *'Management of Portfolios'* (MoP™), *'Management of Value'* (MoV®), *'Management of Risk'* (M_o_R®), *'Portfolio, Programme and Project Offices'* (P3O®) and the *Portfolio, Programme and Project Management Maturity Model* (P3M3®), as well as the APMG-International *'Programme and Project Sponsorship'* and *'Change Management'* qualifications? The answer is that this Guide adds value by:

- Consolidating existing good-practice guidance in one place and making linkages between that guidance.
- Expanding on the existing guidance, by illustrating the theory with practical applications, examples and case studies from a variety of settings. This is important – the Guide emphasizes that benefits management should be based on an understanding of 'what works'. Hence the importance of the research evidence quoted throughout the Guide and the examples and case studies from practitioners and academics from around the world including: Australia, Canada, Germany, Ireland, Japan, New

Zealand, Sweden, the United Kingdom (UK) and the United States of America (USA).

■ Filling in the gaps in coverage to represent a comprehensive statement of current good-practice guidance.

■ Incorporating practices and lessons learned from a variety of disciplines – not only project, programme and portfolio management but also management accounting, economics, behavioural finance, change management, systems thinking and soft skills, psychology and neuroscience.

This Guide therefore represents an authoritative guide to effective benefits management, reflecting not only existing guidance but also academic and industry research, and the collective expertise and experience of a wide range of leading practitioners and thought leaders from across the world (including those listed in the Acknowledgements section).

There are many published approaches to benefits management, and although each has its differences, they do share a fair degree of commonality. This Guide has sought to capture these areas of agreement, while at the same time providing an overview of the alternative approaches available, along with their advantages, and the situations in which each is most appropriate. Rather than prescribing a single solution, the Guide thus provides readers with the insight to enable them to choose the solution most appropriate to their particular circumstances.

There is also one other overriding factor behind the decision to produce this Guide. Benefits are not just another dimension of project and programme management (PPM) – rather, they are the rationale for the investment of taxpayers' and shareholders' funds in change initiatives. As such, benefits should be the driver behind all change initiatives from initiation through to, and indeed beyond, integration into business as usual (BAU). Yet the reality, as we see in the next chapter, is that many organizations still struggle to demonstrate that benefits are realized in practice. This Guide therefore represents a manifesto for change – change in relation to the management and successful realization of benefits from change initiatives. This in turn is dependent on moving:

From – the 'conspiracy of optimism' in forecasting; inconsistent initiative-level approaches to benefits management; passive tracking against forecast; and backward-looking accountability.

To – an approach reflecting:

■ **Realism in planning** based on benefits-led change initiatives, within the context of clearly articulated, but often emergent strategy, consistent portfolio-wide and evidence-based approaches, applied across the business change lifecycle.

■ **Enthusiasm in delivery** based on an active search for benefits, ongoing participative stakeholder engagement, and managed with a forward-looking perspective, based on transparency, insight, learning and continuous improvement.

Important note

The benefits management principles, practices and techniques discussed in this Guide are presented in such a way that where an organization chooses to implement them, it should expect to see significant benefits not only in the medium to longer term, but also in the short term – indeed it should plan to do so. Where an organization is already fairly mature in its use of benefits management (e.g. as assessed using P3M3), this Guide will assist with the attainment of even more effective and efficient practices.

1.3 STRUCTURE OF THE GUIDANCE

Table 1.1 provides a summary of the contents of each chapter.

Table 1.1 – Chapter summary of this Guide

Chapter	Name	Summary
1	Introduction	Introduces the purpose of the Guide; the main areas covered in the subsequent chapters; the fit of the Guide with existing *'Best Management Practice'*; the target audience; and an overview of the main themes addressed.
2	What is Benefits Management?	Defines the terminology used; the track record of change initiatives in terms of benefits realization; and the objectives of benefits management.
3	The Benefits Management Principles	Discusses the seven principles upon which effective benefits management is built.
4	The Benefits Management Cycle	Introduces the Benefits Management Cycle, the organizational context in which it operates, and the constituent practices addressed in the next five chapters. This chapter also addresses the barriers to, and the Key Success Characteristics of, effective approaches to benefits management. It also provides an overview of the main benefits management roles, responsibilities and documentation.
5	Benefits Management Practice 1 – Identify & Quantify	Approaches to identifying benefits, including benefits discovery workshops, benefits mapping and customer insight, as well as forecasting benefits, including problems typically faced and appropriate solutions.
6	Benefits Management Practice 2 – Value & Appraise	Addresses why organizations value benefits in monetary terms; approaches to valuing non-financial benefits in monetary terms; the main approaches to initiative appraisal – cost-benefit, real options, cost-effectiveness and multi-criteria analysis; and the role of value management techniques.
7	Benefits Management Practice 3 – Plan	Covers approaches to validating benefits; prioritizing benefits; managing the pre-transition phase; selecting benefits measures; benefits risk and opportunity management; planning effective stakeholder engagement; and an overview of the main initiative-level benefits management documentation used in planning for benefits realization, and who prepares and maintains them.
8	Benefits Management Practice 4 – Realize	Considers transition management; tracking and reporting, including surveys; and approaches to effective stakeholder engagement to win hearts as well as minds, and so deliver the behavioural change upon which benefits realization is often dependent.

Table continues

Table 1.1 continued

Chapter	Name	Summary
9	Benefits Management Practice 5 – Review	Covers the importance of review as a basis for learning and continuous improvement – before, during and after the initiative.
10	Portfolio-based Benefits Management	Addresses why portfolio-based benefits management is so important and its main elements.
11	Implementing and Sustaining Progress	Includes how to get started with implementing benefits management, and how to sustain progress, including measuring impact and maturity.
12	The Next Steps	Including training, a health-check assessment, recommended further reading, and details of relevant online Communities of Interest and websites.
Appendices		
A – Quantifying and Valuing Benefits – Public-sector Considerations	This appendix includes guidance on quantifying and valuing benefits in relation to: ■ Cross-organizational programmes. ■ Social value benefits. ■ Valuing customer/citizen benefits – the time savings method.	
B – Benefits Management Documentation	The purpose and typical contents of the main benefits management documentation: ■ Portfolio level: Portfolio Benefits Management Framework; Portfolio Benefits Realization Plan; Portfolio Dashboard Report. ■ Initiative level: Benefits Management Strategy; Benefits Realization Plan; Benefit Profile.	
C – Benefits Management Roles and Responsibilities	Descriptions of the key roles and benefits management responsibilities in MoP and MSP environments: ■ Portfolio level: Portfolio Direction Group/Investment Committee; Portfolio Progress Group/Change Delivery Committee; Business Change/Portfolio Director; and Portfolio Benefits Manager. ■ Initiative level: Senior Responsible Owner; Programme Manager; Business Change Manager; Programme Office including the Benefits Manager; and Benefit Owner.	
D – Cognitive Biases Affecting Benefits Management	Description of the main cognitive biases affecting benefits management and forecasting.	
E – Benefits Management Skills and Competencies Log	A Skills and Competencies Log for those whose roles involve a significant focus on benefits management.	
F – Benefits Logic Map for Benefits Management	A Benefits Logic Map for the implementation of benefits management, identifying intermediate and end benefits.	
G – OGC Gateway Reviews – Coverage of Benefits and Benefits Management	Outline of the coverage of benefits and benefits management at each of the OGC Gateway reviews.	

Chapter	Name	Summary
H – P3M3 Benefits Management Assessment	P3M3 assessment of benefits management at portfolio, programme and project levels.
I – Managing Benefits Health-check Assessment	A short 10-question health-check assessment with suggested potential actions to address areas where performance falls below the required standard.
Glossary	Definitions of key terms.
References	Sources of citations/quotes.
Index	Page references for key terms.

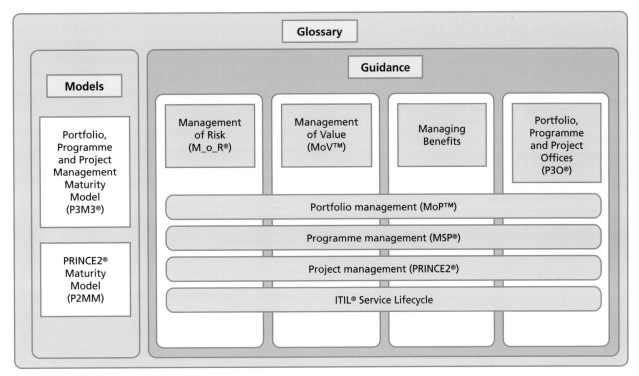

Figure 1.1 – The relationship of 'Managing Benefits' with existing 'Best Management Practice' guidance

Note – To aid understanding, each chapter starts with an overview of the areas covered and finishes with a summary of the key points.

1.4 FIT WITH EXISTING *'BEST MANAGEMENT PRACTICE'* GUIDANCE

This Guide supports the Cabinet Office's existing portfolio of *'Best Management Practice'* by consolidating relevant existing guidance in relation to benefits management. The place of *'Managing Benefits'* within this product portfolio is illustrated in Figure 1.1.

Further information on the relationship between *'Managing Benefits'* and the other guidance shown in Figure 1.1 is contained at relevant points in this Guide.

1.5 TARGET AUDIENCE

This Guide is relevant to all jurisdictions, sectors and types of project or programme – or what we refer to in this Guide as change initiatives. The principles, practices and techniques covered will also be of value to those seeking to optimize benefits realization from an organization's assets and BAU. That said, our central focus in this Guide, consistent with recent Cabinet Office *'Best Management Practice'* publications, is on business

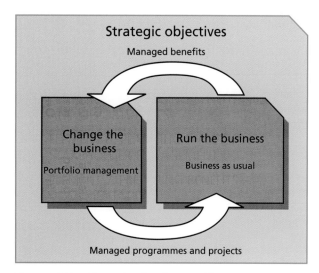

Figure 1.2 – 'Run the business, Change the business'

change initiatives, i.e. those initiatives that come within the 'change the business' category in the 'Run the business, Change the business' model adopted in MoP and P3O (see Figure 1.2).

The target audience therefore encompasses all those with an interest in ensuring the best use of taxpayers' and shareholders' funds and other scarce resources, by optimizing the benefits realized from change initiatives. This multi-disciplinary group includes:

- Change leaders, e.g. Senior Responsible Owners and Directors of Change.
- Change initiators, e.g. Strategic Planners and Policy Leads.
- Change appraisers and evaluators, e.g. Business Case Writers and Appraisers.
- Change implementers/enablers, e.g. Portfolio, Programme and Project Managers, as well as Business Change Managers.
- Change support staff, e.g. Portfolio, Programme and Project Office staff, including Benefits Managers.

1.6 OVERVIEW OF THIS GUIDE

Benefits management extends from identification of desired benefits through to benefits realization and application of lessons learned. The scope of benefits management is illustrated in the Benefits Management Model in Figure 1.3.

What this model highlights is that:

- The Benefits Management Cycle consists of the following **five practices**: Identify & Quantify, Value & Appraise, Plan, Realize, and Review.

- Effective benefits management practices are dependent on the **seven principles** identified: align benefits with strategy; start with the end in mind; utilize successful delivery methods; integrate benefits with performance management; manage benefits from a portfolio perspective; apply effective governance; and develop a value culture.

Nine themes run throughout this Guide:

1. While the approach adopted to meet the seven principles will vary, **the principles themselves are integral to effective benefits management**. For example, some organizations will adopt PRINCE2 and MSP, whereas others will adopt other methods. That is appropriate, but whatever methods are adopted, the principle of 'utilizing effective delivery methods' is fundamental to effective benefits realization.

2. There is no one true way to effective benefits management. **Practices should therefore be tailored to the local circumstances**, reflecting factors such as the organization's strategic objectives; scale of investment in change initiatives; the complexity of those initiatives; existing strategic planning, project and programme, financial, performance and risk management processes; experience and track record in terms of benefits realization; governance structure; and culture. This Guide includes examples of how organizations have adapted these practices in a variety of situations, as well as guidance on when relevant techniques are appropriate.

3. **The five practices in the Benefits Management Cycle are broadly sequential but are characterized by iterative feedback loops**, with learnings being applied throughout the cycle. The emphasis is on actively managing the journey where both the journey itself, and the ultimate destination, are subject to change.

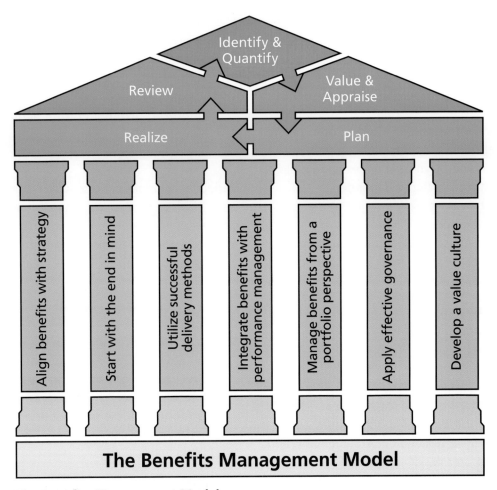

Figure 1.3 – The Benefits Management Model

4. It is crucial that we avoid creating a parallel industry that treats benefits management as a separate discipline. This is costly and ineffective. **Benefits management should be coordinated with, and wherever possible integrated into, the wider organizational context** – and in particular the organization's strategic planning, PPM and performance management systems.

5. **Benefits and value management are mutually supportive disciplines** and are concerned with delivering value for money in relation to ensuring:
   □ Each initiative, and the portfolio as a whole, represents the optimum use of available funds.
   □ The management of these benefits is delivered as cost-effectively as possible. In short, the benefits of benefits management should exceed the costs of benefits management.

6. While **the focus in decision-making should be on realism** (to overcome the twin risks of strategic misrepresentation and cognitive bias), **the approach to benefits realization should be one characterized by enthusiasm**, to help overcome the obstacles that can often arise during initiative implementation and delivery.

7. **Effective management of benefits realization is aided by the selection of appropriate measures** – at least one for each benefit, and preferably a suite of measures, including leading and lagging measures, proxy indicators, evidence events, case studies, surveys and stories, to create a 'rich picture' providing feedback on benefits realization from multiple perspectives; as well as by techniques including 'one version of the truth', 'management by exception' and 'clear line of sight reporting'.

8. The governance structures outlined are based on those that apply in MSP, P3O and MoP environments. Organizations do not need to

follow these to the letter – different job titles may exist and the responsibilities may be shared by more than one person. But **what is crucial is that someone owns the key responsibilities identified,** and in particular that:

☐ Someone is responsible and accountable for delivering each of the enabling products/services and business changes upon which benefits realization is dependent.
☐ Benefit Owners are identified for each significant benefit.
☐ Someone has overall accountability for benefits realization from each change initiative.

9. Effective benefits management is characterized by the following six **Key Success Characteristics** – benefits management should be:

☐ **Active** – rather than passive tracking against forecast, the focus is on an active search for benefits, via ongoing participative stakeholder engagement, and encompasses realizing planned benefits, leveraging emergent benefits, and mitigating the impact of dis-benefits.
☐ **Evidence-based** – forecasts and practices are driven by evidence about what works rather than assumptions and advocacy.
☐ **Transparent** – based on open and honest forecasting and reporting, with a 'clear line of sight' from strategic objectives to benefits forecast and realized.
☐ **Benefits-led** – just as we expect change initiatives and the portfolio to be benefits-led, so too should benefits management be focused on what difference it is making.

☐ **Forward-looking** – with an emphasis on learning and continuous improvement, rather than backward-looking attribution of blame.
☐ **Managed across the full business change lifecycle** – extending from benefits identification through to realization and applying lessons learned.

Various techniques are discussed – they represent ways in which the benefits management practices can be applied, and examples of their use in practice are included throughout the Guide. The main techniques are shown in Table 1.2.

1.7 CHAPTER SUMMARY

1. This Guide is consistent with the existing Cabinet Office *'Best Management Practice'* product portfolio. It builds on existing guidance by including research findings and case studies illustrating how the relevant principles, practices and techniques have been successfully applied in practice.

2. Furthermore, it represents a manifesto for change – calling for an approach that is realistic in planning and enthusiastic in delivery. In so doing, it builds on research from a wide variety of disciplines and the experiences of practitioners and thought leaders from around the world.

Table 1.2 – Key benefits management techniques

Practice	Key techniques	Application
Identify & Quantify	■ Driver-based analysis	Facilitating determination of the strategic contribution of change initiatives.
	■ Investment logic mapping	Applying benefits-led change.
	■ SWOT and PESTLE analysis	Identifying strategic drivers and investment objectives for change.
	■ Benefits discovery workshops ■ Benefits mapping ■ Customer insight	Identifying strategic drivers, investment objectives, benefits, and the business changes and enabling changes on which they rely.
	■ Reference class forecasting ■ Optimism bias adjustments ■ Benefits quantification workshops ■ Stochastic forecasting (including Monte Carlo simulation and three-point estimating) ■ The Delphi technique	Developing accurate and reliable benefits forecasts.
Value & Appraise	■ Willingness to pay and Willingness to accept	Valuing benefits in monetary terms in the absence of market prices/values.
	■ Conversion ratios	Distinguishing between potential and realizable benefits.
	■ Sensitivity and scenario analysis	Determining the margin of safety before an investment decision changes.
	■ Cost-benefit analysis ■ Cost-effectiveness analysis ■ Real options analysis ■ Multi-criteria analysis	Options appraisal, investment appraisal and portfolio prioritization.
Plan	■ The 'dog that didn't bark' test	Ensuring all potential benefits are identified.
	■ Pareto rule ■ Pair-wise comparisons	Prioritizing benefits.
	■ Benefits Measurement Taxonomy	Selecting appropriate benefit measures.
	■ Stakeholder segmentation and analysis	Designing effective stakeholder engagement strategies.
	■ Scout and beacon approach	Identifying emergent benefits.

Table continues

Table 1.2 continued

Practice	Key techniques	Application
Realize	■ Booking the benefits ■ Benefits contracts	Aligning benefits with the HR and operational performance management systems.
	■ Rich picture	Gaining a view on benefits realization from multiple perspectives.
	■ One version of the truth	Consistent and reliable reporting.
	■ Management by exception	Aiding management control by focusing attention on variances that exceed tolerance.
Review	■ Start gate ■ Pre-mortems ■ 'In-flight' benefit reviews ■ Stage/phase gate reviews and 'staged release of funding' ■ Post-implementation review ■ Post-investment review	Confirming the case for moving from strategy to delivery. Continued assessment of the robustness of benefit forecasts and value for money from change initiatives. Identifying lessons learned and collecting a reference class of data.
Across the Benefits Management Cycle	■ Champion-challenger model ■ Journey mapping	Building stakeholder commitment to the Benefits Management Cycle.
	■ Clear line of sight	Transparent planning and reporting.
	■ Decision conferencing	Building senior management commitment to benefits management.
	■ P3M3 ■ Health-check assessment	Assessing practices against recognized good-practice standards.

Chapter 2

Chapter 2 – What is Benefits Management?

2.1 OVERVIEW OF THIS CHAPTER

We start this chapter by defining what we mean by benefits and benefits management, and how they are integral to the successful management of projects, programmes and portfolios. We then review the track record of change initiatives in terms of benefits realization, before considering the objectives of benefits management.

2.2 DEFINITIONS – WHAT ARE WE TALKING ABOUT?

Benefits and benefits management are defined by the Cabinet Office as follows:

- Benefits – the measurable improvement resulting from an outcome perceived as an advantage by one or more stakeholders, which contributes towards one or more organizational objective(s).
- Benefits management – the identification, definition, tracking, realization and optimization of benefits.

The Association for Project Management (APM) has a similar definition of a benefit: "*The positive and measurable impact of change on the performance of the organisation, contributing to one or more strategic objectives.*"

The following points arise from these definitions:

- Benefits are measurable improvements – in terms of, for example, money saved, improved customer satisfaction, increased revenue, reduced risk etc.

- Benefits contribute to organizational/strategic objective(s) – consequently:
  - ☐ The logic and assumptions underpinning the organizational/strategic objectives need to be clearly articulated so that the contribution of benefits from change initiatives to these objectives can be determined reliably and consistently.
  - ☐ Benefits from individual change initiatives should be identified and quantified consistently and in terms that link to the drivers of the organizational/strategic objectives.
  - ☐ Change initiatives should be designed to realize the benefits that enable achievement of the organization's strategic objectives and business priorities.

- Benefits are an advantage to stakeholders, which include those both within and outside the organization – for example, the latter include customers and shareholders (private sector), citizens and other departments and agencies (public sector). An active approach to stakeholder engagement is a Key Success Characteristic of effective benefits management.

- Benefits management extends from identification of desired benefits through to benefits realization and application of lessons learned. While the practices are broadly sequential, they are characterized by iterative feedback loops, with learnings being applied throughout the cycle.

- Benefits management is concerned with informing investment decisions and optimization of benefits realization – consequently, it extends beyond passive reporting against forecast, to active approaches that engage stakeholders in an ongoing search for benefits.

- Benefits management seeks to optimize rather than maximize benefits realization. The difference is that, while maximization seeks the most benefits irrespective of constraints, optimization is about doing the best that can be achieved within constraints (most usually costs but also other constrained resources) and potential other uses of the funds available. Thus, realizing 80% of the potential benefits but for only 60% of the cost may be preferred where the savings can be used to fund other initiatives. So just as we expect change initiatives to deliver value for money, so too with benefits management itself.

Benefits are derived from change initiatives, which include formally constituted projects and programmes. Collectively these initiatives form the organization's change portfolio. The following definitions for portfolios, programmes and projects are drawn from the OGC Common Glossary of Terms and Definitions.

Portfolio/Portfolio Management

■ Portfolio: An organization's change portfolio is the totality of its investment (or segment thereof) in the changes required to achieve its strategic objectives. Note that this does not mean that the portfolio will include all business change, some of which will be delivered via the performance management system (e.g. where managers and staff adapt processes or launch low-risk/less complex initiatives to improve performance). Rather, our focus in this Guide is on the management of benefits from change initiatives that are delivered via formalized project and programme management (PPM) methods.

■ Portfolio management: This is a coordinated collection of strategic processes and decisions that together enable the most effective balance of organizational change and business as usual (BAU). Portfolio management achieves this by ensuring that change initiatives are:
  □ Agreed at the appropriate management level and measurably contribute to strategic objectives and business priorities.
  □ Prioritized in line with strategic objectives and business priorities and in the context of the existing portfolio, affordability, risk, resource capacity and the organization's ability to absorb change.
  □ Reviewed regularly in terms of progress, cost, risk, benefits and strategic contribution.

Further guidance on portfolio management is provided in 'Management of Portfolios' (MoP). Aspects of the MoP guidance that relate to benefits management are covered in Chapters 3 and 10 of this Guide.

Programme/Programme Management

■ Programme: A programme is a temporary, flexible organization created to coordinate, direct and oversee the implementation of a set of related projects and activities in order to deliver outcomes and benefits related to the organization's strategic objectives. A programme is likely to have a life that spans several years.

■ Programme management: This is defined as the action of carrying out the coordinated organization, direction and implementation of a dossier of projects and transformation activities (i.e. the programme) to achieve outcomes and realize benefits of strategic importance to the business.

Further guidance on programme management is contained in 'Managing Successful Programmes' (MSP). Aspects of the MSP guidance, as it relates to benefits management at a programme or individual initiative level, are addressed in Chapters 4–9 of this Guide.

Project/Project Management

■ Project: A project is a temporary organization, usually existing for a much shorter time than a programme, which will deliver one or more outputs in accordance with a specific Business Case. A particular project may or may not be part of a programme. Whereas programmes deal with outcomes, projects deal with outputs.

■ Project management: This is the planning, delegating, monitoring and control of all aspects of the project, and the motivation of those involved, to achieve the project objectives within the expected performance targets for time, cost, quality, scope, benefits and risks.

Further guidance on project management can be found in PRINCE2.

In relation to benefits, the key points to note from the above definitions are that:

■ Programmes and projects are primarily focused on delivery of outcomes/benefits and outputs respectively. The portfolio, in contrast, is focused on the overall contribution of these outcomes, benefits and outputs to strategic objectives.

■ PPM seeks to ensure successful delivery at the individual programme or project level. Portfolio management is concerned with ensuring that the programmes and projects undertaken are the right ones in the context of the organization's strategic objectives and overall risk exposure; delivery is managed efficiently and effectively at a collective level; strategic contribution is optimized; and lessons learned are identified, disseminated and applied in the future.

Another perspective on this is to focus on the relationship between outputs, capabilities, outcomes and benefits. The MSP definitions for these terms are shown in Table 2.1, and their relationship is illustrated in Figure 2.1.

Note – while some benefits are automatic (e.g. where a new contract provides the same service but at lower cost), benefits realization is dependent in many cases on deliberate management action. For example, the outcome of a change initiative might be a reduction in required headcount from a programme encompassing implementation of a new IT system and business process redesign. The benefits then depend on what management action is taken to redeploy or re-use the resulting spare capacity – for example, in reduced budgets, reduced unit costs, or being able to undertake some other value-adding activity. One of the objectives of benefits management is to ensure that this management action happens in practice.

Important note

The description of portfolios, programmes, projects and outputs, capabilities, outcomes and benefits provides a useful logical framework within which to consider benefits and benefits management. It should, however, be recognized that the situation in the real world is not always as clear cut – for example, programmes may be more akin to the description of portfolios, and the management of complex projects has many similarities with portfolio management. That does not devalue the use of a common and consistent framework – but it does emphasize the importance of tailoring solutions to suit the specific circumstances.

Table 2.1 – Outputs, capabilities, outcomes and benefits

Term	Definition	Example
Output	The deliverable, or output developed by a project from a planned activity.	A new just-in-time stock control system, staff training programme and revised processes.
Capability	The completed set of project outputs required to deliver an outcome; exists prior to transition.	The combination of the above outputs ready for 'go live'.
Outcome	A new operational state achieved after transition of the capability into live operations.	The right materials are available, at the right time, and in the right place.
Benefit	The measurable improvement resulting from an outcome perceived as an advantage by one or more stakeholders, which contributes towards one or more organizational objective(s).	Fewer stock-outs and consequent interruptions to production; reduced obsolescent stock and hence lower write-offs; and reduced stock holdings, and so less working capital tied up.

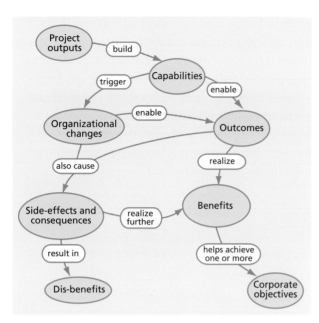

Figure 2.1 – Path to benefits realization and corporate objectives

Dis-benefits

Figure 2.1 shows that as well as realizing intended benefits, initiatives can result in side-effects and consequences and, in turn, in dis-benefits (or what some term a detriment). The issue of unintended consequences is considered further in Chapter 7. For the time being we content ourselves with defining dis-benefits as follows: the measurable decline resulting from an outcome perceived as negative by one or more stakeholders, which detracts from one or more organizational objective(s). Note that a benefit to one stakeholder may be perceived as a dis-benefit by others. One objective of benefits management is to minimize the impact of dis-benefits.

One other thing – management of dis-benefits can be aided by explicitly including them in the benefits categorization framework (see Example 10.2). Alternatively they can be included in the cost base if they are reasonably certain, or treated as a risk if uncertain.

Other relevant terms

- Emergent benefits: Not all positive benefits will be planned from the outset – many will be 'emergent'. These are benefits that are unanticipated, but which emerge as the initiative is developed and, most often, as it is deployed or implemented.

- Intermediate and end benefits: There is often a chain of benefits with intermediate benefits linked to final or end benefits. For example, we might have an initiative that enables earlier invoicing (an intermediate benefit), which results in earlier receipt of income (the end benefit) and so contributes to the objective of reducing working capital. Other intermediate benefits include improved employee morale, more accurate management information and space/accommodation savings. The point to note is that in many cases these intermediate benefits don't automatically lead to the end benefit – that depends on business change or some other management intervention (training, staff re-allocation, process redesign, building sales etc.). Benefits Maps are a useful technique for visualizing this chain, as a basis for tracking benefits realization through to the ultimate end benefit, and for identifying the required enabling and business changes and allocating accountability for ensuring they happen. This is considered further in Chapter 5.

- Tangible and intangible benefits: Some organizations distinguish between tangible benefits (those which are relatively easy to measure) and intangible benefits (those that are not so easy to measure reliably). It should be noted that the definition of benefits shown above refers to a measurable improvement so it can be argued that if a benefit can't be measured it's not a benefit. For example, a report to the US National Electronic Commerce Coordinating Council (NECCC) in 2005 concluded that, "*Justifications for projects usually include a long, predictable list of 'intangible benefits'. The problem here is that there is no such thing ... To call a benefit 'intangible' simply means that nobody has been able – or has done enough analysis – to develop a quantifiable measure.*" The paper goes on to cite the example of "*user friendliness*" where training costs and error rates should be lower, while productivity should be higher. So even with benefits such as improved staff morale and decision-making that might be described as intangible, measurement is often possible via qualitative measures (for example, surveys), proxy indicators, or the Value Index (see Section 6.4).

■ Measurable and observable benefits: The former implies attainment on a scale or by degrees, whereas the latter might be demonstrated by a 'yes/no' observation using a key milestone or evidence event – for instance, the benefit of achieving regulatory compliance is observable, with the evidence event being receipt of a confirmation certificate from the relevant regulatory body.

2.3 VALUE AND VALUE MANAGEMENT

The relationship between benefits and value is also worthy of consideration. We've defined benefits above, but what is 'value' and, more specifically, how does the discipline of value management relate to that of benefits management? The relationship between benefits and value can be approached from two linked perspectives: the value management perspective and the economics perspective.

2.3.1 Improving Value – the Value Management Perspective

The Institute of Value Management (IVM) describes value as follows: *"The concept of Value is based on the relationship between satisfying needs and expectations and the resources required to achieve them. The aim of Value Management is to reconcile all stakeholders' views and to achieve the best balance between satisfied needs and resources."*

In short, value is the extent to which benefits (financial and non-financial) exceed the resources required to realize them – usually costs, including both development costs (for example, asset/system purchase, staff working on the initiative, training, costs of reorganization/redundancy etc.) and running costs (staff to operate the system, licences, ongoing training, maintenance, system refresh etc.).

Value management is considered further in Chapter 6, but what should be noted is that value management and benefits management are mutually supportive disciplines – the techniques of value management enable initiatives to improve benefits for given cost, reduce cost for a given level of benefit, and even to do more for less, by reducing cost and by ensuring functionality is really required by the user.

> **Important note**
> Benefits and value management are mutually supportive disciplines and as such are most effective when they operate in an integrated manner.

2.3.2 Appraising and Evaluating Value for Money – the Economics Perspective

HM Treasury (2004) defines value for money as *"the optimum combination of whole-of-life costs and quality"*. The similarity between this and the definition above from the IVM should be noted. The focus here is, however, less on applying techniques to improve the Value Ratio and more on valuing costs and benefits in monetary terms to enable assessments to be made in terms of:

■ Investment appraisal (undertaken 'ex ante' or prior to investment): to determine whether an investment is justified (i.e. whether the benefits are realistic and worth the cost to realize them), taking into account any previous lessons learned, dis-benefits and the risks and consequences of not undertaking the initiative.
■ Investment evaluation (undertaken 'ex post' or after completion): to determine whether value for money was achieved and to ensure new lessons are learned and applied going forward.

Initiative appraisal is considered further in Chapter 6, while evaluation is examined in Chapter 9.

It should also be noted that value for money is often considered in terms of the 3Es, which are defined as follows:

■ Economy: minimizing the cost of inputs – doing things at lowest cost.
■ Efficiency: the relationship between outputs and the resources required to produce them – doing things right.

■ Effectiveness: the relationship between the intended and actual outcomes achieved – doing the right things.

2.4 WHY DO WE NEED BENEFITS MANAGEMENT?

What we see from the above definitions is that the rationale for investments in change (whether these initiatives are established informally, or formally as projects or programmes) is the realization of benefits. Unfortunately, the evidence paints a disappointing picture as far as this is concerned – for example, the OGC (2003, 2005a) notes that, *"Deficiencies in benefits*

capture bedevils nearly 50% of government projects" and *"30–40% of systems to support business change deliver no benefits whatsoever"*. As Table 2.2 illustrates, this issue extends across the globe, to both private and public sectors, and to many types of initiative.

Such findings should also be seen in the context of change initiatives that not only fail to realize their forecast benefits, but which also cost significantly more than was forecast, further compromising the attainment of value for money. But is this just a list of unfortunate examples, or is it indicative of a wider problem? Unfortunately the answer appears to lie with the latter, as indicated in the research noted below:

Table 2.2 – Benefits realization track record

Type of initiative	Evidence of issues with benefits realization
Corporate business change programmes	*"change remains difficult to pull off, and few companies manage the process as well as they would like. Most of their initiatives – installing new technology, downsizing, restructuring, or trying to change corporate culture – have had low success rates. The brutal fact is that about 70% of all change initiatives fail."* Beer & Nohria (2000)
Information technology	*"even when technically successful, ICT projects do not often deliver the financial and other benefits they promise. It is the remarkable ubiquity of the failure of ICT projects – particularly large ICT projects – and the large sums of money that can disappear as a result that should be of most concern."* Gauld & Goldfinch (2006)
e-government initiatives	In Europe, a report on the results of investment in e-government initiatives (*eGovernment Economics Project, 2006*), concluded that, *"After at least a decade of large investments (running into billions of Euro) [aimed] at digitalizing the public sector, governments in Europe are still mostly unable to objectively quantify and show the benefits and returns of such investments."*
Infrastructure – roads, railways, airports, conference centres	*"a large proportion of recent mega-projects fail any reasonable benefit-cost test"* Altschuler & Luberoff (2003)
Corporate mergers and acquisitions	*"70% to 80% of acquisitions fail, meaning they create no wealth for the shareholders of the acquiring company. Most often, in fact, they destroy wealth"* Seldon & Colvin (2003)
Business process re-engineering (BPR)	*"Unfortunately the number of BPR successes where expectations have been fully realized is said to be quite small."* Cameron & Green (2009)
Total quality management	*"73% of the companies reported having a total quality program underway; but of these, 63% had failed to improve quality defects by even as much as 10%."* Schaffer & Thomson (1992)
Space launches	*"the bottom line – $4.4 billion was spent on these programs, with little to show for it"* Ballhaus (2005)
Business start-ups	*"An analysis of start-up ventures in a wide range of industries found, for example, that more than 80% failed to achieve their market-share target."* Lovallo & Kahneman (2003)

- Lovallo & Kahneman (2003) report that, *"Most large capital investments come in late and over budget, never living up to expectations. More than 70% of new manufacturing plants in North America, for example, close within their first decade of operation. Approximately three-quarters of mergers and acquisitions never pay-off … And efforts to enter new markets fare no better; the vast majority end up being abandoned within a few years."* This might be explained as the result of a competitive market where some degree of failure is necessary. Lovallo & Kahneman come to a different conclusion – they see the scale of failure as being a result of flawed management decision-making. This is discussed further in Chapter 5.

- The NAO (2011) reports that, *"the evidence shows that two-thirds of public sector projects are completed late, over budget or do not deliver the outcomes expected"* and *"The track record of project delivery in the private sector is equally mixed."*

- Flyvbjerg et al (2003, 2005) conclude that, *"At the same time as many more and much larger infrastructure projects are being proposed and built around the world, it is becoming clear that many such projects have strikingly poor performance records"* and *"Our data also show that forecasts have not become more accurate over the 30-year period studied, despite claims to the contrary by forecasters."*

- Research in Australia by Capability Management (2006) found, *"The success ratio of projects has not increased in 15 years – for full delivery of benefits the success figure is still around 5%."*

- A study by Moorhouse Consulting (2009) for the *Financial Times* reported that only 20% of respondents believed their organizations succeed in consistently delivering the planned benefits of change.

So, the fundamental driver for benefits management is the regularly reported poor track record of change initiatives in realizing the benefits they were established to deliver.

2.5 BENEFITS MANAGEMENT OBJECTIVES

Benefits management seeks to address the problems identified above and so optimize benefits realization by ensuring the following objectives are met:

1. Forecast benefits are complete (all sources of potential value are identified), realizable and represent value for money – so we invest in the right initiatives and subsequent efforts to manage benefits are built on the solid foundations of realistic forecasts.

2. Forecast benefits are realized in practice, including by ensuring the required enabling, business and behavioural change takes place – so that performance of the investment matches the 'promise'. That said, in reality not all initially expected results will be realized (because things change and because of forecasting error), but emergent benefits may, and in many cases do, more than balance them out.

3. Benefits are realized as early as possible and are sustained for as long as possible.

4. Emergent or unplanned benefits are captured and leveraged (and any dis-benefits are minimized) – so we optimize the benefits realized and value for money achieved.

5. We can demonstrate the above – not just as part of the framework of accountability but also so that we learn what works as a basis for continuous improvement.

Where progress is made the benefits are significant – a study by Ward et al (2008) found that while the adoption of more structured approaches to initiative delivery had not resulted in increased benefits realization, the adoption of key benefits management-related practices (robust benefits-based Business Cases, planning of organizational change and benefits delivery, and evaluation and review of organizational change and benefits realization) was associated with higher benefits realization.

But achieving these objectives is far from straightforward. A study by Mott McDonald (2002) found, *"some business cases did not give any indication of the benefits estimates. Moreover most projects did not have any post-project appraisal that could provide an indication of how successful the delivery of benefits had been."* Research evidence indicates that many organizations worldwide still struggle to implement benefits management effectively. For example:

■ One Portfolio, Programme and Project Management Maturity Model (P3M3) assessor reports (Aspire, 2010), *"If we look at the evidence from P3M3 maturity assessments, every organisation we have looked at so far has been weak in the area of Benefits Management"*.

■ The report from Moorhouse Consulting (2009) for the *Financial Times* referred to above also found that, *"we still see most organisations struggling to deliver sustainable benefits from their change programmes. There is also scant evidence of any maturation in the discipline of benefits realisation generally."*

■ A survey by the APM in the UK (2009) found that only 38% of respondents had a formal structured approach to benefits management. A more recent joint survey by the APM and Chartered Institute of Management Accountants (CIMA) in Ireland (2012) found that only 45% of respondents described their organization's approach as 'formal/structured' and only 3% indicated that their approach provides value all of the time.

Addressing this calls for effective implementation and operation of benefits management approaches that:

■ Overcome the barriers to effective benefits management discussed in Chapter 4 and so avoid the common misconceptions on what benefits management is about; address the twin dangers of cognitive bias and strategic misrepresentation; and also overcome the 'knowing–doing' gap.

■ Adopt portfolio-wide approaches that manage benefits consistently in the context of current strategic objectives and business priorities.

■ Give due consideration to the Key Success Characteristics of effective benefits management discussed in Chapter 4.

■ Consider not only the practices outlined in Chapters 4–9 but also the principles upon which effective benefits management is based. It is this that we consider in the next chapter.

2.6 CHAPTER SUMMARY

1. Benefits are defined as *"the measurable improvement resulting from an outcome perceived as an advantage by one or more stakeholders, which contributes towards one or more organizational objective(s)"*.

2. Benefits management is process that runs across the full business change lifecycle from benefits identification through to realization and applying lessons learned.

3. The objectives of benefits management are to ensure benefits realization is optimized by the following: forecast benefits are complete, realizable and represent value for money; realization of forecast benefits is maximized; benefits are realized as early as possible and are sustained for as long as possible; emergent benefits are captured and leveraged (and any dis-benefits are minimized); and that we can demonstrate the aforementioned.

4. The case for more effective benefits management is made by the relatively poor track record of many change initiatives in delivering the benefits they were established to realize.

5. Notwithstanding the case for benefits management, many organizations struggle to implement benefits management effectively – this Guide contains solutions to address this issue, starting with the principles discussed in the next chapter.

Chapter 3

Chapter 3 – The Benefits Management Principles

3.1 OVERVIEW OF THIS CHAPTER

The previous chapter demonstrated that there is a strong case for applying effective benefits management practices to address the failure to consistently optimize the realization of benefits from change. The practices that constitute the Benefits Management Cycle (and which are addressed in detail in Chapters 4–9) are: Identify & Quantify benefits, Value & Appraise benefits, Plan for benefits realization, Realize benefits and Review.

However, defined practices are no 'silver bullet' solution. The effectiveness of the benefits management practices depends on a series of enabling factors or principles that represent the

foundations upon which successful benefits management practices are built – these principles, and their relationship with the practices in the Benefits Management Cycle, are illustrated in the Benefits Management Model in Figure 3.1.

These principles are:

1. **Align benefits with strategy** – benefits represent a measurable improvement which contributes towards one or more organizational or strategic objectives and it is therefore important that strategy is clearly articulated so that this contribution can be measured consistently.

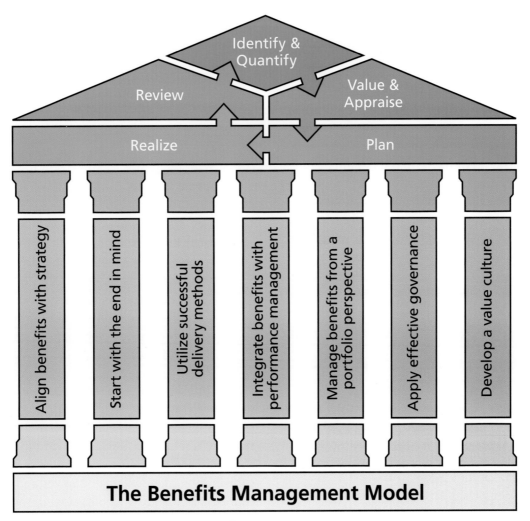

Figure 3.1 – The Benefits Management Model

2. **Start with the end in mind** – with benefits-led change, where initiatives are established to realize the required benefits, rather than benefits being used to justify a pre-selected solution.

3. **Utilize successful delivery methods** – combining appropriately tailored delivery methods, such as PRINCE2 and '*Managing Successful Programmes*' (MSP), with effective approaches to change management, so enabling benefits realization.

4. **Integrate benefits with performance management** – with benefits (and the measures used) being integrated into the organization's operational and HR performance management systems.

5. **Manage benefits from a portfolio perspective** – with consistent approaches applied to all initiatives included within the change portfolio, benefits-led investment appraisal and portfolio prioritization, effective management of dependencies between change initiatives, and tracking benefits realization beyond initiative closure.

6. **Apply effective governance** – including ensuring clear accountability and responsibility for the enabling and business changes upon which benefits realization is dependent, and for realization of the required benefits.

7. **Develop a value culture** – that takes benefits and benefits management seriously, and that focuses on creating and sustaining value from an organization's investments in change.

These principles are considered in turn.

3.2 PRINCIPLE 1. ALIGN BENEFITS WITH STRATEGY

We saw in Chapter 2 that benefits are, "*the measurable improvement resulting from an outcome perceived as an advantage by one or more stakeholders, which* **contributes** *towards one or more organizational objective(s)*".

Understanding the contribution of change initiatives to organizational objectives is consequently at the very heart of effective benefits management. Unfortunately this is not always present in practice – the NAO/OGC's List of Common Causes of Project Failure (2002) includes the following at number 1: "*Lack of clear link between the project and the organisation's key strategic priorities, including agreed measures of success.*"

This can be addressed by establishing a 'clear line of sight' from strategic intent through to initiative benefits and vice versa. This requires:

1. Organizational/strategic objectives being expressed in meaningful, quantifiable terms, or by making clear the implicit assumptions underpinning the logic chain leading to achievement of these objectives. Where this exists there is a consistent basis for assessing the specific contribution of individual change initiatives to the organization's objectives, and this assessment can be used to inform investment appraisal and portfolio prioritization exercises.

2. The benefits from change initiatives being expressed in consistent terms that demonstrate their contribution to the measures and drivers of strategic success. This is facilitated by consistent:
   - Approaches to initiative-level benefits mapping which demonstrate how benefits will be derived from initiatives (and the business and enabling changes on which they are dependent) and, in turn, how these benefits are related to the organizational/strategic objectives. This technique is discussed in Chapter 5.
   - Guidelines providing consistent categorization and valuation of benefits across the change portfolio. This is discussed in Chapter 10.

Where this is in place we have a basis for meaningful assessments of strategic contribution. But a problem regularly faced in practice is that strategy is set at too high a level and this compromises attempts to determine the strategic contribution of individual initiatives and the change portfolio as a whole. Indeed, Sanwal (2007) comments that strategy is too often, *"the justification of last resort or when an investment owner does not want to think about why to do an investment. In essence, strategy is the reason often cited when the benefits of a particular idea cannot be articulated in a more lucid manner."*

Fortunately it need not be so – techniques which facilitate assessment of strategic contribution include driver-based analysis. Here the implicit logic underpinning the strategic objectives is made explicit – by the clear articulation of the beliefs and assumptions that underlie the cause and effect relationships between (and the drivers of) the elements in the organization's business model. For example, in the public-sector Service Value Chain discussed below, one of the elements is 'citizen/client satisfaction' with identified drivers that include timeliness and fairness. This in turn facilitates the assessment of strategic contribution as the benefits of change initiatives can be more reliably linked to the strategic objectives. So, rather than investing in initiatives to improve employee engagement or customer satisfaction for their own sake, such investments can be targeted to address the drivers of the elements in the organization's business model.

But the relationship between driver-based analysis and benefits management is also two-way – since benefits management should provide the data to validate (and refine if necessary) the business model and the assumptions upon which it is based – including the elements in the model, the linkages between them and the drivers of each element. This is another aspect of evidence-based benefits management – and one which is aided where leading as well as lagging benefits measures are agreed (see Chapter 7).

'Management of Portfolios' (MoP) includes reference to the following two generic, high-level examples of driver-based analysis, one suited to service organizations in the private sector and one to the public sector. The outlines contained in MoP have been enhanced here with further information on each technique. But it should be emphasized that these two examples are generic, and it is important that each organization documents its own business model by, for example, adapting one of these approaches or via the Balanced Scorecard and Strategy Map (see Section 3.5).

3.2.1 Private-sector Driver-based Analysis – the Service Profit Chain

Research at Harvard University by Heskett et al (1997) has identified a causal chain from internal service quality to improved profitability and growth. This is what is called the Service Profit Chain, which is illustrated in Figure 3.2.

Starting from the left-hand side:

- Employee satisfaction is based on internal services quality, i.e. high-quality support services that provide staff with the skills and power to deliver results for the customer.

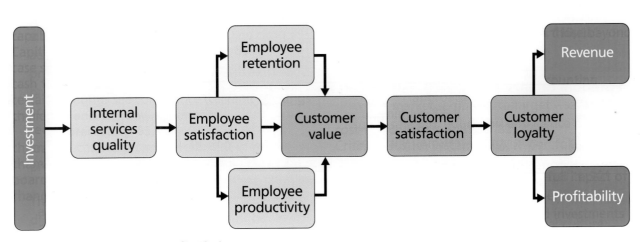

Figure 3.2 – The Service Profit Chain
Source: http://www.livetime.com/wp-content/uploads/2010/05/Service_profit_chain_model.jpg.

■ Employee satisfaction leads to improved retention (with reduced loss of tacit knowledge and costs of replacement) and increased productivity, enhancing external service value for the customer.

■ This results in customer satisfaction and loyalty – which, in turn, drives profits and growth via repeat business and referrals. Research has found that a 5% increase in customer loyalty can increase profits by between 25% and 85%. According to Heskett et al, this led Xerox to focus not on achieving a general across-the-board increase in customer satisfaction, but rather on creating what Cook refers to as "apostles", i.e. customers so satisfied that they convert the uninitiated. Apple is another organization that has reaped the benefits of highly committed customers.

Applying the Service Profit Chain requires organizations to understand the links in their business model, and to measure the relationships between the links by putting hard values on soft measures – for example, via staff exit interviews and regular large sample customer surveys. Taco Bell (an American fast food restaurant chain) has found that stores in the top 25% for customer satisfaction outperform the remaining 75% on all measures, and it has therefore incorporated this perspective into the performance management and reward assessment for store managers. Taco Bell has also discovered that the stores with the lowest staff turnover rates have double the sales and 55% higher profits than those with the highest staff turnover – this acted as a stimulus to targeted initiatives designed to reduce staff turnover. Another company that has used such analysis is Sears (a US department store chain), which has modelled the relationship mathematically – an 8-unit increase in employee attitude was expected to drive a 1.3-unit increase in customer impression and this in turn drives a 0.5% increase in revenue growth. Sears audited the links annually and based its management remuneration on performance across all three factors in the chain (reported in Pfeffer & Sutton, 2000).

What this also means is that the Service Profit Chain can provide an evidence base for identifying areas where change initiatives can be designed to improve service and satisfaction, and so deliver competitive advantage. For example, 'internal service quality', which is measured by "the feelings that employees have toward their jobs, colleagues, and companies" (Heskett et al, 1997), can be enhanced by initiatives in the areas of workplace design, job design, employee training and development, rewards and recognition, and relevant tools for serving the customer, including information systems.

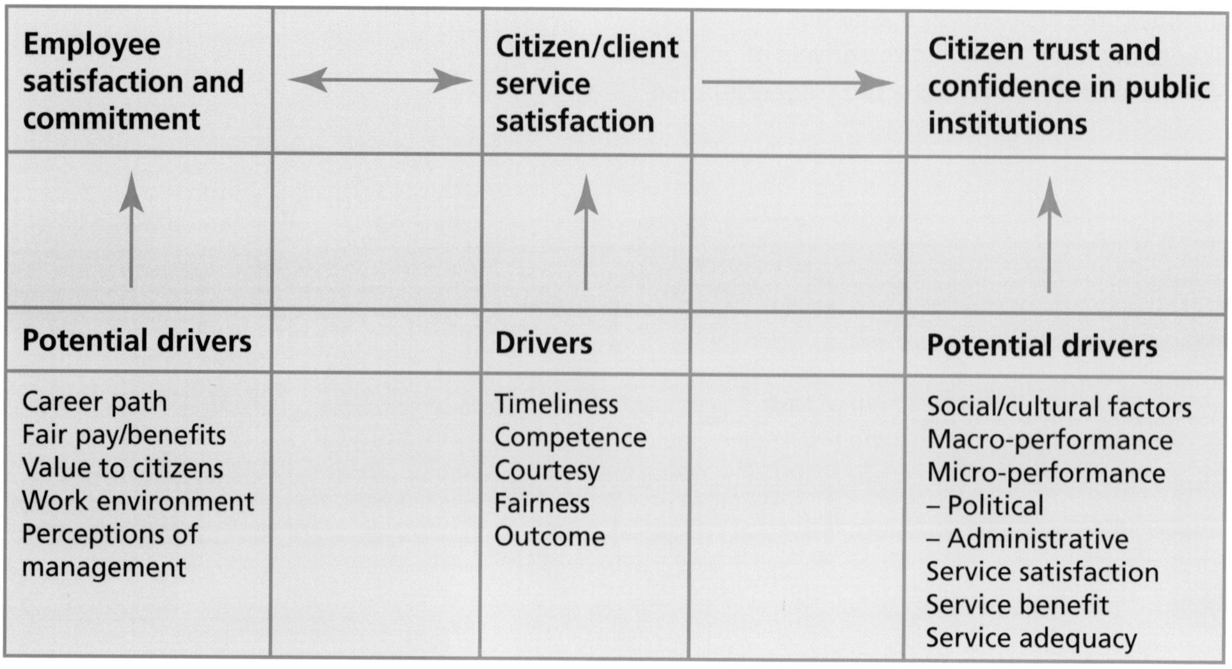

Employee satisfaction and commitment		Citizen/client service satisfaction		Citizen trust and confidence in public institutions
↑		↑		↑
Potential drivers		**Drivers**		**Potential drivers**
Career path Fair pay/benefits Value to citizens Work environment Perceptions of management		Timeliness Competence Courtesy Fairness Outcome		Social/cultural factors Macro-performance Micro-performance – Political – Administrative Service satisfaction Service benefit Service adequacy

Figure 3.3 – The Service Value Chain

3.2.2 Public-sector Driver-based Analysis – the Service Value Chain

Building on the work of Heskett et al outlined above, Heintzman and Marson (2005) in Canada have proposed a Service Value Chain for the public sector. This links employee engagement (satisfaction and commitment) to citizen/client satisfaction and in turn to citizen trust and confidence. This is illustrated in Figure 3.3, which comes from MoP.

Points to note include:

■ The relationship between employee commitment and client satisfaction is based on research from the private sector which consistently finds a strong and two-way relationship – what is referred to as the 'satisfaction mirror'.

■ Based on research from the USA, Sweden and the UK, Heintzman and Marson conclude that there is a casual relationship between service and trust/confidence, but not vice versa, i.e. lack of trust does not cause dissatisfaction with services, but satisfaction with services leads to improved trust.

■ The drivers of each element in the model, as shown in Figure 3.3, are identified as follows:
  □ Potential drivers of employee satisfaction and commitment are derived from research by Erin Research in Canada.
  □ The drivers of service satisfaction are again derived from research in Canada which concluded that the five drivers identified drove 72% of the variance in overall public-sector service satisfaction ratings (note similar research findings are referred to in Section 8.4.4 and in Example A.2 in Appendix A).
  □ Potential drivers of confidence in government are complex and need to reflect wider social factors, but along with service satisfaction, drivers include 'service benefit' (the extent to which people feel they have benefited from services) and 'service adequacy' (the extent to which people feel that services provided meet their needs).

As with the Service Profit Chain, this Service Value Chain can be used to:

■ Identify and design initiatives to enhance satisfaction and commitment (on the part of employees) and satisfaction and hence trust (on the part of citizens).

■ Link the benefits of initiatives to the drivers of employee satisfaction and commitment, citizen satisfaction, and in turn to public trust and confidence.

Important note

To emphasize the point made above – the assumptions about the elements, linkages and drivers in the model need to be validated with evidence. For example, recent research by Hawkins & Matheson (2010) in Canada has confirmed the link between employee engagement and customer satisfaction – but the main factor in this relationship was not job satisfaction, but employees' overall satisfaction with the organization they work for – each two-point increase in organization satisfaction was linked with a one-point improvement in customer satisfaction. Such validation is one valuable output from an effective Benefits Management Cycle.

Note: other techniques that enable assessment of strategic contribution include the Balanced Scorecard and strategy mapping (see Section 3.5); value profiling (covered in Chapter 6); multi-criteria analysis (also covered in Chapter 6); and root cause modelling (mentioned in Appendix A). Consistent assessment of strategic contribution is also facilitated where a design authority has defined the organization's target operating model or has responsibility for its enterprise architecture, which enables consistent appraisal of initiative proposals in the context of their strategic 'fit'.

3.3 PRINCIPLE 2. START WITH THE END IN MIND

In the next chapter we discuss some common misconceptions about benefits management – one of which is that it starts with a given project or programme and then identifies the benefits that will result from that initiative (or, to be more accurate, it often attempts to identify sufficient benefits to justify the cost). This is what Bradley (2010) refers to as *"cart before the horse"* mentality, and Simms (2012) as *"upside-down thinking"*. While this is a misconception, it is one that is too often seen in practice – and the result is wasted effort in managing benefits that are overstated in order to obtain funding.

Schaffer and Thomson (1992) argue that one cause of this failure is that organizations *"confuse ends with means, processes with outcomes"* and pursue *"activities that sound good, look good, and allow managers to feel good – but in fact contribute little or nothing to bottom-line performance"*. Organizations consequently too often make the mistake of investing in activity-centred change initiatives such as management information systems; business process re-engineering; total quality management; enhanced cross-organizational collaboration; staff and management empowerment; customer satisfaction measurement etc. The problem is not

that such initiatives don't or can't add value – they can when implemented as part of an appropriately designed performance improvement programme. Rather, it is that they are implemented without sufficient focus on the ultimate benefits intended because of an assumption (which too often turns out to be an illusion) that improved performance will just happen. The problems are that the linkages between such activities and the organization's objectives are not made clear (hence the need for strategic driver-based analysis mentioned above), and often several (or many) of these initiatives are launched in an uncoordinated manner with all of them claiming to deliver the same benefits. The result is *"Wave after wave of programs rolled across the landscape with little positive impact."* (Beer et al, 1990)

The solution is to adopt benefits-led change initiatives that 'start with the end in mind', and where the scope of the initiative is determined by the benefits required. In short, the benefits required determine the scope (and requirements)

Table 3.1 – Activity-centred and benefits-led change initiatives compared

Activity-centred change initiatives	Benefits-led change initiatives
1. The initiative is adopted because it is 'the right thing to do' or a 'no-brainer'. Where objectives are set, they are defined mainly in long-term, non-specific or process-based terms, with no clear linkage from the activity to strategic contribution.	1. Benefits are identified and the contribution to organizational objectives is clear; and there are measurable, specific, short-term performance improvement goals even when the change effort is long-term.
2. The initiative's champion urges managers and employees to be patient, take a long-term perspective, and 'keep the faith' as the approach will come good in the end.	2. The atmosphere is one of impatience for benefits even when the programme is a long-term change initiative.
3. Progress is measured in terms of measures of activity – people trained, surveys completed etc.	3. Progress is measured in terms of benefits using both leading and lagging indicators.
4. Staff experts and consultants drive the programme.	4. Business managers take the lead with staff experts and consultants helping them to achieve benefits.
5. Substantial investment is required up front before any significant benefits are seen.	5. Incremental and modular approaches are adopted with quick wins being used to generate enthusiasm for the initiative.
6. The approach is based on advocacy rather than evidence. There is no real learning from experience since the solution promoted is accepted as orthodoxy.	6. The approach is driven by evidence about what works – learnings are fed back to provide insight into the design and prioritization of the next phase of the initiative.

of the initiative rather than vice versa. This is far more than semantics – based on the analysis by Scaffer and Thomson we can identify six key differences between these activity-centred and benefits-led initiatives – see Table 3.1.

One benefits management technique that can help in achieving this shift to benefits-led change initiatives is investment logic mapping. This approach was developed by the Victorian Government in Australia and is outlined in Example 3.1.

Example 3.1 – Investment logic mapping

At the heart of the Investment Management Standard adopted by the Victorian Government is the Investment Logic Map (see Figure 3.4). This depicts the story of an investment on a single page in a form that can be easily understood and adapted to represent a changing story. It shows:

1. The drivers or the problem at hand, along with the high-level strategic interventions proposed to address the problem.

2. The benefits to the organization and its customers that result from addressing the problem (these will be supported by at least one or two key performance indicators, with associated targets, for each benefit, which are meaningful, attributable and measurable).

3. The business changes and enabling assets required to realize those benefits.

The Investment Logic Map is the output from a series of three, two-hour workshops focusing on defining the problem, the benefits sought, and the required solution (for small investments this is developed in just one workshop). Fundamental to the success of the process is the engagement of senior executives. The participants will vary between the three workshops, but will include the 'investor' (the person who has identified the business need, who will be making or advocating the decision to invest, and who will be responsible for realizing the benefits), along with relevant internal and external stakeholders. **The crucial point is that the debate starts with the problem faced rather than seeking to justify a solution.**

These are not 'once only' exercises – investment reviews are undertaken at specified intervals where project performance is assessed against cost and schedule and the two-hour workshop is repeated to test the continuing relevance of the investment logic. The outcome of this review is a decision by the governance body to continue, discontinue or vary the terms for implementing the investment. The Investment Logic Map, and supporting Benefits Management Plan, will also be re-endorsed. The key themes underpinning the approach are:

- A clear statement relating strategic drivers to objectives and benefits, and the business and enabling changes required to realize those benefits.
- Short summary documentation focusing on the key high-level benefits and the key performance indicators that will be used to assess benefits realization.
- Regular investment reviews and recommitment to the Investment Logic Map and Benefits Management Plan.

Example continues

Example 3.1 continued

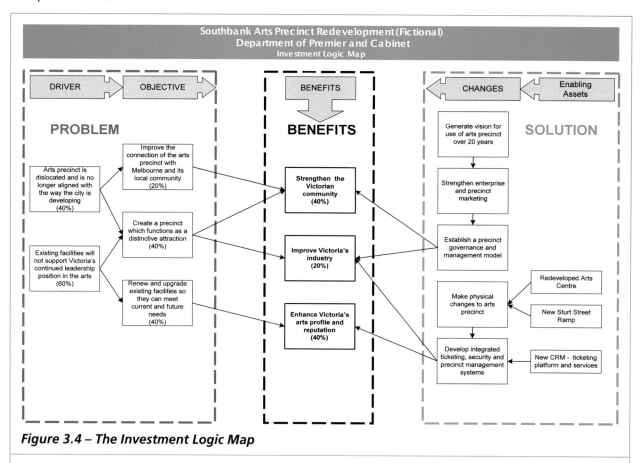

Figure 3.4 – The Investment Logic Map

Provided with the kind agreement of Terry Wright of the Victorian Department of Treasury and Finance. Note that the format of the Investment Logic Map has changed – the original format is shown as it succinctly illustrates the approach. Further information is available at http://www.dtf.vic.gov.au/CA25713E0002EF43/pages/investment-management-home.

Figure 3.5 illustrates the framework adopted for realizing the benefits of e-government in Sweden. This also highlights some of the key themes associated with benefits-led change, including the cyclical nature of benefits management and, significantly, that identification of desired outcomes and benefits should ideally precede the specification of a solution.

Other examples of benefits-led change include what Simms (2008) refers to as *"reverse engineering planning"*, where initiative planning works backwards from 'desired business outcomes' (DBOs) and benefits. This is similar to the 'backcasting' approach advocated by Fowler and Lock (2006). Based on the impressive record of major events, such as the Olympics, political summits and music festivals, being held on the scheduled date with zero delay, Fowler and Lock propose that, in scheduling initiative design and development, we work backwards from the

'wanted by' dates for initiative benefits. In this the 'backcasting' approach uses techniques similar to critical path analysis and agile development methodologies, but always starts with hindsight from the desired state and 'back-plans' from there. Thus the end state is non-negotiable, but there is flexibility in the choice of solutions adopted to get us there. In practice this means that an initiative should clearly identify what Fowler and Lock call 'recognition events®' and 'value flashpoints®' (this is explored further in Chapter 8).

One other point to note – implementing benefits management should itself be seen as a benefits-led initiative (more on this in Chapter 11).

Figure 3.5 – Swedish e-government Delegation Benefits Model

3.4 PRINCIPLE 3. UTILIZE SUCCESSFUL DELIVERY METHODS

If change initiatives are not delivered effectively, or if they are delivered late, there will inevitably be adverse impacts on benefits realization. Consequently, effective delivery methods are enablers for the realization of benefits. *'Best Management Practice'* methods such as PRINCE2 (for projects) and MSP (for programmes) provide a sound basis on which to manage initiatives and so enable effective benefits management:

■ PRINCE2 (PRojects IN Controlled Environments): Since its introduction in 1989, as a UK Government standard for IT project management, PRINCE has been adopted by both public and commercial sectors and is now recognized as a de facto global standard for project management – but one which is flexible enough to be tailored to different organizations and is used successfully for all types of projects. For more information see http://www.prince-officialsite.com.

■ *'Managing Successful Programmes'* (MSP): Large, complex deliveries are often broken down into manageable, interrelated projects.

For those managing this overall delivery the principles of programme management are key to delivering on time and within budget. Cabinet Office *'Best Management Practice'* in this area is found in MSP, which comprises a set of principles and processes for use when managing a programme. It is founded on best practice although it is not prescriptive – rather it is flexible and designed to be adapted to meet local circumstances. For more information see http://www.msp-officialsite.com.

Important note

To emphasize – adoption of methods such as PRINCE2 and MSP does not provide an 'out of the box' solution; indeed, both the above descriptions emphasize that the methods are flexible. Approaches adopted need to be tailored and adapted flexibly to the local circumstances.

These methods also need to be augmented with a range of techniques drawn from other disciplines – many of which are discussed in this Guide. For example, we live in an increasingly complex world characterized by uncertainty, ambiguity, cross-initiative dependencies, a multitude of often conflicting stakeholder interests, emergent strategy and requirements, and transformational rather than incremental change. The consequence of increased complexity, ambiguity and uncertainty is that more attention needs to be given to strategies such as:

■ Adapting traditional delivery methods by applying a 'dolphins not whales' approach: i.e. applying agile, modular and incremental development approaches, and breaking large initiatives down into smaller ones of shorter duration. Two cases of this are outlined in Example 3.2.

■ Combining a rigorous start gate to set things up right from the start with regular review throughout the business change lifecycle.

■ Incremental rather than one-off investment decisions, based on the technique of 'staged release of funding' with funding being linked more closely to confidence in successful delivery (including benefits realization).

■ Ongoing participative stakeholder engagement including bringing the 'voice of the customer' into the design and delivery of change initiatives via customer insight, and leadership based on *"visionaries, storytellers and map makers – the ability to set bold objectives, create compelling narratives to enthuse others and form coherent plans to achieve them"* (Wilford, 2011). This issue of leadership and *"storytellers"* is explored in Chapter 8.

■ Adopting a forward-looking perspective based on learning, feedback and insight throughout the business change lifecycle. The focus should be less on holding people to account for forecast benefits, than a continuous search for emergent benefits and capturing learnings.

Accepting the need for the above does not mean that disciplined delivery methods are no longer applicable – rather, there remains a compelling requirement for standards, rigour and transparency. Consequently, disciplined delivery methods remain a necessary prerequisite for benefits realization; however, such methods are a means to an end, not an end in themselves, and common sense should be used in their application in an environment of uncertainty, opportunity and emergence.

Example 3.2 – Modular projects and programmes – 'dolphins not whales'

Mike Cross (2002) reported that the OECD had called on governments to avoid large IT projects and to create *"dolphins not whales."* An example of this is the Wiring Up Youth Justice programme, which started with the areas identified by the core business as their main areas of concern – making information available on *"who people are, where they are coming from and where they go after they've been with us"* (Veltech, 2009). A series of discrete projects were implemented that minimized dependencies, enabled technical solutions to be proved, and resulted in early realization of benefits. Sir Ian Magee commented in his report on improving Multi-agency Public Protection that, *"In youth justice, very modest investment has been used to make significant incremental improvements in getting critical information to move with the young offender across organizations at the right speed. In the present financial climate, the youth justice system could be useful across the Public Protection Network."*

Another example of creating 'dolphins' rather than 'whales' comes from the cross-government Tell Us Once programme – focusing initially on birth, death and bereavement. The lessons learned from this first phase are being captured and used to inform the future direction and scope of the programme – which includes expansion of current services to include other parts of the public sector, such as the National Health Service (NHS), as well as future service offerings including change of address. Once again, the scale of investment is minimized, risks are controlled more effectively, and benefits are realized earlier.

From: Jenner, S (2010). Reproduced with the kind agreement of the publisher.

Additionally, disciplined delivery methods are necessary but not sufficient to ensure benefits realization. Successful delivery encompasses not only the dimensions of on time/to budget/to specification but also benefits realization – and this often depends on business and behavioural change. This requires:

- Effective planning for business change, including preparing Benefits Dependency Networks/Maps highlighting the business and enabling changes upon which benefits realization is dependent.
- Allocating and documenting responsibilities for delivering the enabling and business changes in Benefit Profiles and a Benefits Realization Plan.
- Ongoing participative stakeholder engagement throughout the business change lifecycle.
- Strategies to achieve behavioural change by winning hearts as well as minds.
- Adopting a portfolio approach to maintain a focus on business change and benefits realization post-initiative closure.

Beyond the above, change management needs to be managed and led consistently, and that is aided by the adoption of a standard approach such as Kotter's (1996) Eight-Stage process:

1. Establishing a Sense of Urgency

2. Creating the Guiding Coalition

3. Developing a Vision and Strategy

4. Communicating the Change Vision

5. Empowering Employees for Broad-Based Action

6. Generating Short-Term Wins

7. Consolidating Gains and Producing More Change

8. Anchoring New Approaches in the Culture

There are many such approaches available, and Kotter's is shown here because it is one of the best known. That said, the selection of an approach to change management needs to be appropriate to the circumstances – as with

benefits management itself, there is no 'out of the box' solution available. For those who wish to explore this further, recommended reading is included in Chapter 12. This includes Cameron & Green's (2009) *'Making Sense of Change Management'*, which forms the basis for accredited examinations in Change Management. (See: http://www.apmg-international.com/APMG-UK/ChangeMgt/ChangeMgt.aspx.)

3.5 PRINCIPLE 4. INTEGRATE BENEFITS WITH PERFORMANCE MANAGEMENT

Wherever possible, benefits (and the measures used) should be integrated into the organization's operational and HR performance management systems. This includes:

Operational performance management

- Wherever possible, linking benefits measures to the organization's key performance indicators (KPIs) and making use of data available from the management information system – this helps minimize the additional costs of new measurement systems to track and report on benefits realization.

- Linked to the above – building benefits into business plans and budgets. This is facilitated by application of the technique of 'booking the benefits' discussed in Chapter 7 whereby benefits are 'booked' in budgets, headcount targets, unit costs and performance targets, including those used as part of the Balanced Scorecard – see Section 3.5.1 below.

HR performance management

- Aligning responsibilities for benefits management with individuals' performance objectives – so that there is clarity about what people are responsible and accountable for, including implementing the changes upon which benefits realization depends.

- Aligning responsibilities for benefits management with the reward and recognition processes. As we see in Chapter 8, financial rewards are not always the best way to motivate people, but inconsistencies between desired behaviours and the organization's reward and recognition systems can be a real obstacle to progress because they send mixed messages about what is regarded as important. So, wherever possible, link incentives (both financial and non-financial) to achievement of the benefits.

It should be noted that integration of benefits with the performance management system does not represent a complete solution to the issue of managing benefits realization. As we see in Section 8.4.1 even where benefits management is integrated into the performance management system, we cannot escape the need to undertake some benefits tracking and reporting (e.g. as a basis for understanding what is actually causing changes in performance and for identifying emergent benefits and mitigating dis-benefits) via development of a suite of benefits measures that include leading as well as lagging measures. But the cost of such activity and its effectiveness is aided where benefits are integrated, as far as possible, with the performance management system. One method which facilitates this is the Balanced Scorecard.

3.5.1   The Balanced Scorecard

Many organizations have adopted the Balanced Scorecard with measures for the four perspectives defined by Kaplan & Norton (1996) – financial, customer, internal business process, and learning and growth. Some organizations have developed their own perspectives – but whichever approach is adopted, the benefits from individual change initiatives can be quantified and expressed in terms of their contribution to these Balanced Scorecard measures – so linking benefits to the organization's performance management system, and in turn to the strategic objectives. Such measures include the following (developed from the generic and core measures identified by Kaplan & Norton):

■ Financial – Measures of financial or 'bottom-line' performance: return on investment/ economic value added, profitability, revenue growth and mix, cost reduction/productivity improvement and level of working capital required.

■ Customer – Measures of customer/client perception of the organization: market share, customer acquisition, customer retention, customer profitability and customer satisfaction.

■ Internal business process – Measures of how efficient the organization is: quality, response time, cost, re-work, bottlenecks and new product introductions.

■ Learning and growth – Measures of employee commitment to the organization: employee satisfaction, employee retention and employee productivity.

Linking benefits from change initiatives to the performance management system is further enabled where the Balanced Scorecard is cascaded down and across the organization – so enabling benefits to be mapped to the measures used at unit or functional level.

It should be noted that the four perspectives and their measures are not independent – as Kaplan & Norton say, *"an entire chain of cause-and-effect relationships can be established as a vertical vector through the four BSC perspectives"* – financial performance resulting from improved new sales and customer retention, which in turn results from improved internal business process quality, which is dependent on skilled and motivated staff. This chain of cause and effects, with the drivers at each stage, is represented in a Strategy Map. This of course sounds very much like the Service Profit Chain discussed above in Section 3.2.1 – and indeed, Kaplan & Norton describe the Service Profit Chain as *"a generic Balanced Scorecard"*.

Whichever Balanced Scorecard is used, it needs to be tailored to the specific organization, and the assumptions and cause and effect relationships underpinning the model should be documented explicitly, and be validated via the Review practice in the Benefits Management Cycle.

Example 3.3 – DfE – Aligning benefits with strategic objectives and the performance management system

The Department for Education (DfE) was formed on 12 May 2010, with the vision of creating, *"… a highly-educated society in which opportunity is more equal for children and young people no matter what their background or family circumstances".*

Central to achievement of this vision is the Education Single Programme (ESP). Crucially, at the time of designing the programme benefits management approach, the Departmental Vision, Aims and Objectives had not yet been formally agreed. As an interim solution, and to ensure the benefits work was not held up, it was decided that the draft Departmental Performance Report objectives and business plan, along with success measures identified by some sub-programme project initiation documents, would be amalgamated to form an initial set of high-level benefits for the programme.

The ESP sub-programmes are designed to ensure these benefits are realized, and so each sub-programme was commissioned to produce an evidence of impact (EoI) assessment. An EoI states the aims of the sub-programme and records the indicators that it is proposed be used to assess achievement of those aims, as well as the forecast trajectory. This was the first time that sub-programmes had been asked to define benefits and indicators in quite this way, and so time was taken to explain the approach and get sub-programme staff 'on-side'.

In measuring progress, the DfE was aware that, while in some cases reliable EoI would not be seen for several years, it could not wait for this as feedback on progress against the vision was required in the interim. A set of four high-level checks were therefore designed to provide feedback on progress against the vision:

1. A listening task – to see if partners, stakeholders and clients see the programme as having the desired effect. This involved a customer clinic where officials spoke to parents and young people aged between 5 and 18 to hear their perspectives.

2. A reality check – to check the evidence (via the high-level benefits and indicators) that the department's 'big ticket' policies really were delivering for children.

3. An exploratory 'deep-dive' operation – the first 'deep-dive' focused on school governance, covering all aspects of maintained-school, academy and free-school governance policy. It involved an exploratory review of school governing bodies, with a view to maximizing their effectiveness in discharging their duty to hold schools to account for performance in raising attainment of all pupils and narrowing achievement gaps between children from poor backgrounds and their wealthier peers.

4. A financial test – to review two areas of the ESP (nominated every six months) to estimate its value for money, suggest ways to improve efficiency and consider the relative value of alternative approaches.

Example continues

Example 3.3 continued

As stated above, the benefits management regime was introduced as the departmental objectives were being developed. Once these objectives were confirmed, it was vital to ensure that the high-level benefits were explicitly linked to the agreed departmental objectives – to provide a 'clear line of sight' between activity and the strategic objectives. The original high-level benefits were therefore reviewed and amended using data from the current Departmental Performance Report and sub-programme EoI statements. An example is shown below.

DfE objective	High-level benefit	High-level benefit indicators
4. To improve school performance so that no school is allowed to fail its pupils and all strive towards better levels of attainment for all.	4a. Increased performance of pupils in all state-funded schools.	a) Improving rates of progression at Key Stage (KS) 2 and KS4.
		b) Improving results in Age 6 phonics test.
		c) Improving attainment at KS2 (e.g. increasing % of children reaching Level 4 in English and Maths at age 11).
		d) Improving attainment at KS4 (e.g. increasing attainment in the EBacc and those achieving 5 A*–Cs).
		e) Improving attainment at KS1/Early Years Foundation Stage Profile.
		f) Increased % of pupils gaining good A-Levels in 'facilitating subjects' for Russell Group Universities.

It was also essential that the data required to assess progress against the high-level benefit indicators was readily available, as additional research burdens of new indicators and the associated cost implications were not appropriate. Programme staff therefore worked closely with policy analysts as well as the Performance Unit (PU) to ensure that this work complemented a more streamlined quantitative version of the Departmental Performance Report. The resulting high-level benefit indicators are designed to support the strategic focus of the ESP and will be used by the Programme Boards to assess progress and to inform decision-making.

The department's strategic-level board will be the forum for consideration of these indicators as a whole. It will report any issues or concerns about progress of the overall programme towards delivering the department's objectives.

These high-level benefits and their indicators remain under review – to see if there is any potential for further streamlining, and, fundamentally, to ensure they continue to reliably measure strategic contribution.

Provided with the kind assistance of Steve Oram and Charlotte Eales, DfE.

3.6 PRINCIPLE 5. MANAGE BENEFITS FROM A PORTFOLIO PERSPECTIVE

Benefits are derived from change initiatives so it might be wondered why a portfolio-based approach to benefits management is necessary. The reasons why this is so important are because it helps ensure:

- Consistent alignment of change initiatives with the organization's strategic objectives and performance management system.
- Good practice is repeatable across all initiatives within the change portfolio – with consequent efficiency savings and enhanced effectiveness in terms of benefits realization.
- Double counting (i.e. where the same benefits are claimed by, and used to justify, more than one initiative) is minimized.
- Lessons are learned and applied more widely.
- Benefits realization and value for money from available resources is optimized.

Important note

Managing benefits at a portfolio level does not mean you can dispense with doing it on individual change initiatives, although a portfolio-based approach helps ensure consistency, a 'clear line of sight', efficiency in the use of resources, and effectiveness in terms of optimizing benefits realization.

The six main elements of portfolio-based benefits management identified in MoP are as follows:

1. Benefits eligibility rules including a consistent approach to benefits categorization.

2. A portfolio-level Benefits Realization Plan, including consideration of dependencies and portfolio-level benefits risks and opportunities.

3. Inclusion of re-appraisal of the benefits from change initiatives at stage/phase gates and portfolio-level reviews.

4. Effective arrangements to manage benefits post-project/programme closure.

5. Clear arrangements for benefits tracking and reporting at a portfolio level, including via the Portfolio Dashboard Report.

6. Regular and robust post-implementation reviews and feeding lessons learned back into forecasting and the benefits management practices.

In addition to further consideration of the above, including practical examples, Chapter 10 also considers the roles and responsibilities for benefits management at a portfolio level, along with the main portfolio-level benefits management documentation.

3.7 PRINCIPLE 6. APPLY EFFECTIVE GOVERNANCE

The importance of governance in relation to benefits has been highlighted by the NAO (2011), who reported that *"weak governance structures and poor performance management systems have resulted in missed benefits"*.

But what is governance? It is defined as encompassing the structures, accountabilities and policies, standards and process for decision-making within an organization for business change to answer the four key strategic questions of 'Are we doing the right things?', 'Are we doing them the right way?', 'Are we getting them done well?' and 'Are we getting the benefits?'.

Accountability lies at the heart of effective governance. Where there is no clear means of determining who is accountable for an initiative, for the enabling and business changes upon which benefits realization is dependent, and for realization of the required benefits, the result can be what is termed moral hazard. This is a situation in which people's behaviour is altered because they are insulated against an outcome, such as non-realization of planned benefits (just as those with insurance may not take as much care of their belongings as they would without insurance). As we shall see, this does not mean that we seek to attribute blame, rather we seek to influence behaviour by ensuring clear allocation of accountabilities and transparent reporting of performance, as a basis for learning and continuous improvement.

In relation to benefits management, the four key characteristics of effective governance are that it is clear, aligned, consistent and active. These characteristics are addressed in turn.

3.7.1 Clear Governance

There should be clarity/transparency about:

■ Who is responsible for what, and accountable to whom – at both the portfolio level and the individual initiative level – and that includes clear business-based accountability for the change initiative, as well as accountability for all enabling and business changes, and both the intermediate and end benefits.

■ What decisions are made, where, when, by whom and using what criteria – and that includes:
   ☐ Clear lines of delegated responsibility.
   ☐ Rules and routes for escalation where variances from plan arise.
   ☐ Regular reviews of progress via initiative reporting, stage/phase gates and portfolio-level reviews.

■ How benefits are categorized and managed, and how they contribute to the organization's objectives by explicitly describing the assumptions underpinning the organization's business model.

This is aided by documenting the governance structures, including key roles and decision rules, and benefits management practices in a Portfolio Benefits Management Framework (see Chapter 10).

3.7.2 Aligned Governance

Responsibilities and accountabilities for benefits management should be aligned:

■ Top down and bottom up, i.e. from the portfolio to the individual initiative and vice versa.
■ With the organization's wider governance framework – so that board members see benefits realization from the change portfolio as a priority.

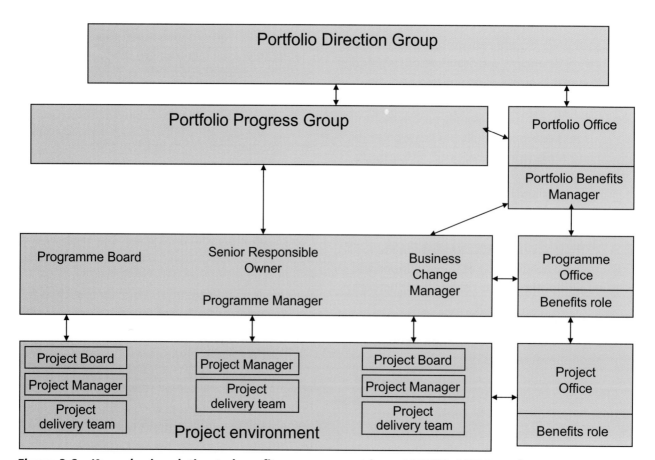

Figure 3.6 – Key roles in relation to benefits management in an MSP/MoP/P3O environment

An overview of the key benefits management roles at initiative and portfolio level, and their relationships based on the guidance in MSP, *'Portfolio, Programme and Project Offices'* (P3O) and MoP, is shown in Figure 3.6. Further information on the key roles and their responsibilities is contained in later chapters and in Appendix C.

What is emphasized is that:

- In addition to the roles shown in Figure 3.6, Benefit Owners, in the business areas affected, should be identified – they are responsible for the realization of individual benefits.
- This Guide reflects the governance recommended in MSP, MoP and P3O, but organizations do not need to follow this to the letter – different job titles may exist and the responsibilities identified may be shared by more than one person. What is important is that someone owns the responsibilities identified in Appendix C.
- Whoever performs these roles, their responsibilities should be reflected in the relevant role profiles/job descriptions and/or performance agreements.

3.7.3 Consistent Governance

Governance should be premised on consistent application of the benefits management practices to effectively address the issue of 'box ticking', where people adhere to the letter rather than the spirit of the law, and prevent by-passing of agreed processes on the pretext of operational necessity.

This does not mean that benefits management practices should be applied inflexibly – but variations from agreed processes should be subject to approval by the appropriate authority (the Portfolio Direction Group/Investment Committee or Progress Group/Change Delivery Committee in an MoP environment), and the rationale for such decisions should be recorded and communicated to all those involved.

Consistent governance is aided by the agreement of an escalations process and application of the technique of 'management by exception' whereby variances from plan that exceed a pre-set control

limit are escalated to the next governance level for consideration as to what action is appropriate (e.g. where the benefits forecast or benefits realization varies from plan by +/–10%).

3.7.4 Active Governance

Effective governance depends upon an active rather than passive approach based on:

- Ongoing engagement of business managers, staff and users in change initiatives from the start. What we are talking about here is more than just regular communication until the initiative is completed and handed over to business as usual (BAU). Rather we mean the business taking real ownership of change initiatives and realization of the anticipated benefits, via the Senior Responsible Owner and Business Change Manager, agreeing Benefit Owners, and bringing the 'voice of the customer' into the very heart of the development of the initiative via customer insight.

- Planning for success rather than detecting failure and attributing blame; with an emphasis on an active search for emergent benefits throughout the business change lifecycle; and creating value by leveraging existing capability rather than passive tracking to check that planned benefits have been realized.

- What Thorp (2003) calls activist accountability – *"which goes beyond traditional notions of passive accountability. It includes the concept of 'ownership' – meaning active, continuous involvement in managing a program and, most importantly, clear ownership of each measurable outcome and the associated benefits"*. Significantly, it is also based on willing acceptance by the individual that *"the buck starts here"*.

This last point highlights that governance mechanisms need to be allied to appropriate changed behaviours if we are to achieve the results required. This is addressed in the next principle.

3.8 PRINCIPLE 7. DEVELOP A VALUE CULTURE

Effective benefits management is enhanced by the shift from a delivery-centric culture, where the focus is on delivering capability to time, cost and quality standards, to a value-centric culture, where the primary focus is on delivering value (APM, March, 2011). In short, we need a culture that takes benefits and benefits management seriously, that focuses on creating and sustaining value from an organization's investments, and that extends beyond initiative closure.

Unfortunately, research finds that there is often room for improvement in this regard, with many focusing on process rather than outcomes. For example, a report by Moorhouse Consulting for the *Financial Times* (2009) found that only 20% of respondents believe their organizations succeed in consistently delivering the planned benefits of change, and research by Ward (2006) found that, *"The data also indicates that organisations have undue faith in the business cases and that the deployment of formal methodologies gives managers a false sense of security, and perhaps an excuse for not becoming sufficiently involved."* The bottom line is clear – business managers must take active responsibility for benefits realization.

How to address this? Well, firstly, we should recognize that successful implementation of benefits management and sustaining progress is a business change programme in its own right – further guidance on this issue is included in Chapter 11.

Secondly, don't be too impatient. New behaviour won't happen overnight, but if you adopt effective benefits management practices consistently and for all change initiatives, then behavioural change will follow particularly among the project and programme management (PPM) professionals and business managers directly involved. Beer et al (1990) argue that most change programmes fail because they are premised on the flawed belief that changing individual's attitudes will lead to changed behaviour, which when repeated across many people results in organizational change. In fact they argue the reverse is true and that, *"individual behaviour is powerfully shaped by the organizational roles*

that people play". The most effective way to achieve the desired cultural and behavioural change is therefore to start with revised governance, roles and benefits management practices – and this in turn will result in changed behaviours. Beer and his colleagues emphasize that achieving behavioural change is facilitated by three interrelated factors. These are the three Cs of:

1. **Coordination** – ensuring sufficient attention is given to opportunities for sharing and disseminating lessons learned across the organization. A Benefits Management Forum can be useful here.

2. **Commitment** – to drive *"the effort, initiative and cooperation that coordinated action demands"*.

3. **Competencies** – ensuring sufficient and ongoing training to build and enhance the competencies and capabilities within the organization.

Addressing all three of the above is crucial – many change initiatives fail because they address only one or two of these factors. We will revisit these factors, and in particular 1 and 3, in Chapter 11 when we consider how to implement and sustain benefits management, but for the time being we focus on the issue of commitment and, in particular, senior management commitment.

Thirdly, one of the keys to rapid progress in developing a value culture is senior management commitment – not curiosity or interest, but commitment. This is because there is nothing more effective in demonstrating to everyone that benefits are taken seriously and to help address the obstacles that usually arise at some point. Strategies to build senior management commitment include:

■ Nomination of a board-level champion – in an MoP environment this will be the Business Change/Portfolio Director. In other organizations it could be the Finance Director (depending on the importance of financial benefits), the Director of Strategic Planning, or indeed an influential non-executive director.

But whoever it is they must lead by example in taking a visible and active role driving the benefits management agenda forward.

■ Winning the support of influential non-executive directors who are able to encourage their executive colleagues to take benefits management seriously.

■ Demonstrating the benefits others have achieved (an application of social proof discussed in Chapter 8).

■ Communicating benefits and benefits management in a language that makes sense to senior managers – so communicate clearly and consistently, and ensure the contribution of change initiatives, and the portfolio as a whole, to organizational objectives and business priorities is clear.

■ Align senior management responsibilities for benefits management with the performance management, reward and recognition systems – financial rewards are not necessarily the best way to motivate people, but inconsistencies between desired behaviours and the organization's reward and recognition systems can be a real obstacle to progress because they send mixed messages about what is regarded as important.

■ Expect senior management to actively engage in the process. This doesn't mean we necessarily expect senior managers to track individual benefits, but they should actively and collectively debate the merits of all initiatives in the change portfolio. The technique of 'decision conferencing', as developed by Professor Larry Phillips at the London School of Economics, can play a key role in building commitment to benefits management – an application of the argument above that the roles people play can lead to attitudinal and behavioural change. So what is 'decision conferencing'? It is a technique whereby managers consider and debate, in a facilitated workshop, the:

☐ Relative weightings to attach to the organization's objectives.

☐ Percentage of available funds to allocate to each objective in the context of current business priorities.
☐ Criteria to be used to assess strategic contribution in each case.
☐ Scores/ratings to allocate to individual change initiatives.

In this way senior management comes to a collective decision on the composition of the portfolio. This has been found to be very effective in terms of optimizing portfolio returns, and also results in enhanced commitment to the portfolio management practices, including benefits management.

3.9 CHAPTER SUMMARY

The benefits management principles represent the foundations upon which effective benefits management practices are built. The seven principles are:

1. **Align benefits with strategy** – via, for example, driver-based analysis, so that we can assess the strategic contribution of individual change initiatives in a meaningful and consistent manner.

2. **Start with the end in mind** – with benefits-led rather than activity-centred change. Benefits should determine the solution rather than vice versa.

3. **Utilize successful delivery methods** – benefits realization is dependent on effective initiative delivery and change management. '*Best Management Practice*' methods such as PRINCE2 and MSP provide flexible solutions to achieve this. However, we also live in an increasingly complex world characterized by uncertainty and ambiguity – and this calls for the adoption of agile and modular approaches to initiative development; tight control over the start of initiatives; regular independent review to ensure the initiative is still strategically aligned and represents value for money; and effective approaches to achieve the business and behavioural change upon which benefits realization is dependent.

4. **Integrate benefits with performance management** – including linking benefits measures to the organization's KPIs and making use of data available from the management information system; 'booking' benefits into budgets, headcount targets, unit costs and performance targets (including those contained in the Balanced Scorecard); aligning responsibilities for benefits management with individuals' performance objectives; and aligning responsibilities for benefits management with the reward and recognition processes.

5. **Manage benefits from a portfolio perspective** – so ensuring consistent approaches to assessing strategic contribution; good practice is repeatable across all initiatives within the change portfolio; double counting is minimized; lessons are learned and applied more widely; and benefits realization and value for money from available resources is optimized.

6. **Apply effective governance** – the characteristics of which are that it is clear, aligned, consistent and active.

7. **Develop a value culture** – which can be achieved by managing the implementation of benefits management as a business change programme; recognizing that active engagement in the process can lead to behavioural change, with a focus on coordination, commitment and competencies; and building senior management commitment by their active involvement via techniques such as 'decision conferencing'.

Chapter 4

Chapter 4 – The Benefits Management Cycle

4.1 OVERVIEW OF THIS CHAPTER

In this chapter we begin our examination of the Benefits Management Cycle and its constituent practices, which will be covered in detail in the next five chapters. We also consider the context within which it operates; some of the barriers to effective practice and how to overcome them; the Key Success Characteristics of benefits management; and an overview of the key benefits management roles, responsibilities and documentation.

4.2 THE BENEFITS MANAGEMENT CYCLE

The Benefits Management Cycle is applied at an individual initiative level. Coverage of benefits management from a portfolio perspective is addressed in Chapter 10.

The Benefits Management Cycle used by 'Managing Successful Programmes' (MSP) represents a generic approach for programme management and consists of the following four stages: identify, plan, deliver and review. For the purposes of this Guide we have:

■ Expanded this cycle to encompass the five practices illustrated in Figure 4.1. The reasons for this expansion are to provide more in-depth and benefits-focused coverage of the key benefits management practices.

■ Replaced the term 'stage' with 'practice' – the use of the term 'practice' rather than 'stage' emphasizes the iterative rather than fixed sequential nature of the Benefits Management Cycle.

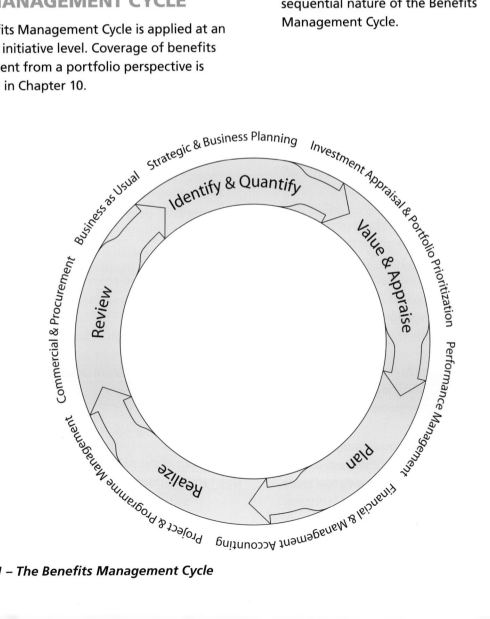

Figure 4.1 – The Benefits Management Cycle

These practices are covered as follows:

- **Chapter 5. Identify & Quantify** – here we consider approaches to identifying benefits (including benefits discovery workshops, benefits mapping and 'customer insight') as well as forecasting the scale of improvement anticipated, problems typically faced and relevant solutions.

- **Chapter 6. Value & Appraise** – next we address why organizations value benefits in **monetary** terms (to inform options and investment appraisal, and portfolio prioritization); approaches to valuing non-financial benefits in monetary terms; the role of value management techniques; and the main approaches to initiative appraisal – cost-benefit, real options, cost-effectiveness, and multi-criteria analysis. Note – our focus here is less on independent appraisal of the Business Case than the approaches to appraisal used in developing the Business Case.

- **Chapter 7. Plan** – having identified, quantified, valued and appraised the benefits to confirm the rationale for investment, we need to plan for benefits realization. This encompasses approaches to validating and prioritizing benefits; managing pre-transition activities; selecting benefits measures; benefits risk and opportunity management; planning stakeholder engagement; and bringing all the aforementioned together in the main initiative-level benefits management documentation and the Business Case.

- **Chapter 8. Realize** – covering transition management; tracking, reporting including collecting survey evidence, and taking corrective action; and effective approaches to stakeholder engagement to achieve behavioural change by winning hearts as well as minds.

- **Chapter 9. Review** – the importance of review as a basis for learning and continuous improvement before, during and after the initiative.

It should be noted that while this cycle is broadly sequential, it incorporates iterative feedback loops throughout the cycle – so, for example, as we shall see in Chapter 9, we shouldn't wait until after benefits realization to review progress.

Important note

Managing benefits is **not** a **fixed** series of staged practices, one following the other in strict sequence. Rather it is based on a series of practices with iterative feedback loops so that, for example, plans are updated in the light of experience throughout the cycle.

What Figure 4.1 also highlights is that the Benefits Management Cycle doesn't operate in isolation. As a recent APM thought leadership report (May, 2012a) says, we *"need to avoid deploying a silo-based approach; especially one which only focuses on project and programme management"*. Indeed, benefits management operates within a wider organizational context encompassing coordination with the key functions and activities identified in Figure 4.1:

- Strategic & Business Planning
- Investment Appraisal & Portfolio Prioritization
- Performance Management
- Financial & Management Accounting
- Project & Programme Management
- Commercial & Procurement
- Business as Usual.

Important note

It is crucial that we avoid creating a parallel industry that treats benefits management as a separate discipline. This is costly and ineffective. Benefits management should be coordinated with, and integrated into, the organization's strategic planning, PPM and performance management systems in particular.

The main areas of common concern between benefits management and the key functions/activities in this wider organizational context are shown in Table 4.1.

Table 4.1 – Integration of benefits into the wider organizational context

Key activities/functions	Main benefits-related areas of common concern
Strategic & Business Planning	■ Benefits are related to strategic objectives so that strategic contribution can be clearly identified. ■ Benefits reviews are used to validate the business model (the elements in the model, their respective drivers and linkages between them). ■ Information on what works is fed back to strategic planners and policy-makers.
Investment Appraisal & Portfolio Prioritization	The importance of this is shown by research from McKinseys (2012), which found that organizations that are good at capital allocation and management are worth on average 40% more over a 15-year time span than those who perform less well. So ensure: ■ Benefits are clearly and consistently articulated to provide a 'level playing field' for investment appraisal and portfolio prioritization. ■ Benefits are incorporated into assessments of both return/attractiveness (the scale of the benefits over costs required to realize those benefits) and risk/achievability (i.e. how likely is it that those benefits will be realized).
Performance Management – encompassing operational and HR performance management	Operational performance management ■ Linking benefits measures to the organization's key performance indicators (KPIs) and making use of data available from the management information system. ■ Ensuring planned benefits are reflected in business unit plans, performance targets and budgets where appropriate. HR performance management ■ Aligning responsibilities for benefits management with the reward and recognition processes. ■ Reflecting responsibility for benefits realization in individuals' performance targets.
Financial & Management Accounting	■ Consistent rules for valuing benefits in monetary terms. ■ 'Booking' cashable benefits in budget baselines.
Project & Programme Management	■ 'Starting with the end in mind' – ensuring benefits-led change. ■ Ensuring successful delivery as an enabler for benefits realization.
Commercial & Procurement	■ Incentivizing suppliers to realize benefits by arrangements that include: gain-sharing arrangements (where both parties share the benefits realized); risk-reward (where the supplier is paid to take on the risk of benefits not being realized); and transaction-based charging (where the supplier bears the risk that demand won't be as great as intended). ■ Payment by results (dependent on those results being clearly defined and attributable). ■ Savings from outsourcing – ensuring quality standards don't suffer.

Table continues

Table 4.1 continued

Key activities/functions	Main benefits-related areas of common concern
Business as Usual	■ Business change is appropriately scheduled. ■ Benefit Owners are identified in the affected parts of the business. ■ Planned benefits are realized. ■ Emergent benefits are fully leveraged. ■ Dis-benefits are mitigated as far as is possible.

4.3 THE BARRIERS TO EFFECTIVE AND EFFICIENT BENEFITS MANAGEMENT AND OVERCOMING THEM

We saw in Chapter 2 that not only do many organizations struggle to realize the benefits forecast but they also have problems in implementing effective benefits management regimes. Why might this be?

4.3.1 Difficulties in Determining Benefits Realization

One explanation concerns the very real difficulties organizations sometimes face in determining whether benefits have been realized due to:

■ The (often long) time lag between a decision to invest in an initiative and the benefits actually being realized. Solutions – break the initiative down into modules, and track lead indicators and intermediate benefits so that early feedback on impact is collected.

■ The loss of learning as staff and Senior Responsible Owners (SROs)/sponsors move positions within the organization and take with them the tacit knowledge they have acquired. Solutions – retain staff for the duration of the change initiative, shorter and modular developments, and effective handover arrangements including formal sign-over of commitment to benefits realization.

■ The desire to get started with the initiative, which means that baseline data against which to measure the realization of benefits is not available. Solutions – start measuring from an early stage and relate benefits to existing performance measures in the management information system.

■ Existing performance measures are not utilized, meaning that benefits measurement comes with an unwelcome price tag. Solutions – relate benefits to existing performance measures in the management information system wherever possible, and build benefits data collection into the system design where applicable.

■ The outcomes of an initiative are a combination of intended and unintended consequences, with often ambiguous causes. Consequently, it can be difficult to determine what caused what – the attribution problem. Solutions – benefits mapping, tracking lead indicators and intermediate benefits to provide confidence in the realization of end benefits, and the use of confidence ratings.

■ Some benefits and outcomes are difficult to measure reliably. Solutions – track lead indicators, intermediate benefits and use proxy indicators.

■ The common problem that change initiatives are closed down before the changes have been embedded as BAU and benefits have been fully realized. This is one of the eight reasons identified by Kotter (1995) as to why transformational change initiatives commonly fail. Solutions – don't declare victory too early, effective handover of responsibility for benefits management when the initiative closes, and continuing to monitor benefits post-initiative closure at a portfolio level.

Beyond the factors identified above, there are an additional three barriers to effective benefits management: common misconceptions about what benefits and benefits management are really about, what has been referred to as the 'knowing–doing' gap, and a series of cognitive biases. We consider each of these in turn.

4.3.2 Common Misconceptions

There are a number of common misconceptions that often compromise the effectiveness of benefits management and the realization of benefits in practice. Arising from the discussion in Chapter 2 it can be seen that benefits management is **not**:

1. A 'silver bullet' – Processes and practices, no matter how well designed, cannot compensate for ineffective governance and lack of management commitment. We therefore need to combine benefits management practices with effective governance and a value culture.

2. An 'out of the box' solution – The approaches adopted need to be tailored to the local circumstances and specifically the organization's:
   - ☐ Strategic objectives.
   - ☐ Scale of investment in change initiatives.
   - ☐ The complexity of those initiatives.
   - ☐ Existing strategic planning, investment appraisal and portfolio prioritization, project and programme, financial, performance and risk management processes and practices.
   - ☐ Experience and track record in terms of benefits realization.
   - ☐ Governance structure.
   - ☐ Culture.

   For example, in relation to the last point – the approach to benefits management needs to align with the culture and values of the organization including the degree of centralization/decentralization of authority, approach to accountability and delegation of responsibility, and commitment to front-line empowerment.

So, there is no 'one true way' to effective benefits management. The adoption of consistent approaches is crucial, but the determination of exactly which approaches to adopt should reflect the above factors. Consequently, rather than prescribing a single solution, this Guide provides an overview of various techniques available, and examples illustrating how organizations have adopted the practices in real life. Guidance is included to assist the practitioner in determining when each technique is most appropriate.

3. An approach that identifies and manages benefits from a pre-identified solution (or at least it shouldn't be) – One indicator that something is wrong is when teams struggle to identify the benefits from an initiative. The solution is to take a benefits-led approach and start with the benefits required. To emphasize – benefits should be the rationale for investment not a means to justify a pre-selected solution.

4. About managing benefits from an initiative perspective with at best limited consideration given to what is going on elsewhere in the portfolio – The results are seen in double counting of benefits, ineffective dependency management and poorly scheduled business change – and so the failure to optimize benefits realization from the available funds. The solution is to adopt portfolio-based benefits management.

5. A linear, bureaucratic process concerned with passive monitoring against forecast – As stated above, and repeated throughout this Guide, it is crucial that iterative feedback loops are applied all the way through the Benefits Management Cycle with lessons being actively sought throughout as a basis for learning and continuous improvement. It is also crucial that monitoring is active with the aim of taking effective intervention when things are not on track.

6. A specialism – That's not to say that there isn't a place for benefits management specialists, but rather to emphasize that such specialists should clearly support business managers in the delivery of benefits-led change initiatives.

7. An additional bureaucracy or new 'cottage industry' – Yes, benefits management comes with a price tag and needs to be appropriately resourced, but it's one that should be more than paid for by the improvements in benefits actually realized. Indeed, applied with intelligence, effective benefits management can be achieved with less effort than is currently expended as long as change initiatives are set up to succeed from the start, focus on the key benefits, and if we integrate the approach more effectively with the functions and activities identified in Table 4.1.

8. Concerned with making the inevitable happen – Too often it is assumed that benefits just happen (i.e. all we need to do is to complete the initiative and the benefits that were included in the Business Case will be automatically realized). This misconception manifests itself in the confusion of business and enabling changes (a new IT system and training programme for example) and the benefits that arise from those changes (realization of time savings and productivity improvements etc.). This misconception also results in an underestimation of the focus required to realize the benefits. For example, research undertaken by Donald Marchand at IMD (Marchand, 2004), shows that IT can deliver business value, but the key is usage not deployment. He argues that while organizations devote 90% of their efforts to deployment this only accounts for 25% of the business value, and relatively little effort is directed at realizing the 75% of value that derives from increased usage of information. The coverage of ongoing participative stakeholder engagement in Chapter 8 is of relevance here.

Beyond difficulties in measuring benefits realization and the misconceptions outlined above, there is also evidence that people in a wide variety of managerial disciplines suffer from what has been termed the 'knowing–doing' gap.

4.3.3 The 'Knowing–Doing' Gap

Pfeffer & Sutton (2000) argue that there is a paradox in many areas of management in that good practice is known, but rarely applied. There is evidence that this applies to benefits management in that much of the current guidance has been around for at least a decade, and yet, as we saw in Chapter 2, many organizations struggle to implement it effectively. Reasons for this failure to apply known good practice include: talk is a lot easier than action; the tendency to fall back on old habits (note the status quo bias in Appendix D); and not taking benefits seriously enough. For example, research in the area of project portfolio management has found that:

- Benefits management rated 25th out of 27 portfolio management office functions in one report (Hobbs).
- Across 10 dimensions of project portfolio management, perceptions of maturity were lowest for benefits management, with an average rating of 3.83 out of 10 (Jenner & Byatt, 2012).

This is partly due to the multi-disciplinary and cross-functional nature of benefits management requiring extensive coordination. But another explanation is that we suffer from a range of cognitive biases that negatively affect benefits management in practice.

4.3.4 Cognitive Biases Affecting Benefits Management

Psychologists have identified that we use unconscious routines and shortcuts to cope with complexity in daily life. These routines are called 'heuristics' and for the most part they serve us well – for example, Hammond et al (1998) cite the example of how, in judging distance, our minds frequently rely on a heuristic that equates clarity with proximity. Yet these heuristics are not without issue, and psychologists have identified a series of flaws, or cognitive biases and illusions, that can cause managers to violate the principles of rational decision-making. We shall see in Chapter 5 that these cognitive biases can affect the accuracy and reliability of our benefits forecasts. We will also see in Chapter 9 that they can limit our ability to learn from experience, but for now we concentrate on some cognitive biases that can limit the effectiveness of benefits management more generally – by skewing investment decision-making, or by negatively influencing the practices we adopt to manage benefits.

The most powerful of such biases is simple over-confidence. The result is what is termed the 'planning fallacy', or the tendency to believe that our change initiative will proceed as planned, even when knowing that many similar initiatives have been delivered late, cost more than planned, and failed to realize the forecast benefits. In this regard it is interesting to note the conclusions of a research study into SRO attitudes by Moorhouse Consulting (2009): *"Only 10% of SROs feel business cases and benefits realisation are adequately understood on programmes across Government and industry, however over 60% feel the understanding on their own programmes is adequate."*

Cognitive biases that negatively impact the effectiveness of benefits management also include: the illusion of control, the status quo bias, the sunk cost effect, confirmation bias, framing, mental accounting, ignoring regression to the mean, the endowment effect and the affect heuristic. A description of these biases, and their impact on benefits management, is included in Appendix D.

4.3.5 Addressing These Cognitive Biases

The biases outlined above are described as 'illusions' because, as with many optical illusions, they persist even when we are aware of them. The solution is therefore to not only be aware of them, but also to take deliberate steps to guard against them by:

- Senior management acceptance that some change initiatives will fail. As Hammond et al (1998) say, *"By acknowledging that some good ideas will end in failure, executives will encourage people to cut their losses rather than let them mount"*.

- Post-implementation and post-investment reviews examining not only the results that occurred but also the quality of the decision-making.

- Exposing the benefits forecasts included in Business Cases to independent challenge. As Kahneman (2011a) says, *"it is much easier to identify a minefield when you observe others wandering into it than when you are about to do so"*. So apply regular independent stage/phase gate reviews and the technique of 'staged release of funding'.

- Training and developing staff so that they are aware of the cognitive biases that influence decision-making.

- Addressing the need not only for repeatable processes (as detailed in Chapters 5–9) but also the principles in Chapter 3 that underpin their effective operation.

One other thing – in applying the practices outlined in the following five chapters (and the seven principles in Chapter 3), keep in mind the Key Success Characteristics of effective benefits management listed below in Section 4.4.

Example 4.1 – Avoiding confirmation bias

The Tell Us Once programme has sought to avoid the risk of seeking confirmatory evidence and discounting anything else. The programme has therefore officially adopted a policy of *'all feedback is good feedback'* – benefits reports include provision for feedback on areas in which improved performance is required. Engagement activities with local authorities also stress this point (see the survey in Example 8.5), and the case studies that are prepared also include sections on what didn't go as anticipated.

Provided with the kind agreement of Matthew Briggs, Programme Manager, Tell Us Once.

4.4 THE KEY SUCCESS CHARACTERISTICS OF EFFECTIVE BENEFITS MANAGEMENT

Beyond the consistent operation of the practices contained within the Benefits Management Cycle, and the principles discussed in the previous chapter, we can also identify the following Key Success Characteristics of effective benefits management:

■ **Active** – rather than passive tracking against forecast, the focus is on an active search for benefits, with ongoing participative stakeholder engagement. As Thorp (2003) says, *"Benefits realization is a continuous process of envisioning results, implementing, checking intermediate results and dynamically adjusting the path leading from investments to business results."* This is reflected in the title of this Guide – *'Managing Benefits'* is an active process.

■ **Evidence-based** – forecasts and practices are driven by evidence about what works rather than assumptions and advocacy. In many cases such an evidence base will be lacking and so one benefit of implementing benefits management will be the development of an evidence base to inform and guide investments going forward.

■ **Transparent** – based on open and honest forecasting and reporting, and a 'clear line of sight' from strategic objectives to benefits forecast and realized.

■ **Benefits-led** – focusing less on the activities undertaken to realize benefits and more on the actual realization of those benefits, i.e. just as we expect change initiatives to be benefits-led, so too should benefits management be focused on what difference it is making.

■ **Forward-looking** – with an emphasis on learning and continuous improvement, rather than backward-looking attribution of blame.

■ **Managed across the full business change lifecycle** – extending from benefits identification and quantification through to

realization and capturing and applying lessons learned. As Glynne (2012) says, *"Benefits realisation can no longer be considered an add-on at the tail end of project delivery"*.

These characteristics should run throughout the Benefits Management Cycle and its constituent practices.

4.5 OVERVIEW OF THE KEY ROLES, RESPONSIBILITIES AND DOCUMENTATION

Before we begin our more in-depth consideration of the benefits management practices, it is worth having in mind an overview of the key roles involved, their responsibilities and the main benefits documentation where much of the analysis and activity will be recorded.

In an MSP environment responsibility for benefits management sits with the following:

■ The **Senior Responsible Owner** (SRO) – the single individual who is accountable for the programme, with overall responsibility for ensuring that it meets its objectives and delivers the projected benefits. As such, the SRO represents a single point of (business-based) accountability.

The effectiveness of the SRO role has been the subject of some debate, not least in relation to a failure to ensure benefits realization post-transition and initiative closure. The problem, however, seems to lie less in the concept of a single point of business-based accountability than in its application. Too often SROs are selected rather than volunteer, don't have the authority to ensure all required changes happen, and have to fit the role into their existing responsibilities. The NAO (2006) found that half were in their first SRO role and, *"around half spend less than 20 per cent of their time on the role. This lack of experience and focus is compounded by the limited amount of support given to Senior Responsible Owners, with a striking 38 per cent of Senior Responsible Owners having no involvement with a Centre of Excellence and 20 per cent rating their support as poor."* The solutions lie in benefits-led change initiatives, where the benefits are clearly aligned with the business objectives for which the SRO is responsible; where these benefits are related to the SRO's personal objectives; and more effective support from Programme and Portfolio Offices. To emphasize – aligning benefits with the performance management regime includes the SRO's personal objectives and the objectives of the business unit or function for which the SRO is accountable. One other thing – the SRO should be the SRO for the benefits, rather than the initiative designed to deliver those benefits.

■ The **Programme Manager** – responsible for developing the Benefits Management Strategy and the Benefits Realization Plan in consultation with the Business Change Manager and business managers, preparing the Business Case and initiating benefits reviews.

■ The **Business Change Manager** – a 'business-side' role whose responsibilities extend beyond the life of the initiative, and who reports to the SRO. Responsible for identifying and quantifying the benefits with support from business stakeholders and PPM staff; establishing benefits measures, producing the Benefit Profiles and agreeing them with the Benefit Owners; monitoring the delivery of the required enabling and business changes; reporting on benefits realization; updating the Benefit Profiles and Benefits Realization Plan when required; and initiating benefits reviews after the closure of the initiative. Note they represent, *"the bridge between the programme and business operations, since the individual(s) will be an integral part of business operations."* (MSP).

■ The **Benefit Owner** – the individual responsible for the realization of a benefit and who agrees the Benefit Profile prepared by the Business Change Manager. The OGC's (2005b) short guide to managing benefits emphasizes that *"The SRO must assign responsibility to named individuals in the business area with a clear statement of the benefits they are to deliver"*.

From the above it can be seen that much of the detailed work undertaken as part of the Benefits Management Cycle addressed in the next five chapters, will fall to the Business Change Manager. But note that MSP does not see the role being filled by a single individual – indeed, the role is typically allocated to more than one person. The Business Change Manager will also be assisted by the Programme/Project Office in facilitating agreement of the Benefits Management Strategy, the Benefits Realization Plan and the Benefit Profile; tracking benefits realization against plan; collating benefits data for reporting purposes; gathering information for the benefits reviews; and maintaining benefits information under change control.

'Portfolio, Programme and Project Offices' (P3O) also envisages a benefits role within a portfolio (see Chapter 10 in relation to the Portfolio Benefits Manager role), programme or project office (referred to as a Benefits Manager in this Guide). This role provides a benefits realization support service to Programme Managers, Business Managers and Business Change Managers and encompasses the following responsibilities: leading benefits and dis-benefits identification activities; developing and maintaining the Benefits Map; assisting the Programme Manager in developing the Benefits Management Strategy; tracking and reporting on the realization of benefits by the business; and working with the Business Managers and/or Business Change Managers to identify additional opportunities for benefits realization, and to minimize dis-benefits.

Further guidance on benefits management roles and responsibilities is contained in Appendix C.

Important note

This Guide reflects the governance recommended in MSP, MoP and P3O, but organizations do not need to follow this to the letter – different job titles may exist and the responsibilities identified may be shared by more than one person. What is important is that someone owns the responsibilities identified here and in Appendix C.

The key initiative-level benefits management documents are:

■ **Benefits Management Strategy** – This details how and by whom benefits will be managed on an initiative throughout the Benefits Management Cycle. It should be consistent with the Portfolio Benefits Management Framework and will guide activity undertaken throughout the Benefits Management Cycle.

■ **Benefits Map/Dependency Network** – This shows how project outputs combine to create capabilities, which transition into outcomes, and which in turn enable the realization of benefits, which contribute to organizational objectives; or how enabling and business changes combine to realize benefits that contribute to investment objectives.

■ **Benefit Profile** – This is the document that identifies the details associated with each benefit (and dis-benefit) including: when it will be realized, the measures that will be used and who is responsible for its realization – the benefit 'owner'. The Benefit Profile will therefore contain much of the information collected during the Identify & Quantify and Plan practices.

■ **Benefits Realization Plan** – This provides the baseline against which performance in terms of benefits realization can be tracked.

■ **Benefits Realization Report** – This provides information on benefits realization against the Benefits Realization Plan, emergent benefits and dis-benefits, and revised forecast. It can be reported in a variety of formats – see Section 8.4.3.1.

More detailed advice on the typical contents of these documents and an example Benefit Profile are contained in Appendix B.

4.6 CHAPTER SUMMARY

1. The Benefits Management Cycle consists of five practices: Identify & Quantify, Value & Appraise, Plan, Realize and Review.

2. While these practices are broadly sequential, their effective operation requires iterative feedback loops throughout the cycle.

3. Barriers to effective benefits management include the difficulties sometimes associated with measuring benefits; some common misconceptions about benefits and benefits management; the 'knowing–doing' gap; and a series of cognitive biases.

4. Addressing these barriers calls for us to address not only the practices of benefits management but also the principles discussed in Chapter 3. We also need to apply the Key Success Characteristics so that benefits management is active, evidence-based, transparent, benefits-led, forward-looking, and managed across the full business change lifecycle.

Chapter 5

Chapter 5 – Benefits Management Practice 1 – Identify & Quantify

5.1 OVERVIEW OF THIS CHAPTER

This chapter covers the first practice in the Benefits Management Cycle: Identify & Quantify. The objective of this practice is to lay the basis for: informed options analysis, investment appraisal, and portfolio prioritization; and the management of benefits realization in due course. Much of the analysis undertaken during this practice will be captured in the Benefit Profiles, Benefits Realization Plan and Business Case that are considered in Chapter 7.

This practice includes:

- The identification of benefits – primarily via benefits discovery workshops, benefits mapping and customer insight.
- Quantification of benefits – here we are concerned with forecasting/estimating the scale of benefits anticipated. We address the main problems faced in developing reliable benefits forecasts and the solutions.

The importance of this practice cannot be overstated because it lays the basis for all that follows. If we start off with inaccurate and unreliable benefits forecasts then subsequent management of these benefits is severely compromised.

5.1.1 Benefits Identification and Benefits-Led Change

One point should be emphasized – the focus in this practice should be less on identifying the benefits from a formally established initiative than, as was highlighted in our consideration of principle 2 in Chapter 3, on identifying the benefits required and then ensuring the solution is designed to realize these benefits, i.e. 'starting with the end in mind' with benefits-led change.

That said, we need to recognize that in many cases the initiative will have been established before detailed work on benefits commences – but this only emphasizes the importance of starting this practice as early in the business change lifecycle as possible – by identifying the 'end in mind' and working back to complete the picture, and, often, in the process redefining the opportunity or problem, and sometimes, even the solution itself.

5.2 IDENTIFY BENEFITS

We firstly consider the advantages of, and key factors to be considered in, running a benefits discovery workshop. We then examine some of the popular approaches to benefits mapping that are applied at such workshops, before considering approaches to customer/user engagement.

5.2.1 Benefits Discovery Workshops

Benefits discovery workshops are an effective method for:

- Identifying the strategic drivers, investment objectives and benefits for/from an initiative.

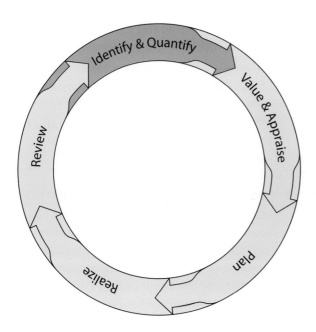

Figure 5.1 – The Identify & Quantify practice in the Benefits Management Cycle

- Ensuring the benefits identified are sound.
- Identifying the enabling and business changes required to achieve the outcomes and benefits desired.
- Establishing a 'clear line of sight' from investment objectives through to the required solution.
- Engaging stakeholders and building consensus around, and commitment to, an initiative, and so improving the likelihood of benefits realization.
- Building commitment to the Benefits Management Cycle itself.

As indicated above – the first step that should precede the identification of benefits is to consider the strategic drivers behind a change initiative and the investment objectives that follow from them. In short, we need clarity on what exactly the problem is that we are trying to solve, or what the opportunity is that can be exploited. These strategic drivers and investment objectives are then used to guide the identification of benefits. This is aided where driver-based analysis, as discussed in Chapter 3, has been undertaken. Another technique that is useful in identifying strategic drivers is 'SWOT' analysis. This encompasses:

Internal appraisal

- **S**trengths – to be leveraged/exploited
- **W**eaknesses – to be circumvented

External appraisal

- **O**pportunities – to exploit using our strengths
- **T**hreats – to be avoided

The external/environmental appraisal can be informed by using PESTLE analysis, i.e. considering the Political, Economic, Social, Technological, Legal and Environmental factors.

The main factors to consider in setting up a benefits discovery workshop are:

- **Membership** – this should include all affected stakeholders: the business sponsor, subject-matter experts, representatives from the business areas affected, initiative team members including the Programme/Project Manager and Business Change Manager, the Portfolio Benefits Manager (to ensure the approach adopted is consistent with the Portfolio Benefits Management Framework and to help identify dependencies and potential double counting with other change initiatives), and other stakeholders affected both positively and negatively by the change. Crucially, those present need to have the expertise and experience to identify the potential business benefits and dis-benefits (with appropriate support from the facilitator). Senior management involvement also pays dividends in demonstrating the importance of the activity.

- **Authority to act** – those present should have the authority to represent their part of the business (or other stakeholder group) and to agree the resulting analysis.

- **Duration** – experience shows that, while it may be tempting to try to cover everything in one go, anything more than half a day can be counter-productive. It is better to hold a series of workshops than risk disengaging key stakeholders with a session that runs for too long.

- **Agenda** – the workshop agenda should include:

  1. Introductions – so everyone knows who everyone else is and which part of the business or external stakeholder group they represent.

  2. Purpose – to develop a shared understanding of the objectives of the workshop. For example, *'to identify the key benefits from the initiative, the cause and effect chain underpinning the realization of those benefits, and any required business change'*.

  3. The 'rules of the game' – it is essential that all involved understand the protocols to be applied during the workshop – for example, *'no talking over others'*.

  4. Summary of the organization's approach to benefits management as defined in the Portfolio Benefits Management Framework.

5. Background briefing – including the desired contribution to strategic objectives: what problem is the initiative being designed to solve or what opportunity is it designed to exploit? This can be crucial – it is essential that the problem or opportunity is framed in a way that ensures the workshop focuses on the real issue at hand and considers all relevant factors. On the other hand it needs to be bounded appropriately – balancing the risk of attempting to 'boil the ocean' with the trap of developing sub-optimal solutions. It is also important that any assumptions are surfaced – so that participants are clear about the lines of demarcation between assumptions and evidence (between what we know and what we think we know), and between advocacy and analysis. The role of the facilitator is crucial in this regard. Note also that the Results Chain™ discussed below is one approach to benefits mapping that can assist with surfacing assumptions.

6. Production of a Benefits Map, open discussion or brainstorming to capture potential benefits – using the benefits categorization specified by the Portfolio Benefits Management Framework. Guidance on approaches to categorization is included in Chapter 10.

7. Conclusions, actions arising and next steps, with allocated responsibility and timescales for each action. This will include the date by which the draft Benefits Map will be circulated to participants for validation.

Note – don't waste time at the workshop 'dotting all the Is and crossing all the Ts' – the facilitator needs to know when enough is enough, call time, go away and tidy things up ready for the next round.

■ **The facilitator** – the success of the workshop is heavily dependent on a skilled and motivated facilitator. Their job is to ensure that the workshop achieves its objectives, while ensuring that everyone present is sufficiently involved. This calls for an active but impartial approach – active in the sense that the role requires that the workshop is steered towards its objectives, and impartial

in the sense that the facilitator's role is to help the attendees reach a shared understanding of the investment case, but not to impose their views on the group. A key aspect of the role is to play back the conclusions to the group at regular points throughout the workshop, and to capture key decisions as they arise. The essential features of effective benefits workshop facilitators are that they should be:

☐ Informed – facilitators should have an appreciation of the strategic drivers and investment objectives, where the initiative fits with the existing change portfolio, and any constraints affecting the initiative – so they can effectively steer the workshop towards its objectives.

☐ Intelligent – so they have the respect of those present.

☐ Impartial – so they are not associated with partisan views or special interests. This is where an external resource can be invaluable, either external to the organization, or to the areas impacted, so that they are not perceived as having a hidden agenda (and are also not afraid to ask 'foolish' questions).

Beyond these three features, effective facilitation also requires leadership – to guide and motivate those present to commit to the process. For example, skilled facilitation is crucial in ensuring an appropriate balance between the tendency for project team members to be overly optimistic about the potential benefits, and business representatives to be more pessimistic. What we want are views that are realistic, but which, at the same time, do not underestimate the potential benefits.

5.2.2 Benefits Mapping

The second approach to identifying benefits is benefits mapping. Various approaches to benefits mapping are in common use, but they usually fit into one of the following categories:

■ Logic chain approaches – where the focus is on showing how the initiative will result in benefits, which in turn contribute to strategic objectives via the drivers of each element in the organization's business model. Note that this chain may often be more assumed than factual – and the objectives of benefits management include:

☐ Testing the model – by surfacing assumptions, e.g. by asking: *'what would need to be true for this cause and effect relationship to hold?'.*

☐ Validating the assumptions underpinning the map or model by tracking and monitoring a suite of leading and lagging measures.

■ Business change approaches – where the focus is on identifying how enabling and business changes can be combined to deliver benefits.

■ A combination of the above.

Ultimately the choice of approach should reflect local needs (and be consistent with guidance in the organization's Portfolio Benefits Management Framework) but, whichever approach is adopted, it should be applied in a disciplined and rigorous manner so that the benefits identified (and in due course, quantified) provide a reliable basis for investment decisions and subsequent management through to realization. The other point to bear in mind is that much of the value lies in the process of completing the map, rather than in the map itself.

The following sub-sections outline four of the most common approaches to benefits mapping:

1. The *'Managing Successful Programmes'* (MSP) Benefits Map

2. The Results Chain™

3. The Benefits Dependency Network/Map

4. The Benefits Logic Map

Additionally there is the Investment Logic Map approach described in Chapter 3. Another approach – root cause modelling – is referred to in Appendix A.

5.2.2.1 The MSP Benefits Map

MSP states, *"Programme outputs, capabilities, outcomes and benefits are interrelated … and corporate objectives are not achieved by accident. It is important for programmes to carefully model the flow between these elements and monitor and manage their interdependencies thoroughly."* The approach suggested by MSP supports this by showing how project outputs combine to create capabilities, which transition into outcomes, and which in turn enable the realization of benefits, which contribute to corporate objectives. This is illustrated in Figure 5.2.

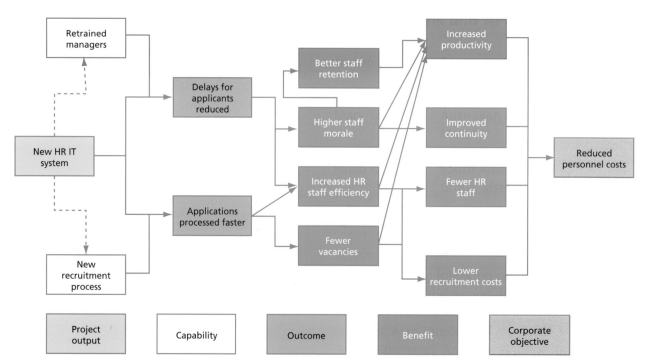

Figure 5.2 – The MSP Benefits Map: new HR system example

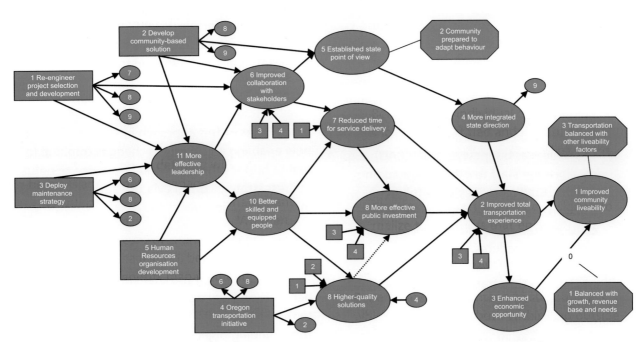

Figure 5.3 – Oregon Department of Transportation Results Chain (Source: Thorp, 2003)

It should be noted that it is recommended that the map be completed from right to left or, in an emergent programme for example, from both sides. In an MSP environment, the Benefits Map will be produced by the Business Change Manager (usually following a benefits discovery workshop), will be reviewed by the Programme Manager, and will be approved by the Senior Responsible Owner. This approach is obviously particularly suited to programmes being managed in accordance with MSP.

5.2.2.2 The Results Chain™

This benefits mapping technique was developed by the DMR Group (now part of Fujitsu Consulting), and described by Thorp (2003) in *The Information Paradox*. It provides a graphical representation of the events and conditions required to achieve stated business outcomes. It has four components:

- Outcomes – results sought including intermediate and ultimate outcomes (shown as circles).
- Initiatives – actions that contribute to one or more outcome (shown as squares).
- Contributions – by initiatives or intermediate outcomes in contributing to other initiatives or outcomes (shown as arrows).
- Assumptions – hypotheses about the realization of outcomes (shown as hexagons).

This is illustrated in Figure 5.3.

Advantages of this approach include that its completion at a workshop promotes discussion, consensus, commitment and shared understanding about how an initiative will add value. A particular strength is that by surfacing assumptions (the hexagons) it focuses on making implicit thinking explicit.

5.2.2.3 The Benefits Dependency Network (BDN)/Map

The BDN approach was developed by Cranfield University's Information Systems Research Centre (Ward & Daniel, 2006) and maps:

- Left to right – the enabling and business changes on which benefits realization from an initiative is dependent. Enabling and business changes are distinguished as follows:
  - Enabling changes are the necessary prerequisites for a business change to happen and are usually one-off – such as the implementation of a new IT system. Bradley (2006) sees enabling changes as something that can be developed, built or acquired, normally from outside the area where the benefits will be realized. Bradley also suggests enabling changes can be categorized as: people, process, information or technology.

☐ Business changes are the new ways of working needed in order that benefits will be realized – for example adoption of revised processes. Bradley (2006) sees these as changes to the business operations that utilize the enabler. They are usually ongoing and can take time to embed themselves as business as usual (BAU), e.g. re-allocating staff to other value-adding activity. Bradley suggests the following categorization for business changes: culture, strategies/policies, processes and practices/procedures.

■ Right to left – the strategic drivers and investment objectives to which the benefits contribute:

☐ Drivers represent senior management's views as to what is important and where change must occur within a given timescale, e.g. the need to increase market share, reduce costs, or improve services provided. As such they exist independently of any initiative.

☐ Investment objectives are an organizational target for achievement agreed for an initiative in relation to the drivers.

Note that an effective way of identifying drivers and investment objectives is via driver-based and/ or 'SWOT' analysis as referred to above.

The BDN approach is illustrated in Figure 5.4.

Advantages of this approach include the focus on how enabling and business changes combine to realize business benefits and how these benefits address strategic drivers via the agreed investment objectives.

Bradley (2006) suggests a variation (the Benefits Dependency Map). Firstly, a Benefits Map is completed showing the chain of intermediate benefits (and any dis-benefits) and how they lead to the end benefits, and in turn to achievement of the bounding objectives, i.e. the objectives (usually limited to three or four) that define the boundary of the initiative (the investment objectives in the BDN approach). As a second step, the enabling and business changes on which benefits realization is dependent are added to the map. The result is a comprehensive and detailed visualization of the intermediate to end benefits chain, and the business and enabling changes upon which realization of these benefits are dependent.

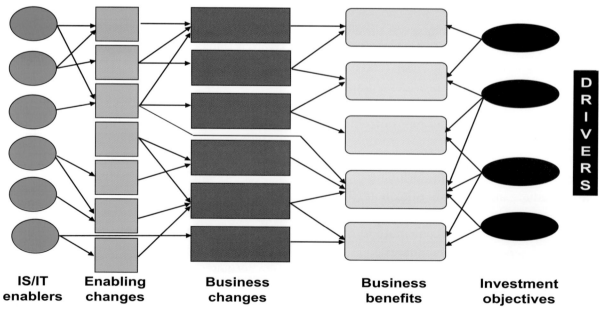

BENEFITS DEPENDENCY NETWORK

IS/IT enablers | Enabling changes | Business changes | Business benefits | Investment objectives

DRIVERS

Cranfield UNIVERSITY
School of Management

JW113

Figure 5.4 – The Benefits Dependency Network (Source: Ward & Daniel, 2006)

5.2.2.4 The Benefits Logic Map

This approach was derived from the Investment Logic Map (ILM) approach discussed in Chapter 3. The main differences are: the problem to be solved is re-stated in positive terms (psychological research indicates change is facilitated where the goal is expressed in 'moving towards', rather than 'away from', terms), and the benefits are split into intermediate and end benefits. As with the ILM, the Benefits Logic Map is the outcome from a workshop, or short series of workshops. The approach is illustrated in Example 5.1.

Advantages of this approach include the focus on 'starting with the end in mind' with the problem to be solved or opportunity to be exploited;

Example 5.1 – Benefits Logic Maps on the Tell Us Once programme

Tell Us Once (TUO) is a cross-government programme with a wide reach. As such it faced the challenge of how to effectively communicate the value proposition to stakeholders that included central government departments, local government and citizens. One solution was to develop a series of Benefits Logic Maps, one for each service – the map for the Birth service is illustrated in Figure 5.5. This then provided the basis for further work to identify a suite of measures for the benefits identified in the Benefits Logic Map.

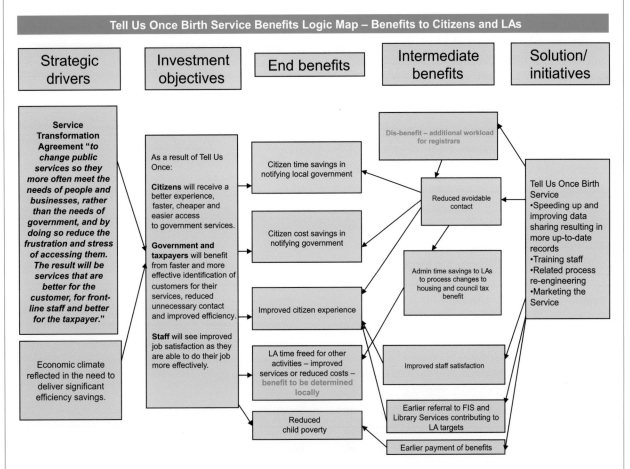

Figure 5.5 – The Tell Us Once Birth Service Benefits Logic Map

This was found to be an effective approach, not only as a basis for subsequent benefits management but also by providing an overview of the rationale for the service on a single page, as a means of benefits-led stakeholder engagement. It should also be noted that it did not shy away from recognizing the dis-benefit to registrars of an increased workload.

Provided with the kind agreement of Matthew Briggs, Tell Us Once Programme Manager.

mapping the chain of intermediate and end benefits; and, by capturing the 'story of the change', providing a basis for benefits-led stakeholder engagement.

5.2.3 Customer/User Insight

One of the Key Success Characteristics of effective benefits management identified in Chapter 4 was ongoing participative stakeholder engagement throughout the Benefits Management Cycle. A key element of this is informing the design of an initiative with an understanding of user needs, wants and desires. In short, we bring the 'voice of the customer' into the design of the initiative via the technique of 'customer insight'. This is defined (by the Government Communication Network's Engage Programme) as, *"A deep 'truth' about the customer based on their behaviour, experiences, beliefs, needs or desires, that is relevant to the task or issue and 'rings bells' with target people."* An important element about this truth is that it is powerful enough to bring about behavioural change. Techniques that can be used to achieve 'customer insight' include:

1. Segmentation, i.e. breaking users into groups with common characteristics to explore and gain insight via focus groups, interviews and surveys. Common approaches to customer segmentation are by usage, demographics (e.g. age, gender, employment, location etc.) and attitudes. The resulting insight should be used in designing the solution, for forecasting and quantifying the benefits, and, in due course, in evaluating whether the benefits have been realized and those needs and wants met.

2. Customer journey mapping, which describes the customer experience of a service or set of services from need to outcome. As we shall see in Chapter 8, stories can be a powerful means of stakeholder engagement to win hearts as well as minds, and customer journey mapping is a useful tool in this regard. Guidance from the Cabinet Office ('*Customer Journey Mapping Guide for Practitioners*'; and '*Customer Journey Mapping Guide for Managers*') notes that, *"Mapping the experience brings the story to life and engages your audience"*. In this way narrative is used to engage the user on an emotional level in the need for, and scope of, the change required to realize the potential benefits.

3. Focus groups to explore directly with customers and users their needs, wants and desires. Another related option is user experience audits – see Example A.3 in Appendix A. It is important to note that user needs and wants are not always obvious – as Mark Pearson, Head of Research at Egg, is quoted as saying in the Cabinet Office's primer on customer insight, *"People can't always articulate what they want or need … You can't expect them to just give you the answers"*.

4. One answer to the above problem is ethnography, which observes users in real-life situations to understand their behaviour. Cooper & Edgett (2007) point out that, *"If you want to study gorillas, a couple of focus groups with gorillas, an e-mail survey and a few interviews probably won't be enough. You must buy a tent and move into their village site – and camp out with them. And so it is with gaining real customer insights: You must move into their home, office or business and spend time observing and gaining insights."* The point is that by observing users in practice you can gain insights that just don't emerge from more formal consultation. This is illustrated in Example 5.2.

5. Other methods include: gathering feedback from front-line/customer-facing staff; monitoring call volumes and website statistics; market research using surveys to confirm insight into customer needs is sound; customer endorsements and complaints; and 'mystery shopping' data.

So far we have identified benefits using benefits discovery workshops, benefits mapping and 'customer insight'. The next step is to quantify those benefits.

Example 5.2 – Ethnographic research: the design of a new breathalyzer

Draeger Safety is a major German manufacturer of safety, emergency and firefighting equipment. One of their product lines is breathalyzer testing devices used by police forces to test alcohol levels in suspected drunk drivers. A new product line in Europe was the goal, but the project needed direction and lacked blockbuster ideas.

Two VoC study teams were formed and, after some training on how to do ethnographic research, the teams began their camping-out exercises in England and Sweden. In both countries, the teams spent time at police stations, conducting interviews with police officers and their supervisors. But the real learning and aha's came from their night-time vigils – the camping-out exercise – where the VoC teams worked beside the police officers as they ran their night-time road-spot checks on drivers. These learnings provided the key to a new product with significant competitive advantage. For example, the British VoC team soon realized how difficult a job the police officers had in maintaining order and control over a carload full of exuberant young drivers fresh from the nearby pub. The police order to the suspected drunks is always: "Remain in the car!" The breathalyzer test device is passed through the driver's window by the officer (who wears latex gloves for fear of HIV), and the driver is commanded to blow into the mouthpiece. It takes two minutes to get a full reading. Meanwhile the other officer has pulled over another car, so now there are two carloads of drunks to manage. Quite clearly, the police officers are somewhat intimidated by the task of crowd control – they're outnumbered, and many of the lads in the cars are twice the size and half the age of the officers. Note that officers never admitted to intimidation during the formal daytime interviews!

One solution the team came up with to overcome the problem of crowd control and intimidation was to speed up the process. The goal became to substantially reduce the two-minute wait-time for test results that was creating the queue. And they did achieve this by developing a ten-second test device.

A second observation was that because of the dials on the UK version of the instrument, it could only be used on right-hand-side drivers in the UK. Thus, when a car from France or Germany, driving in the UK, was pulled over … the police could not conduct the test. And they had no option but to simply wave the car through. This behaviour was never revealed to their supervisors nor in the formal interviews. The solution was to design an ambidextrous testing instrument – an arm with the mouthpiece attached that could be swung over the top of the test device depending on whether a right-hand or left-hand side drive car was pulled over.

From Cooper, R.G. & Edgett, S.J. (2007*) Generating Breakthrough New Product Ideas,* Product Development Institute. Reproduced with the kind agreement of the authors.

5.3 QUANTIFY BENEFITS

We saw in Chapter 2 that many organizations struggle to demonstrate that the forecast benefits used to justify an initiative in the Business Case are actually realized. Why might this be? Possible explanations are shown in Table 5.1.

But, in addition to these factors, psychologists and other researchers have identified a number of cognitive biases and organizational factors that adversely impact our ability to produce accurate and reliable benefits forecasts. **The cause of the** **failure to realize benefits is thus, in many cases, because the benefits were overstated to start with**. Indeed, research finds that the causes of failure can usually be traced back to the Business Case:

- A study by Mott McDonald (2002) concluded that, "*the most important contributing factor to optimism bias was the inadequacy of the business case*".
- A research study in Australia by Capability Management (2006) found that, "*Of the business cases reviewed, over 65% misrepresented the benefits*".

Table 5.1 – Causes of the failure to realize planned benefits

Cause	Solution
The initiative is set up to fail from the start in relation to benefits.	The answer here is to take a benefits-led rather than activity-centred approach (principle 2 in Chapter 3).
Failure to surface, mitigate and manage assumptions.	Regular review and validation of the evidence underpinning such assumptions. Appropriate use of Benefits Maps can be a powerful tool to assist in addressing this.
Delivery failure – the project or programme fails to be implemented as planned.	The answer in this case lies in more effective delivery methods (principle 3 in Chapter 3) and regular stage/phase gates to ensure that, when required, failing or non-strategically aligned change initiatives are terminated.
The initiative is delivered but things have changed in the interim so, while the initiative is delivered successfully, the anticipated benefits are not realized, or at least not to the scale planned.	The answer in this case is to ensure change initiatives are designed in a modular way, so that long time spans between initiative design and delivery are minimized, and to subject the investment rationale to regular review so that if things change appropriate action is taken.
Business change failure – the initiative is successfully delivered but the business changes on which benefits realization is dependent don't occur.	The answer here is to ensure an appropriate focus on business change throughout the business change lifecycle, including by: the use of Benefits Dependency Networks as outlined above; ensuring responsibility for the required changes is clearly assigned; and not declaring victory too early.
The benefits are realized but we either can't or don't collect sufficient evidence to demonstrate benefits realization.	The answer here is to apply an effective benefits management regime as outlined in this Guide; undertake baselining; develop a suite of benefits measures, and relate those measures wherever possible to the existing measures used by the organization's performance management system.

This needs to be addressed if we are to have a solid foundation on which to base our benefits management practices. Cognitive biases are firstly examined, before we consider the organizational factors that can also work against accurate and reliable forecasting. We then review strategies and techniques that can be used to overcome both factors.

5.3.1 Cognitive Biases Affecting Benefits Forecasting

We saw in Chapter 4 that there are a number of cognitive biases that can compromise effective benefits management. This is also true in relation to the specific area of benefits forecasting. In regard to the public sector, the NAO (2011) reports that optimism bias is, *"endemic."* In a similar vein,

in relation to the private sector, Lovallo & Kahneman (2003) say that executives suffer from *"Delusional optimism: we overemphasise projects' potential benefits and underestimate likely costs, spinning success scenarios while ignoring the possibility of mistakes."*

The consequence for benefits forecasting is clear – benefits forecasts are overstated and in due course realization falls below what was anticipated – with consequent loss in faith by key stakeholders, so putting future investment at risk.

At the root of this optimism bias or over-confidence are a series of cognitive biases. These include: expectation or confirmation bias; the planning fallacy; availability bias; groupthink; the framing effect and loss aversion; anchoring and adjustment; biases affecting our ability to handle probability; confusing correlation and causation; and assuming the 'arrow of causation'. A description of these biases and their impact on benefits forecasting is included in Table D.2 in Appendix D.

What makes such cognitive biases so powerful is that:

- Firstly, despite the evidence of past forecasting errors, we are often unaware of these biases (or believe that they affect others rather than ourselves).
- Secondly, many of these biases are linked and reinforcing.
- Thirdly, they affect experts as well as the general population.
- Fourthly, many assessments of probability appear counter-intuitive – for example, the odds that at least two people in a room of 24 people will share the same birthday are better than one in two, and the odds rise to over 90% when as few as 36 people are present (this is the so-called 'Birthday paradox').

But another explanation for forecasting errors has been proposed – and it is one where the cause lies less in cognitive biases that affect us as individuals, and more in organizational factors that mitigate against accurate and reliable forecasting.

5.3.2 Organizational Pressures Affecting Benefits Forecasting

Professor Bent Flyvbjerg at Oxford University has undertaken extensive research of transportation infrastructure projects – research with a global reach. He and his colleagues concluded (2005) that forecasts are *"highly, systematically and significantly misleading (inflated). The result is large benefit shortfalls"*. The cause is what he terms *"strategic misrepresentation"*, which is defined as *"the planned, systematic, deliberate misstatement of costs and benefits to get projects approved"*. This is not restricted to transportation initiatives – comparative research (Flyvbjerg, 2006) finds a similar picture applies in a wide range of initiatives: concert halls, museums, sports arenas, convention centres, urban renewal, power plants, dams, IT systems, oil and gas exploration, aerospace projects, new product development etc.

Other academics have reached similar conclusions – for example, in Australia, Lin et al (2005) report that 26.2% of respondents admitted to regularly overstating benefits in order to get their Business Cases approved. Ward et al (2008) report an even more depressing situation in Europe, with 38% of respondents in one survey undertaken by Cranfield University openly admitting to overstating benefits to get funding. Peppard et al (2007) find that the traditional investment appraisal process is *"seen as a ritual that must be overcome before any project can begin"*.

The cause is, according to Flyvbjerg et al (2006), either because it is in the economic interests of those making the case, or because it is expected by the project sponsor. In short, benefits are used to help justify the investment in a preferred solution – and so the emphasis is on identifying benefits, not as a basis for managing their realization, but in order to justify the costs required. The result is a series of 'tricks of the trade' that are used to maximize the benefits in the Business Case, but with little attention being given to whether these benefits are actually realizable. These 'tricks of the trade' include:

- Ignoring risks and assumptions, even officially recorded ones, in calculations, and using best case benefits and costs to calculate the return on investment.
- Deliberate double counting of benefits (i.e. including in the forecast, benefits that will be realized from other initiatives).
- Forecasting benefits to stakeholders without validating them with those stakeholders – ultimately benefits are *"the measurable improvement resulting from an outcome perceived as an advantage by one or more stakeholders"* – consequently validating benefits with the relevant stakeholder is essential.
- Claiming staff time savings in full, but with no indication as to how the time saved will be redeployed to value-adding activity.
- Overvaluing benefits – by, for example, including overhead costs (e.g. accommodation, lighting and heating) even when there will be no reduction in those overheads.
- Failing to account for dis-benefits.

■ Ignoring some of the costs required to realize the benefits (e.g. counting the salary costs saved from staff redundancies, but not including the costs of the redundancy payments).

Why is all of this important? Some say as long as all Business Cases are based on equally inaccurate forecasts it doesn't matter. But it is important and not just because inaccuracies are rarely equal, but also because:

■ Firstly, if we don't know the benefits to be realized from our investments, we cannot make best use of the resources at our disposal – the good lose out to the bad but well-presented proposals.

■ Secondly, it is taxpayers' and shareholders' money, and it is therefore incumbent upon those making investments that they are able to demonstrate effective stewardship of the funds entrusted to them – by providing a sound rationale for investment and a commitment to realizing all potential benefits to optimize the return on investment.

■ Thirdly, if we don't know where the benefits are we cannot manage them – and so the benefits management regime is built on unstable foundations.

Whether the cause is cognitive bias or strategic misrepresentation (or indeed both in combination – the so-called 'conspiracy of optimism') the result is benefits forecasts that are unlikely to ever be realized in practice. So, the relevant question is how can we address this and what techniques can be applied to ensure benefits forecasts are reliable and so lay the basis for their realization in practice?

5.3.3 Setting the Organizational Context for More Reliable Benefits Forecasting

The first step is to be aware of the psychological and organizational traps that can compromise forecasting accuracy. The trouble is that even when we are aware of these issues we can fall victim to them. Consequently, more formalized strategies are also required. Fortunately, there are

a range of techniques available that can help promote more accurate and reliable benefits forecasts.

5.3.3.1 Organizational and Cultural Factors

1. 'Start with the end in mind' with benefits-led change initiatives. Here there is less incentive to overstate benefits as they are the rationale for the investment rather than being used to justify a preferred solution.

2. Stronger leadership. The NAO (2011) highlights the importance of senior management *"setting the tone by encouraging honesty in estimates, challenging optimism bias and assumptions and being willing to stop projects which no longer make sense"*.

3. Effective accountability frameworks that hold people to account for results, by tracking performance through to benefits realization. If forecasters know that robust post-implementation and post-investment reviews will compare forecast with actual performance, then there is more of an incentive for them to ensure their forecasts are realistic. Similarly, if forecasters and sponsors know that future forecasts will be adjusted based on their track record (what is termed 'reference class' forecasting), there is a greater incentive to ensure today's forecasts are more accurate – otherwise future investments will be put at risk.

4. Requiring benefits forecasts to be validated with the recipients/beneficiaries prior to investment, and, wherever possible, 'booked' in budgets, plans, performance targets etc. More on this issue of validation and 'booking the benefits' is given in Chapter 7.

5. Dan Ariely (2009) found that asking people to sign an honour code meant that they were less likely to subsequently be dishonest. So ask forecasters to put their name on the Business Case along with an ethical statement about their commitment to reliable forecasting.

5.3.3.2 *Challenge and Scrutiny*

1. Deliberately seek disconfirming evidence and ensure Business Cases include both evidence for and against the case – with credible alternative options being included wherever possible. In this way we can overcome expectation or confirmation bias.

2. Linked to the above – ensure forecasts are subject to robust and independent challenge and scrutiny. A diversity of perspectives is crucial to help overcome 'groupthink'. Internal audit and non-executive directors can play an important role here, but of most importance is senior management commitment to a culture of open scrutiny and challenge – not one based on 'points scoring', but one in which honest examination of the Business Case from multiple perspectives is valued.

3. Regular review – ensure regular stage/phase gates are held at which benefits are subject to review and are re-forecast if required. Similarly, ensure regular portfolio-level reviews encompass examination of trends in accurate forecasting – is performance matching the promise?

5.3.4 Evidence-based Forecasting

The first point to make is that if we adopt benefits-led change there is less scope for optimism bias and strategic misrepresentation because we start with the benefits required and then work back from them in determining the scope of the initiative. The key questions to ask here are less about the accuracy and reliability of the benefits forecast, and more about whether the scope of the initiative is sufficient to realize those benefits, i.e. are all required enabling and business changes included within the initiative scope?

Accepting that the above won't always be possible, the recommended approach is to adopt evidence-based or **'reference class' forecasting**. This approach is recommended by both Kahneman and Flyvbjerg and is based on the following five-step process (Lovallo & Kahneman, 2003):

- Firstly, select a reference class of comparable projects – one that is broad enough to provide meaningful data, but one that is also comparable to the initiative under review.
- Secondly, assess the distribution of outcomes of the reference class including the average (or 'mean') and measure of variability (e.g. via the standard deviation).
- Thirdly, make an intuitive prediction as to where on the distribution the current initiative should sit.
- Fourthly, assess the reliability of your prediction above – for example by assessing past performance or by making an assessment of how confident you are on a scale of 0–10.
- Fifthly, correct the intuitive estimate made at step 3, by adjusting it towards the average for the reference class based on the analysis undertaken at step 4.

Taking such an 'outside view' (as opposed to an 'inside' view where forecasts are built bottom up by considering the initiative in detail) has been found to produce more accurate forecasts, by avoiding both the cognitive and organizational biases associated with 'inside view' forecasts. The use of 'reference class' forecasting has been found to be particularly valuable in novel, non-routine change initiatives (like many transformational change programmes), where the scope for optimism bias and strategic misrepresentation is the greatest. It does, however, depend on sufficient data on past initiatives being available to provide statistically representative data – an example of how tracking initiative data at a portfolio level can deliver added value going forward.

A similar approach is to apply **optimism bias adjustments**. The HM Treasury *'Green Book'* (2003a) recommends that estimates included in Business Cases should be empirically based using data from past projects or projects elsewhere. Where such data is not available, departments are encouraged to collect it. In the meantime departments are required to use the optimism bias adjustments on the HM Treasury *'Green Book'* home page. This is similar to 'reference class' forecasting, but rather than starting with a reference class of similar change initiatives, the approach takes the 'inside view' forecast and then adjusts it to reflect the organization's track record in realizing benefits. For example, if an organization only realizes 80% of its forecast benefits and with a six-month delay on average, then it would adjust forecasts accordingly – by reducing and delaying the receipt of forecast benefits. The risk of course is that those making the forecasts realize this and adjust their forecasts to take this into account – the 'Green Book' therefore recommends that adjustments for optimism bias should be independently reviewed, including at Gateway reviews and by internal audit. The availability of such empirically derived adjustments can however be an issue – the HM Treasury 'Green Book' includes no optimism bias adjustments for benefits because the data collected by the original Mott McDonald (2002) study was insufficient for this purpose. A more recent study (Communities and Local Government, 2007) also found, *"both appraisal and out-turn data was far more difficult to extract ... such is the paucity of this data, and such are the difficulties surrounding output assessment in these areas, that there is considerable doubt surrounding the efficacy of these figures in any systematic investigation of optimism bias"*. The absence of such data means that, at least in relation to benefits forecasts, optimism bias adjustments need to be based more on intuitive judgement (which has been proven to be an unreliable basis for benefits forecasting) rather than empirical evidence.

The reality is therefore that in many cases a reference class of benefits data, or empirically derived optimism bias adjustments, will not be available. How then should those involved in forecasting proceed?

5.3.5 A Practical Approach to Benefits Forecasting

5.3.5.1 Baselining Current Performance

The first challenge is to ensure that we understand the current level of performance. In short, we need to understand the 'as is' performance so that we have a baseline against which to forecast the improvement anticipated in the 'to be' state. The trouble is, managers are often so keen to get an initiative started that insufficient attention is given to baselining current performance – and the results are seen later in an inability to manage benefits effectively and to demonstrate benefits realization. But baselining is of fundamental importance – as illustrated in Example 5.3.

In baselining current performance, the following should be taken into consideration:

- Wherever possible relate baseline measures to existing data from the organization's management information system – this minimizes the cost associated with benefits measurement and helps demonstrate strategic contribution. For example, the lessons learned in the DVLA Case Study (2005) for the OGC noted that, *"Baseline data for benefits was difficult to find. It became apparent that baseline data should always be sourced from statistics routinely collected wherever possible"*.

- Start benefits tracking as early as possible during development and delivery so that data against which to measure benefits realization is available. As the Public Sector Programme Management Approach (PSPMA) guide states,

---

Example 5.3 – Baselining in Standard Chartered Bank

The Benefits Management guidelines from Standard Chartered Bank include the following: Obtaining appropriate baseline data is critical to demonstrating improvements in performance. The baseline position for tangible financial measures, tangible non-financially quantifiable measures and key performance indicators needs to be identified and agreed at the commencement of a project. This will, as benefits are realized, enable the improvements in performance ('deltas') to be calculated, help validate the assumptions on which the benefits case was based, and aid ongoing tracking and validation during the scheduled periodic and post-implementation reviews.

Source: *'Management of Portfolios'*. Provided with the kind agreement of Tim Carroll.

"The current or baseline value, together with the target value to be achieved, should be stated for all benefits. In some cases for example, with a new benefit, or one that is hard to quantify, there may not be an easily identifiable current value, or target value. In these cases, it is still important to list the benefit. It is vital that work is done up front to identify which key benefits do not have any baseline data and put actions in place to identify the baseline information needed. This will ensure that benefits can be measured during and following programme delivery." Provision for the costs of this activity should be included in the initiative's budget.

■ Watch out for seasonal trends and normal variation in data – trend analysis should be used to help ensure that reliable baseline measurements are taken.

■ Also take into account the impact on performance of change initiatives delivered or due to be delivered, i.e. use forecast baselines where relevant rather than historical ones. This means you should use as the baseline what performance will be in the future without the proposed initiative, not always what it was last year. This can be helped by reviewing the organization's business plan, forecast performance targets and future year budgets.

Baseline performance should be recorded as part of the 'as is' information in the programme blueprint along with the 'to be' state, which should include the planned improvement and the performance measures that will be used to determine whether the benefits have been achieved. But how do we forecast the scale of benefits in the 'to be' state?

5.3.5.2 Forecasting the Scale of Improvement

Techniques to assist benefits forecasting include:

1. **Benefits quantification workshops** – building on the benefits mapping and the benefits discovery workshop, they are undertaken with subject-matter experts to agree the scale of improvement that can be realistically

attributed to the initiative, taking into account current performance and other planned change initiatives.

2. **Pilot studies** – base forecasts on evidence from pilot studies, although this can be problematic as evidence collected from pilots may not be representative of what can realistically be achieved from wider roll-out because:

   ☐ Resources and support devoted to pilots often far exceed that provided to other sites during full roll-out.
   ☐ The famous Hawthorne experiments demonstrated that when we pay close attention to something, performance tends to improve – so improved performance at pilot sites can derive not just from the new ways of working but also from their selection as pilot sites.

3. **The Delphi technique** – as Surowiecki (2004) has demonstrated, groups often make better estimates than individuals – the so-called 'wisdom of crowds' effect. The 'Delphi' technique makes use of this by seeking consensus from a panel of subject-matter experts over several rounds of questioning, with the results of the previous round being fed back to the panel anonymously. In this way the members of the panel are able to revise their conclusions in the light of the views of others. But in order to guard against 'groupthink' it is crucial that:

   ☐ The group making the forecasts are diverse and independent – as Surowiecki says, *"the best collective decisions are the product of disagreement and contest, not consensus and compromise"*.
   ☐ The group should make their forecasts anonymously – as Solomon Asch demonstrated in a classic psychology experiment, there is a strong pull towards conformity and this can influence people's judgements. So ensure the initial forecasts are made without knowledge of what others are estimating.

In refining the benefits forecast specific consideration needs to be given to the following factors:

■ **Leakage** or positive **spill-over** effects, i.e. benefits that arise to those beyond those the initiative is intended to benefit.

■ **Attribution**, i.e. how much of the outcome can be attributed to the initiative compared with other initiatives.

■ **Deadweight**, i.e. benefits that would have occurred in any case.

■ **Displacement**, i.e. the extent to which benefits are offset by dis-benefits resulting elsewhere – for example where factory discharge contributes to environmental damage.

■ **Ramp up**, i.e. the trajectory to full benefits realization, making allowance for familiarization with the new ways of working. In practice this rarely follows a linear path (0% to 50% in the first six months and then 100% thereafter) and instead follows something more akin to an 'S' curve – reflecting a dip in performance at first, as people adjust to the new ways of working, followed by slow improvement as they settle in, and then a faster rate of increase until full realization and then tail-off sets in.

■ **Drop or tail-off**, i.e. as time passes other factors will emerge that influence the system and so the effect of the initiative on operational performance will tail off.

5.3.5.3 Enhancing the Accuracy and Reliability of Forecasts

Confidence in the accuracy and reliability of the resulting forecasts can then be enhanced by the following techniques:

Example 5.4 – Bronze, Silver and Gold benefits certainty ratings

A Scottish Council adopted the use of bronze, silver and gold certainty ratings reflecting the fact that confidence in benefits forecasts should improve as initiatives advance through the business change lifecycle. These ratings are shown in Table 5.2.

Table 5.2 – Benefits certainty ratings

Features of bronze estimates	Features of silver estimates	Features of gold estimates
■ Are high-level estimates provided at the start of a project. ■ Have not been broken down by service/team/individual. ■ Are not rigorous enough to be factored into budgets.	■ Are provided once the scope of a project has been agreed. ■ Will have been discussed with services and/or team managers but not necessarily signed off. ■ Are not broken down to individual level as selection process may still have to be agreed. ■ Can be factored into budgets but expectation should be that they can change as the project develops. Any changes would be managed through change control process.	■ As the project develops, the assumptions and plans will become further refined resulting in the benefit projections being firmed up. ■ Gold estimates are still in advance of the project being implemented. ■ Services and managers have signed off the figures and they are built into budgets.

Sourced from the benefits realization case studies on the Scottish Programme and Change Management Group Community of Practice at http://www.communities.idea.gov.

1. Stochastic (probability-based) estimating. Rather than using single-point or deterministic forecasts, probabilities can be assigned to a range of outcomes or can be calculated using 'Monte Carlo' simulation. Alternatively, we can avoid the issues around assessing probabilities, while still recognizing the uncertainty inherent in forecasting, by estimating using optimistic, pessimistic and most likely scenarios. These estimates can then be simply combined using the Project Evaluation and Review Technique (PERT) formula: [Optimistic Outcome + Pessimistic Outcome + four times the Most Likely Outcome] divided by six.

2. Apply sensitivity analysis to identify the factors and assumptions on which forecasts are most dependent. This technique is explained further in the next chapter.

3. Recognize uncertainty with the use of confidence or certainty ratings, i.e. how confident/certain are we that the benefits forecast will actually be realized? See Example 5.4.

5.4 CHAPTER SUMMARY

1. The first practice in the Benefits Management Cycle concerns the identification and quantification of benefits. The objective is to lay the basis for informed options analysis, investment appraisal and portfolio prioritization; and the management of benefits realization in due course.

2. Approaches to benefits identification include benefits discovery workshops, benefits mapping and 'customer insight'.

3. Benefits forecasts provide the foundation upon which the subsequent practices in the Benefits Management Cycle are built. Research indicates that benefits forecasts are often neither accurate nor reliable due to a combination of cognitive bias and strategic misrepresentation.

4. There are a range of strategies and techniques that can be used to promote more accurate and reliable benefits forecasting including: strategies that address organizational and cultural factors; regular and independent challenge; and more reliable forecasting methods including 'reference class' forecasting.

5. Where a reference class of data is unavailable, the following techniques can be applied to improve the reliability of benefits forecasts: benefits quantification workshops, pilot studies and the Delphi technique.

6. The reliability of forecasts can be further enhanced by stochastic rather than single-point estimates, sensitivity analysis and confidence/certainty ratings.

Chapter 6

Chapter 6 – Benefits Management Practice 2 – Value & Appraise

6.1 OVERVIEW OF THIS CHAPTER

The objective of the Value & Appraise practice is to ensure resources are allocated to those change initiatives that individually and collectively represent best value for money.

This practice encompasses:

- The valuation of benefits in **monetary terms** – the reasons for doing so (to facilitate options analysis, investment appraisal and portfolio prioritization) and approaches to doing it (using market prices where possible and, where not, the alternatives that are available such as 'willingness to pay' and 'willingness to accept').

- The four main methods of **investment appraisal**: cost-benefit, real options, cost-effectiveness and multi-criteria analysis. Note that our focus here is less on independent appraisal of the Business Case, than using the most appropriate approach to support the preparation of the Business Case.

We also review techniques that can be used not only to value the benefits of change initiatives but also to improve the value to be derived from those initiatives by using value management techniques.

Note – sections of this chapter may appear to be relatively technical but it is important that those involved in benefits management have at least an awareness of the wider context within which it operates and, specifically, an understanding of the techniques applied to investment appraisal and portfolio prioritization.

6.2 VALUING BENEFITS

6.2.1 Why Value?

Chapter 5 examined the identification and quantification of benefits. The next step is to value these benefits in monetary terms. The reason for doing this is that monetary value provides a 'level playing field' or consistent basis on which to undertake:

- Options analysis – to compare the various options or alternative ways of achieving the desired outcomes and benefits.
- Investment appraisal – to assess whether the benefits justify the costs required.
- Portfolio prioritization – to rank potential investments in priority order where resources are limited.

> **Important note**
>
> Not all organizations seek to value all benefits (i.e. both financial and non-financial benefits) in monetary terms – but many do. Organizations that employ this approach include the UK Central Government, where HM Treasury's 'Green Book' (2003a) requires all benefits to be valued wherever feasible and Net Present Value (NPV) is the preferred/ recommended decision criterion.

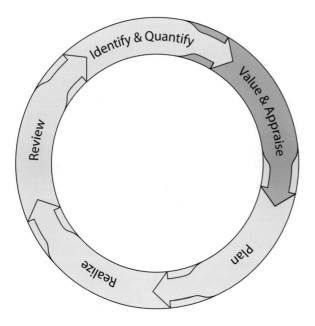

Figure 6.1 – The Value & Appraise practice in the Benefits Management Cycle

6.2.2 How to Value?

We consider this topic in relation to financial benefits, efficiency improvements (which may or may not result in financial benefits) and non-financial benefits.

6.2.2.1 Financial Benefits

Approaches to valuing benefits vary with the nature of the benefit under consideration. For example, cashable financial benefits (e.g. cost savings, increased revenue and reduced unit costs) are relatively easy to value in monetary terms since the benefit is financial in nature. Such benefits will normally be valued using guidance in the organization's financial policies and should be agreed with the relevant budget holder and the finance department.

One type of financial 'benefit' that needs particular consideration concerns cost-avoidance benefits. Business Cases should reflect the costs associated with not taking action, but the subsequent treatment of costs avoided as part of the benefits management regime will depend on the nature of these costs. Costs avoided can come in many forms and the appropriate treatment will depend on the circumstances. For example:

- The running costs of existing legacy systems replaced by a new system – such costs avoided should either be recycled to help fund the new system (so appearing as a reduction in the costs required rather than as a benefit) or alternatively they should be realized by extracting them from the operating budgets as cashable efficiency savings.

- Improved service reliability resulting in less system outages or downtime – for example, internal systems which when down result in people having to do slower, manual workarounds. Such benefits are not really cost/efficiency savings but time savings, and consequently the focus should be on determining how the time saved will be used.

- Uncertain future costs associated with the failure of legacy systems – unless provision for such costs is already built into operating budgets, benefits realization cannot be tracked in any meaningful sense. Such potential benefits are appropriate to the options appraisal, but are generally no longer relevant once the decision to invest is taken.

- The benefits of choosing one project option over another in achieving a given policy objective – for example, where an IT system to meet an objective costs £100,000 compared with £150,000 for a manual system. These notional costs avoided (i.e. £50,000 in this example) are relevant in the options appraisal, but the notional incremental costs associated with pursuing the next best alternative are not relevant once the investment decision has been made. They should therefore not be included in the benefits management regime.

Similar issues apply to revenue retention benefits – the argument being that if you don't do something such as invest in a system refresh, then your existing revenue predictions will have to be revised downwards. In such cases investment requires confirmation that this is indeed the case in the near future (e.g. what failures have occurred to date and with what impact?) and that the proposed solution represents the most cost-

---

Example 6.1 – Revenue protection and cost avoidance benefits in Standard Chartered Bank

Revenue protection – revenue protection should not be included in the financial benefits case, because it is unable to be tracked and validated. However, this should be included when providing a holistic description of the benefits.

Cost avoidance – cost avoidance should not be included in the financial benefits case. However, it should be included when providing a holistic description of the benefits.

Source: 'Management of Portfolios'. Provided with the kind agreement of Tim Carroll.

effective way of maintaining current revenues. The Benefits Management guidelines from Standard Chartered Bank include the guidance shown in Example 6.1.

This area is one in which organizations need to pay particularly close attention to ensure that they understand the true nature of the benefits claimed and whether they will be realized in any meaningful sense.

6.2.2.2 *Efficiency Improvements*

While efficiency improvements can be relatively easy to value this is not always the case. For example, where staff time savings are concerned, we need to consider what value to attribute to the time saved. The basic principle should be that the value should not be based on the cost of that time, but rather reflect the use to which the time savings are put:

- If staff leave the organization without being replaced then there will be a budget saving and this saving will be the financial benefit derived, net of any redundancy costs.
- If staff are able to undertake more of the same type of work, then the unit costs should fall – and this will be the financial benefit derived.
- If staff time is redirected to some other activity then the benefit will be this other activity. Valuing this (in monetary terms) will depend on the nature of this activity and whether it has a readily available market price.

> **Important note**
>
> The value of staff time savings is not the cost of that time, but rather the value of the use to which the time savings are put. Benefits mapping can help here by surfacing assumptions about how time saved will be used.

All this means that valuing efficiency improvements is not always entirely straightforward. For this reason, and particularly early on in the business change lifecycle, it is common to value staff time savings at cost rather than the value to be derived (which may be uncertain at that point). It should be noted that there are some very real risks associated with this approach:

- The value attributed may be overstated compared to the benefits that are realistically realizable.
- The work to value benefits in terms of their true nature (whether that be budget savings, unit cost reductions or improved operational performance) can be forgotten once the Business Case has been approved.
- Referring back to those cognitive biases considered in Chapters 4 and 5, we can 'anchor' on the original value (based on the cost of time saved) and adjust insufficiently when considering the value of the benefits that can actually be realized.

Accepting that valuation of efficiency time savings based on cost is a reality in many situations, we can mitigate these risks by:

- Valuing staff time saved at the marginal cost of labour, i.e. with no provision for overheads unless it is clear that these overheads will reduce.

- Applying a realistic 'conversion ratio' based on the assumption that not all the time saved will be redeployed. Here the time savings are multiplied by a factor ranging from 0 to 1 depending on the ability of the organization to realize the time savings – and ideally this should reflect the organization's track record in realizing such benefits in the past. Curley (2004) suggests adjusting the time saved forecast to reflect two factors – firstly, the Hawthorne effect (*"the tendency of a group under study to over-perform"*), which may account for pilot studies overestimating potential time savings, and, secondly, that not all the potential time saved will be redeployed to value-adding activity. Curley cites the adjustments used in a Business Case in a London Council, where the time savings were divided by half (for the Hawthorne effect) and then by half again (to reflect management's ability to realize the time saved) – and it was this revised time saving (25%) that was used in valuing the benefit. In another example, a council agreed that where productivity gains exceeded £20,000, then half was retained by the service and the other half was converted into a cashable saving that was released from the relevant budget.

- Ensuring the Benefits Management Strategy (see Chapter 7) includes provision for work to identify the end benefits that will be derived from the staff time savings.

- 'Booking' efficiency savings in budgets, headcount targets, performance targets etc. (see Chapter 7).

- Including guidance on the valuation of such benefits in the Portfolio Benefits Management Framework.

6.2.2.3 Non-financial Benefits

If valuing efficiency savings in monetary terms is not always straightforward this is doubly so in relation to other types of non-financial benefit (improved staff engagement and customer satisfaction for example), i.e. benefits that are quantified in non-financial terms. But monetary valuations can be elicited by determining end-users' or customers' 'willingness to pay' or 'willingness to accept' the outcomes of an initiative. Techniques available include:

- Revealed preferences – where values are inferred from observed behaviour in a similar or related situation.
- Stated preferences – here questionnaires are used to elicit estimates of willingness to pay or accept via contingent valuation (where estimates are derived from direct questions) or choice modelling (where estimates are based on selecting a preferred option from a range of alternatives).

The use of such econometric measurement techniques are, however, not without issue. For example, where people are not aware of the benefits, it is difficult for them to say how much they would be willing to pay to receive them, and what people say they would do does not always accurately reflect what they actually do in practice. Research also finds that estimates are not always logically consistent – for example Kahneman (2011a) quotes the following example. After the Exxon Valdez oil disaster people were asked how much they would pay for nets to protect migratory birds from an oil spill. Different groups were asked to say how much they would be willing to pay to protect 2,000, 20,000 and 200,000 birds. If saving birds is an economic good

one would expect some logical relationship between the amount people were willing to pay and the number of birds protected – but the average amount each group were willing to pay was US$80, US$78 and US$88 respectively.

'Anchoring' (see Appendix D) can also affect estimates made. People in a similar study to the one above were asked how much they would be willing to pay annually to help protect seabirds from oil spills. Some were first asked *'would you be willing to pay $5'*, before being asked how much they would be willing to pay. Others were first asked whether they would be willing to pay $400, and a final group were just asked how much they would be willing to pay. The results – those with the $5 'anchor' said they would pay $20 on average. When no 'anchor' question was asked, the average was $64 and when the $400 'anchor' was used, the average was $143 (Kahneman, 2011a).

Partial solutions to the above issues associated with valuing non-financial benefits in monetary terms include:

- Informing estimates with the views of experts – particularly where valuations are derived from a panel of experts using the 'Delphi' technique rather than valuations derived from a single expert.
- Combining cost-effectiveness and 'willingness to pay' analysis – there is more on this below (see Section 6.3.3.1).

Guidance on valuing specific types of benefit and categories of initiative is included below (for mandatory initiatives) and in Appendix A (in relation to the public sector and benefits from cross-organizational programmes, social value and valuing customer/citizen benefits).

6.3 APPRAISAL

Having valued the benefits of an initiative in monetary terms, the next step is to appraise the initiative to determine whether the benefits to be realized exceed the costs required to realize those benefits, and whether those benefits are realizable, i.e. in short, whether there is a compelling case for investment. There are four main approaches to this: cost-benefit analysis, real options analysis, cost-effectiveness analysis and multi-criteria analysis – each with their own advantages and disadvantages that should be borne in mind by those undertaking the appraisal and feeding the results into the Business Case. We consider each of these approaches in turn.

Note – our focus here is less on independent appraisal of the Business Case than the approaches to appraisal used in developing the Business Case. The first step for those involved is therefore to confirm what approaches are mandated by the organization – the Centre of Excellence, Portfolio Office or finance department should be able to answer this. Those involved, including the Business Case Writer and Benefits Managers, should also consider which approach to appraisal is most appropriate given the type of initiative and benefits anticipated. Guidance on the appropriateness of each approach to appraisal is included below.

6.3.1 Cost-benefit Analysis

Cost-benefit analysis quantifies in monetary terms as many of the costs and benefits of an initiative as possible to determine whether the benefits exceed the costs and hence whether investment is justified. Traditionally, the most popular financial appraisal techniques were payback (how long will it take before the total cash inflows repay the total cash outflows – a *time* measure), and accounting rate of return, i.e. average annual accounting profit (total profits divided by the number of years) divided by the initial cost or average cost (i.e. initial cost divided by 2) of the investment – a *percentage* measure. The calculation of payback is illustrated in Table 6.1. Accounting rate of return is calculated as follows:

An investment of £100,000 is expected to generate annual cashable benefits of £20,000 (year 1), £30,000 (year 2), £40,000 (year 3), £40,000 (year 4) and £10,000 (year 5). Depreciation charges are £20,000 per annum.

So, average annual profits are £140,000 cashable benefits less £100,000 depreciation, divided by 5 = £8,000 per annum. Average investment cost would be £100,000 divided by 2 = £50,000. So the accounting rate of return is £8,000/£50,000 x 100 = 16%.

These techniques are widely used and have the advantage that they are relatively easy to calculate and understand. Payback also has the advantage that it takes some account of risk by rating earlier (and hence normally more certain) cash flows more highly than later cash flows. Both methods do, however, have a number of serious disadvantages:

■ Payback – ignores cash flows after the break-even point and therefore doesn't consider total profitability; it also ignores any salvage value at the end of the asset life.
■ Accounting rate of return – it is based on accounting profits (rather than cash flows), which are influenced by changes in accounting policy and which can lead to sub-optimal decisions from the perspective of maximizing shareholder value.

Fundamentally, both methods also take no account of what is termed the time value of money, i.e. a pound sterling, dollar or euro is worth more today than in the future. For example, with inflation of 5%, £100 will only be worth £78 in five years' time (although this can be accommodated in the case of payback, by calculating the discounted payback, i.e. how long it takes in present value terms to pay back the original investment – see Table 6.1).

Consequently, modern finance theory recommends the use of Discounted Cash Flow (DCF) techniques whereby the future incremental cash flows are discounted to calculate the Internal Rate of Return (IRR) and/or the NPV – and these are then used to determine whether the initiative represents value for money:

■ NPV is a statement of the value of future costs and benefits, expressed at today's value. It is a *monetary* measure.
■ IRR is related to NPV as it is the discount rate that expresses future costs and benefits at a zero NPV – in short, the annual percentage return that it is forecast the initiative will achieve. It is a *percentage* measure.

It should also be noted that:

1. Past investments are regarded as 'sunk' and are consequently excluded from the calculation – in other words, the decision to invest, or to

continue to invest, should be based on future cash flows only (which include the costs of stopping the initiative) and exclude all previous costs incurred and benefits realized.

2. Appraisal is concerned with the forecast outcome after adjusting for what would have happened without the initiative – this is termed 'additionality'.

3. Cash flows exclude accounting adjustments such as depreciation, accruals and prepayments, as well as any allocation of fixed overheads to the initiative. But they include the opportunity cost of assets – for example, if land that could be sold for £500,000 is to be used for an initiative, then the £500,000 should be included as a cash outflow reflecting the income foregone. Similarly, if stock cost £100 to produce but now only has a £10 sales value, the value to include in the appraisal is £10.

4. Tax can normally be excluded from an appraisal where the different options have similar tax implications. Where this isn't the case, the tax implications need to be reflected in the analysis. This can be a highly technical area and advice should be sought from the organization's finance function.

5. While IRR has some advantages (e.g. you don't need to select a discount rate and it is usually easier for managers to understand) the theoretically correct approach is to rank change initiatives according to their NPV. This is because IRR has a number of theoretical faults – for example:
   □ Where the cumulative net flow changes sign from negative to positive more than once, an initiative can have more than one IRR.
   □ IRR also includes the unrealistic assumption that cash inflows can be reinvested at the IRR, whereas NPV assumes (more realistically) that they are reinvested at the discount rate.
   □ In the case of mutually exclusive initiatives (i.e. the acceptance of one precludes acceptance of others), IRR can provide sub-optimal decisions. While NPV is an absolute measure, IRR is a relative one and as such

ignores the size of investments. For example, it ranks a 20% return on £100 (£20) higher than a 10% return on £1,000 (£100).

6. Where there is a constraint, the NPV should be divided by the unit of the constraining or limiting factor – this is the so-called 'Productivity Index' and shows how much money at today's value will be delivered from a unit of the limiting factor, such as funding, availability of skilled resources or the business change capacity of the organization. In this way the combined NPV within the constraint of the limiting factor is optimized. Where there is more than one limiting factor or constraint, mathematical modelling approaches (linear programming) may be applied – this is aided by relevant software programs and it is recommended that advice is sought from a qualified management accountant.

7. The NPV is dependent on the costs and benefits, their timings and the discount rate selected. In selecting the discount rate various approaches are open to us – but the objective remains the same: to help determine which change initiatives provide a return on investment, within an acceptable time limit, that exceeds the cost of acquiring the funds required for that investment:
   □ Some organizations will specify a hurdle rate of return that all change initiatives are expected to pass. This means that to be considered for funding, an initiative's IRR needs to exceed the hurdle rate and/or the NPV should be positive when the costs and benefits are discounted at the hurdle rate of return.
   □ The organization may use its Weighted Average Cost of Capital (WACC) – this is the average cost of finance (from equity and debt capital) weighted to reflect the proportion of each form of financing used. For example:

Capital	Market value	Rate of return
Equity	£5,000,000	8%
Debt	£3,000.000	6%

The WACC in this case would be 7.25% ([5/8 x 8%] + [3/8 x 6%]).

☐ One objection to the use of a standard hurdle rate of return (either determined as a target rate or using the WACC) is that it makes no allowance for the relative risk of different initiatives unless the cash flows have been adjusted for risk by, for example, optimism bias adjustments. An approach that seeks to address this is the Capital Asset Pricing Model (CAPM), which adjusts the required rate of return to reflect relative risk as follows:

Required return = Rf + β (Rm – Rf)

Where:
- Rf = the risk free rate, e.g. the return you could get by investing in government gilts. Note for simplicity this is often assumed to be the average historical risk free rate of return.
- β = beta, i.e. a measure of the volatility of the company's share price compared to the market, where 1 = the volatility of the market as a whole.
- Rm = the rate of return on the market as a whole. This is usually estimated using the historical returns on a market portfolio such as the FTSE 100.

So, for example, if a company's share price is more volatile than the market as a whole it will have a beta of >1 and vice versa. Let's say a company has a beta of 1.2. The long-term market premium (the return required for investing in shares rather than gilts) in the UK has been around 5.3% – so this represents Rm – Rf in the CAPM formula. Let's say the relevant risk free rate is 2%. So in this case the required rate of return for this company will be 8.36% (2% + [1.2 x 5.3%]).

The advantages of the CAPM include its simplicity (it only requires three pieces of information that can be estimated relatively easily at least on a historical basis) and the fact that risk (variability in return) is explicitly taken into consideration. On the other hand, the data used tends to be based on historical data that may no longer be relevant (past performance is not necessarily an accurate predictor of future performance). Also, while the company's beta may be readily available (they are widely published in company directories around the world) it may not be appropriate if an initiative's risk varies from that of the company as a whole. This can be addressed by adjusting beta up or down

Table 6.1 – DCF calculations

	Year 0	Year 1	Year 2	Year 3	Year 4	Year 5
Costs (£m)	70	10	10	10	10	10
Benefits (£m)	0	15	25	35	35	25
Annual net flow (£m)	-70	5	15	25	25	15
Cumulative net flow (£m)	-70	-65	-50	-25	0	15
Discount factor	1	0.9524	0.9070	0.8638	0.8227	0.7835
Annual NPV (£m)	-70.0	4.762	13.605	21.595	20.5675	11.7525
Cumulative NPV (£m)	-70.0	-65.238	-51.633	-30.038	-9.4705	2.282
IRR						6%

Notes:
1. The above analysis follows the 'point in time' convention that year 0 represents the point in time when the initial cash flows occur and all future cash flows are assumed to occur on the last day of the year for ease of calculation purposes.
2. The annual net flow row represents the excess of benefits over costs in that year.
3. Discount factors are based on a discount rate of 5% and are obtained from a table of discount rates.
4. Annual NPV represents the NPV of that year's cash flows (benefits less costs).
5. Discounted payback occurs when the cumulative NPV reaches zero and turns positive.
6. The IRR can be found by interpolation (trial and error) or more easily by the IRR function in a spreadsheet.

– for example, by using the beta of a proxy company. Estimating beta for public-sector change initiatives is clearly problematic.

8. The choice of discount rate applied to the cash flows can include or exclude inflation – as long as the cash flows are stated in similar terms. 'Real' cash flows are expressed at today's valuation with no adjustment for general inflation, whereas 'nominal' cash flows include inflation, in which case the discount rate needs to also include inflation.

DCF calculations are illustrated in Table 6.1 for an initiative with a cost-benefit profile over a five-year life.

The analysis in Table 6.1 shows that over a five-year life, the initiative has an NPV of £2.282 million, an IRR of 6% and pays back (in current value terms) in year 5, and in undiscounted terms by the end of year 4.

Two other comments are worth making on cost-benefit analysis. Firstly, we have already seen in Chapter 5 that forecasts of benefits (and costs) are subject to a number of cognitive biases and organizational pressures which can compromise their accuracy and reliability. The IT adage 'GIGO' (garbage in, garbage out) applies here. Solutions discussed included the use of 'reference class' forecasting, adjusting forecasts for optimism bias and stochastic forecasting.

Secondly, there is a difference in the way economists and management accountants approach DCF. This is more than a technical difference and is one that has significant implications for benefits management.

■ The economists' approach – here cost-benefit analysis *"quantifies in monetary terms as many of the costs and benefits of a proposal as feasible, including items for which the market does not provide a satisfactory measure of economic value"* (HM Treasury 'Green Book', 2003a), i.e. both financial and non-financial benefits are valued in monetary terms and are included in the appraisal. The result is that the NPV derived from the economists' cost-benefit appraisal includes both financial benefits (where there is a direct impact on cash inflows or outflows) and what may be termed 'economic' value (i.e. non-financial benefits such as improved customer satisfaction with an attributed monetary value).

■ In contrast, the management accounting approach to cost-benefit appraisal only takes into account cash flows (both costs/cash outflows and benefits/cash inflows), i.e. there is no attempt to value non-financial benefits in monetary terms. This results in an NPV that represents the current value of financial benefits over costs, or the Net Present Cost (NPC), i.e. a negative NPV which represents in current value terms the cost of realizing the non-financial benefits.

It is emphasized that neither approach is right or wrong – they both serve different purposes. The economists' approach is used to inform assessments as to whether an intervention is justified in economic terms. The management accountants' approach is used to inform assessments of:

■ Change initiatives with a financial investment objective – do the financial benefits exceed the costs in current value terms?
■ Change initiatives with a non-financial investment objective – what is the cost in current value terms (NPC)? Management can then come to a view as to whether this is a price worth paying to realize the non-financial benefits on a 'willingness to pay' basis.

From the above, it should be clear that the management accountants' approach is more suitable for benefits management purposes as it treats benefits in accordance with their nature by only applying monetary values to cashable financial benefits. That's not to say we should not also use the economists' approach – organizations can use both, although it is important to remember when each approach is being used and the assumptions on which they are based.

6.3.1.1 Problems with Cost-benefit Analysis and Accommodating Risk

The issue of risk (that cash flows, including benefits, may turn out to be different from those forecast) can be accommodated, at least in part, by a number of techniques. These include:

- Adjusting the discount rate to reflect the degree of risk – for example, by using the CAPM or by setting progressively higher hurdle rates for initiatives allocated to low, medium and high risk categories. The issues here are how to decide what premium is required for each category and on what basis initiatives are allocated to each category?

- Adjusting the cash flows for optimism bias, using 'reference class' forecasting or three-point estimating (pessimistic, optimistic and most likely) and combining these estimates via the PERT formula (see Section 5.3.5.3).

- Sensitivity analysis whereby changes are made to the variables to determine which have the most significant effect on the outcome and hence those that we may wish to study in more detail. This can be done in two ways:
  - □ Determining what are termed switching values, i.e. by how much each variable needs to change (usually in percentage terms) before the investment decision is changed, i.e. what is termed the margin of safety.
  - □ Carrying out 'what if' or scenario analysis – e.g. what would happen if demand fell by 20% and the price by 10%? The advantage here is that changes to more than one variable can be combined to assess the impact of different scenarios.

- Using probability distributions for the range of possible NPVs to calculate Expected Net Present Value (ENPV). Probabilities can be objective (based on past experience) or subjective (based on management judgement). The calculation of ENPV is shown as follows:

NPV	Probability	Outcome
£10,000	0.4	£4,000
£20,000	0.25	£5,000
£30,000	0.35	£10,500
Expected NPV (ENPV)		£19,500

One issue with expected value (aside from the problem of estimating reliable probabilities) is that it represents the average return that would be achieved if the initiative were repeated many times – it doesn't represent an actual return from an initiative being undertaken once. It also fails to take account of what risk actually represents, i.e. variability in return. For example, the two initiatives shown in Table 6.2 have the same ENPV but are they equally risky?

The problem is that ENPV fails to take into consideration the distribution of possible returns – the returns on initiative A in Table 6.2 vary between £450 and £-150, whereas initiative B only varies between £120 and £200 and hence is less risky. This can be accommodated by calculating the standard deviation.

- Standard deviation is a measure of the dispersion of possible outcomes. It is calculated as the square root of the mean of the squared deviations from the expected value. Table 6.3 shows the calculations for a company that is considering investment in initiative A or initiative B.

Both initiatives have an expected value of £8,000,000 – but initiative A has a standard deviation of £1,095 compared with a standard deviation for initiative B of £2,280. Standard

Table 6.2 – ENPV calculations

Initiative A			Initiative B		
NPV (£)	Probability	Outcome (£)	NPV (£)	Probability	Outcome (£)
£1500	0.3	450	600	0.3	180
£500	0.4	200	500	0.4	200
(£500)	0.3	(150)	400	0.3	120
	ENPV	£500		ENPV	£500

Table 6.3 – Calculation of standard deviation

		Initiative A			
Column 1	Column 2	Column 3	Column 4	Column 5	Column 6
NPV	Probability	Col 1 x Col 2	1 – EV	4 squared	Col 5 x Col 2
(£000)		(£000)	(£000)	(£000)	(£000)
6,000	0.1	600	-2,000	4,000,000	400,000
7,000	0.2	1,400	-1,000	1,000,000	200,000
8,000	0.4	3,200	0	0	0
9,000	0.2	1,800	1,000	1,000,000	200,000
10,000	0.1	1,000	2,000	4,000,000	400,000
			Sum of squared deviations		1,200,000
			Standard deviation		1,095.45
			Expected value		8,000
			Coefficient of variation		0.14

		Initiative B			
Column 1	Column 2	Column 3	Column 4	Column 5	Column 6
NPV	Probability	Col 1 x Col 2	1 – EV	4 squared	Col 5 x Col 2
(£000)		(£000)	(£000)	(£000)	(£000)
4,000	0.1	400	-4,000	16,000,000	1,600,000
6,000	0.25	1,500	-2,000	4,000,000	1,000,000
8,000	0.3	2,400	0	0	0
10,000	0.25	2,500	2,000	4,000,000	1,000,000
12,000	0.1	1,200	4,000	16,000,000	1,600,000
			Sum of squared deviations		5,200,000
			Standard deviation		2,280.35
			Expected value		8,000
			Coefficient of variation		0.29

deviation is an absolute measure of risk and as such it ignores the relative size of each initiative. So, in comparing change initiatives we should also consider a relative measure of risk – and this is provided by the 'Risk Index' or 'coefficient of variation', which is the standard deviation divided by the expected value. In Table 6.3, initiative A has a 'coefficient of variation' of 0.14 whereas initiative B has a 'coefficient of variation' of 0.29. So initiative A is less 'risky' than initiative B.

However, even with the above, the approaches to cost-benefit analysis discussed so far can be criticised in that they:

■ Assume an investment decision now is followed by a certain stream of costs and benefits. This ignores the reality that in many cases decisions will be adjusted in the light of experience – to leverage emerging opportunities or to reflect a less favourable future than was originally intended.

- Assume management is passive and recognizes risk by increasing the discount rate – but risk also has an upside, and management concerns not only minimizing downside risk but also leveraging the upside opportunity. DCF techniques fail to adequately recognize this upside potential.

- Treat the discount rate/cost of capital as being unchanged throughout the life of the initiative.

- Treat as a cost, initiatives that can be seen as value-adding from a strategic perspective. For example, a proof of concept is treated as a cost by DCF with its benefits (in providing a more informed basis for an investment decision) being ignored. The risk is that an over-reliance on DCF techniques may act as a disincentive for investment in such initiatives.

A potential solution to the above criticisms is real options analysis, which seeks to place a value on flexibility in conditions of uncertainty where decisions can change as new information becomes available.

6.3.2   Real Options Analysis

The origins of real options analysis (ROA) lie in the world of financial options where purchasing an option provides the right but not the obligation to buy (a call option) or sell (a put option) a specific share at a set value (the exercise price) on a defined date ('European' option) or at any time up to that date ('American' option). Financial options enable investors, for the price of the option, to limit their downside risk (that share prices will fall) while retaining their exposure to upside risk (to enjoy the benefits of a rise in the share price).

Examples of real options (as opposed to financial options) include the option to:

- Expand – for example a project is built with excess capacity which can be utilized if demand grows.
- Contract – for example a project is built so that if demand is less than anticipated output can be reduced.
- Switch – for example the project is built so that capacity can be expanded or contracted as required.

- Upgrade – for example this is of particular value in those initiatives with long lifecycles and in fields with a high rate of technology development.
- Defer – for example the start date of a project can be delayed until market conditions change.
- Abandon – for example to cancel a project during its life.
- Staging or sequencing – for example the option to deliver a series of initiatives in parallel or in sequence, as the outcome of the earlier projects becomes known. Another example would be the option to acquire goods incrementally rather than in one order.

Several methods of valuing real options have been developed, including the Black Scholes formula (as used for financial options) and binomial trees/ binomial lattices. There are, however, a number of issues with the application of such methods:

- The mathematics underpinning the approach can be complex (particularly with the calculus-based Black Scholes formula) – although this can be offset by the use of software solutions. Alternatively, binomial models can be used which are based on algebra and can consequently be built using spreadsheets.

- Unlike financial options, real options are rarely traded – and hence market values for the model's variables (the current value, the exercise price and the volatility of the underlying asset) are not available. Techniques such as 'Monte Carlo' simulation can partly address this by calculating probability estimates for a range of potential outcomes.

- Beyond the technical issues, there is the behavioural issue that ROA will only work if options are actually exercised when they should be – which requires projects to be stopped when the data indicates this is appropriate. Unfortunately, there is sometimes a 'conspiracy of continuation' that compromises the value that the ROA approach can provide.

The reality is that applying ROA is problematic – if only because managers have not been trained to understand it. That said, ROA does rightly emphasize the importance of recognizing the value of flexibility and it is particularly suited to organizations operating in highly uncertain environments, such as oil and gas exploration, and pharmaceuticals, and those with a strong finance background to draw on specialist knowledge and experience. In practice, however, flexibility and uncertainty is often recognized in practice by other simpler techniques such as regularly updating the NPV at each stage/phase gate, and by including qualitative ratings for such factors in a multi-criteria analysis approach (see Section 6.3.4 below).

6.3.3 Cost-effectiveness Analysis

In cost-effectiveness analysis (CEA), the costs of alternative ways of realizing the desired benefits are compared. The decision rule is, all other things being equal, to accept the option with the lowest NPC. If applied appropriately this approach has some real advantages and can help overcome some of the difficulties associated with valuing non-financial benefits in monetary terms. This is illustrated by considering the issue of mandatory initiatives.

6.3.3.1 CEA and Mandatory Initiatives

Some change initiatives won't necessarily be able to demonstrate a positive financial return on investment, at least in part because of the difficulty in quantifying and demonstrating the benefits. These include those driven by the following investment objectives:

- To meet legal or regulatory requirements – where the investment rationale is the avoidance of the consequences of not complying with the law or regulatory requirements, both financial and non-financial, including fines and damage to organizational reputation.

- The need to maintain business-critical operations – and so avoid, or lessen the risk of, the costs of failures in key operational and support systems.

- In the public sector especially, politically mandated projects, including those designed to avoid, or that are in response to, a major system or policy failure – the investment rationale being to prevent or reduce the likelihood of systemic failures including failures in the organization's purpose, core mission or duty of care.

Given the nature of the investment rationale, many of these initiatives will proceed, with or without a positive financial return on investment, and this reality should be reflected in the investment appraisal and benefits management approaches adopted. So, what options are open to us?

Firstly, there is the option of ignoring the benefits on the basis that the initiative will go ahead in any case. This approach is insufficient because:

- Many initiatives have claimed a mandatory justification only for it to become all too clear with hindsight that the initiative had little chance of actually meeting the original mandate, or that it would only partly address that mandate.

- 'Must do' projects and programmes can also easily become the 'Trojan horse' for a whole load of other functionality that would otherwise fail the investment test. For example, many IT projects were funded under the mandate of addressing the Year 2000 issue – it only became apparent later that many of these initiatives were not required to address that particular issue.

- On occasions, the mandate that originally arose in response to a real or perceived threat no longer applies with the passage of time – and yet the initiative ploughs on without regularly reaffirming that the mandate is still current.

- How do you know that the mandate could not be achieved more cost-effectively?

It is therefore recommended that even with initiatives classified as mandatory, there should be a focus on articulating and, where possible, quantifying the anticipated benefits. Two approaches are outlined below.

Mandatory Initiatives – the Expected Value Approach

One option is to value benefits on the basis of the cost of not investing. This is achieved by adopting an expected value approach, as follows:

Benefits of a mandatory project = the probability of the undesired event occurring x the cost or impact of that event.

According to Curley (2004), Deutsche Bank used a variation of this approach to value reductions in business risk. The risk of an 'event', which was defined as something that could negatively affect the bank, was the product of the probability the event would occur, the likelihood that the bank would be exposed to that event, and the impact of that event. Costs were then estimated both with and without the investment, and in this way a value for the reduction in risk could be assessed.

While this approach is intuitively appealing, there are several issues with the expected value approach:

■ How do we assign a value to an uncertain future event?
■ How to measure things that don't happen and how to attribute their avoidance to specific initiatives, i.e. just because something doesn't happen does not necessarily mean the initiative was successful – another failing may be just around the corner.
■ How do we assess the probability of the event occurring? As noted in Chapter 5 the evidence suggests that even experts can be remarkably poor at estimating probabilities.

Nevertheless, the expected value approach can be useful in informing investment decisions on mandatory initiatives. There is, however, another option that offers a way around some of the above issues by combining cost-effectiveness analysis with 'willingness to pay' analysis.

Mandatory Initiatives – the 'Willingness to Pay' Approach

There is an implicit assumption that the value of compliance with laws and regulations and avoidance of a policy failure represents, at a minimum, the net cost of the initiative designed to address this risk – if not we would not invest.

We can take this a step further by making this implicit cost explicit, based on a 'willingness to pay' approach, i.e. requiring whoever is funding the initiative to formally agree that the cost of the initiative, net of any financial benefits, represents the value placed on compliance with laws and regulations and avoidance of a policy failure. This should be supported by:

■ Firstly, a detailed cause and effect analysis (supported by a Benefits Map) to demonstrate the rationale for linking the initiative to the business requirement (approved by the Senior Responsible Owner) along with an assessment of the degree of confidence that the initiative will address the issue at hand effectively.
■ Secondly, an options analysis demonstrating that the selected solution represents the most cost-effective solution to the issue.

In this way the non-financial benefits can be valued in monetary terms on a 'willingness to pay' basis.

6.3.4 Multi-criteria Analysis

Cooper and Edgett (2006) argue that *"The best project-selection system in the world is worthless unless the data are sound."* But the problems of inaccurate forecasting and difficulties in valuing non-financial benefits mean that the data is often far from sound (although we have discussed solutions to this in the last chapter). Cooper and Edgett therefore argue that, in relation to investment appraisal and portfolio prioritization, *"all methods are somewhat unreliable; so consider using multiple selection methods in combination"*.

Multi-criteria analysis seeks to overcome the problems of unreliable forecasts by examining an initiative from more than one perspective. *'Management of Portfolios'* (MoP) contains further guidance on multi-criteria analysis, but in summary the approach:

■ Identifies the factors to consider in making a decision, i.e. choosing between options or between initiatives. Typically these factors will be listed under the twin headings of 'Attractiveness' (factors such as financial return on investment, scale of non-financial benefits, strategic contribution etc.) and

'Achievability' (factors such as technical challenge, scale of business change required, user commitment etc.).

- Weights these factors to reflect their relative importance.
- Scores options and initiatives against the weighted factors to calculate an overall score of 'Attractiveness' and 'Achievability'. These scores can then be combined and divided by the cost to provide a relative strategic 'bang for your buck' assessment.

Note that from a benefits perspective, multi-criteria analysis combines consideration of financial and non-financial benefits without attempting to value the latter in monetary terms, and combines consideration of the benefits (under the 'Attractiveness' heading in the context of the costs required to realize those benefits) with consideration of how likely it is those benefits will actually be realized (under the 'Achievability' heading). Portfolio Maps/Bubble Charts are a popular way of presenting the findings (as illustrated in Figure 10.2).

Important note

There is a risk that weightings and ratings will be set so that a preferred option scores highest. This can be mitigated by:

- Developing portfolio-wide factors and weightings.
- Independent investment appraisal, i.e. appraisals under each heading are made by subject-matter experts independent of the initiative.
- Including in the appraisal the views of those who would benefit from initiatives that are foregone or delayed should the initiative under review be approved.

The application of multi-criteria analysis is illustrated by two examples – the first comes from the world of e-government initiatives. Several frameworks have been developed to help articulate and value the benefits of these initiatives over recent years (e.g. also see the description of the US Value Measuring Methodology and Australian Demand and Value Assessment Methodology in Appendix A) but few have been applied over an extended period of

time. A notable exception in this regard is the WiBe® framework used in Germany, as described in Example 6.2.

The next example of multi-criteria analysis comes from the Obayashi Corporation in Japan, which tailors consideration of qualitative and quantitative factors to the relevant portfolio category of ICT investment (see Example 6.3).

6.4 VALUE AND BENEFITS MANAGEMENT

Alongside benefits management there is the related discipline of value management (VM), which is defined by *'Management of Value'* (MoV) as a systematic method to define what value means for organizations, and to communicate it clearly and provide methods to maximize value across portfolios, programmes, projects and operations.

Originating mainly in the manufacturing and construction industries, the discipline has been extended to projects and programmes more widely. The tools and techniques of value management include:

- Generic tools and techniques that are common to benefits and value management, as well as other related disciplines, and which are addressed elsewhere in this Guide – for example, cost-benefit analysis, multi-criteria analysis, pair-wise comparisons, the Pareto rule, risk analysis, root cause analysis, stakeholder analysis and SWOT analysis.
- Tools and techniques specific to value management, such as function analysis and value engineering and analysis.

6.4.1 Function Analysis

Function analysis is a method of analysing functions to show appropriate linkages (MoV). The two main methods of function analysis are:

1. **Function Analysis System Technique (FAST)** – FAST is a diagrammatic representation of functions and their hierarchy, expressed in one direction to address 'how' they are delivered, and in another to address 'why'. Costs are also

---

Example 6.2 – The WiBe® Framework – Germany

The WiBe framework is concerned with the ex ante appraisal and ex post evaluation of ICT project proposals (although it can also be applied to other types of initiative). It was developed by Dr Peter Röthig, from the WiBe-TEAM, as a consulting project for the German Ministry of the Interior. It has been regularly refined and updated since being first published in 1992 and is widely used at federal, state and municipal level in Germany. WiBe (the German abbreviation for economic efficiency assessment) is an interesting example of how traditional cost-benefit analysis can be combined with non-financial assessment to provide a more holistic appraisal.

The framework encompasses assessment of monetary (quantitative) and non-monetary (qualitative) impacts as follows (see Figure 6.2):

■ Monetary economic efficiency [WiBe KN] – development and operating costs and benefits expressed in NPV terms.
■ Extended economic efficiency – non-monetary factors including:
  □ Urgency of the measure (e.g. replacement of the existing system) – [WiBe D]. Assessed using 11 weighted criteria, including the stability and flexibility of the current system and compliance with the law.
  □ Qualitative strategic importance (the benefits to be realized by the proposed new system) – [WiBe Q]. Assessed using 13 weighted criteria, including impacts on strategy, task fulfilment, staff and job performance.
■ Economic efficiency from an external point of view focusing on the benefits to other institutions, companies and to the user/citizen – [WiBe E]. Assessed using 11 weighted criteria, including user friendliness and any direct economic gain to the user.

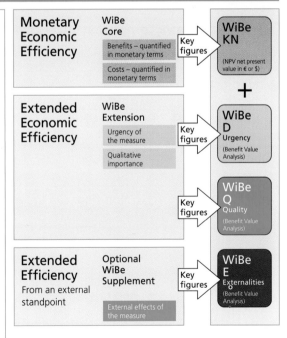

Figure 6.2 – WiBe Economic Efficiency Assessment

Example continues

Example 6.2 continued

What this means is that an initiative may have a negative NPV, and still be classified as 'efficient' (i.e. worthy of investment) in the extended sense. The approach requires some training to be most effective and is supported by a dedicated software tool. The verified results are seen in:

- More balanced Business Cases that demonstrate the full range of benefits anticipated, and, consequently, improved decisions about where to invest.
- A comprehensive framework for considering and, if necessary, modifying requirement specifications.
- A consistent methodology for evaluating the impact of projects post-implementation.

Provided with the kind agreement of Dr Peter Röthig. More information is available at http://www.eu.wibe.de/.

Example 6.3 – Benefits visualization in the Obayashi Corporation, Japan

The Obayashi Corporation is one of the world's leading construction contractors. Among its many achievements is the Tokyo Sky Tree, the world's tallest self-supporting tower at 634 metres.

Obayashi has developed a series of 'cost-benefit visualization' check sheets to provide consistency and transparency in the appraisal and evaluation of potential ICT investments – with a particular focus on ensuring forecast benefits are robust and realizable. Separate check sheets have been developed for each of four portfolio categories: Enhance Competitiveness, Support Governance, Improve Business Processes, and Modernize IT Infrastructure.

The cost-benefit visualization check sheet includes both quantitative and qualitative cost-benefit measures, and is applied as part of the investment appraisal and post-project evaluation processes. Extracts from one of the check sheets are shown in Table 6.4.

Table 6.4 – Obayashi Corporation benefits visualization check sheet

Key factor	Sub-factors	Check points
Aim/objective		Background to the project and the appropriateness of the aim/objective in the context of the Strategic Plan.
Benefits	Financial	Sales increase, profit increase, cost reduction.
	Non-financial (quantitative)	Existence of relevant key performance indicators (KPIs).
	Non-financial (qualitative)	Evaluation of qualitative benefits – how will they be realized/what difference will they make?
Risk	Project	Risks to benefits realization, functional and non-functional requirements.
	The 'do nothing' option	Implications of the project not being implemented.

Example continues

Example 6.3 continued

Key factor	Sub-factors	Check points
Cost	Initial capital investment	Initial capital investment required (CAPEX).
	Operation/running costs	Operating costs (OPEX).
Schedule		Completion date; expected time to full benefit realization.
External situation		Competitors' actions/responses, market trends.
Alternatives		Potential alternatives not requiring investment in ICT.
Implementation	Deployment/'popularization' of the new project	Process for managing deployment and 'popularization' of the project to realize the initial aim and planned benefits.

Provided with the kind assistance of Professor Hirokazu Okumura, The University of Tokyo.

added to assist in identifying any value management mismatches or areas of over-engineering.

2. **Value trees and derivatives** – a value tree is a diagram that shows the relationship between, and hierarchy of, value drivers, which can be both financial and non-financial. This can be further enhanced by prioritizing the primary value drivers to create a Value Profile.

Further analysis can then be undertaken in the form of:

■ The Value Index – this provides a method for assessing the performance of an option or initiative against the organization's Value Profile. This enables effort to be directed into underperforming areas of the initiative to improve value or expected benefits. As noted in MoV, the Value Index is relevant where additional funding can be raised.

■ The Value for Money (VfM) Ratio – this divides the Value Index by the resources/costs required to deliver that value at the value driver and initiative levels. As noted in MoV, this is relevant where available funding is limited – in such cases the decision rule is to maximize the VfM Ratio from the available funds. Note: the use of resources is usually represented as cost, but may be measured in other ways if appropriate – for example, the NASA space programme has used weight as a measure, and an oil production facility used time, because in these instances weight or time were more critical than cost.

6.4.2 Value Analysis/Engineering

Value analysis (VA) is a structured team-based approach that reviews the design and material composition of a product, building or process so that modifications can be made that reduce cost but do not reduce value to the customer.

Value engineering (VE) is a method of maximizing value within a design. It can be distinguished from VA by when it occurs: VE is concerned with reducing or avoiding costs before the production phase, whereas VA is concerned with reducing or avoiding costs during production.

6.4.2.1 Application of Value Management throughout the Benefits Management Cycle

Value management tools, techniques and studies/reviews can be usefully applied throughout the Benefits Management Cycle in ensuring that initiative development, design and delivery is aligned with the objective of optimizing benefits.

Use of value management in the Identify & Quantify practice

By starting with the objectives or required outcomes of an initiative, function analysis can help identify the value drivers needed to achieve these objectives, which can help identify the required benefits. Function analysis goes on to explore how each of these value drivers may be delivered, identifying secondary, tertiary drivers etc. The output is normally captured in a function diagram, for example a value tree. This value tree provides a succinct way to articulate an organization's objectives in terms that all can understand.

Use of value management in the Value & Appraise practice

Techniques such as paired comparisons can be used to weight attributes and assess their relative importance. This technique can also assist in the development of a robust Value Profile, showing the relative importance of each of the primary value drivers to the organization. This in turn helps appraise strategic contribution by linking benefits to strategic objectives. Further analysis in the form of the Value Index and VfM Ratio can be used to inform investment appraisals and portfolio prioritization.

For an example of the above, see the discussion of the US Government's Value Measuring Methodology in Appendix A.2.1.

Use of value management in the Plan practice

Application of value management techniques can assist in the Plan practice by, for example:

- Validation of benefits using a verb-noun description to describe the benefit unambiguously.
- Prioritization through the use of a Value Profile to align with an organization's priorities.

- Engaging stakeholders to reconcile differences in requirements and gaining their support and commitment to the delivery of the benefits via techniques such as paired comparisons.

Creative activities based on function analysis ask not *'what other benefits are there?'*, but *'how else can we achieve the benefits we seek?'*. This can be a very powerful way of uncovering innovative ideas.

Use of value management in the Realize practice

Value management can support the realization of benefits by, for example:

- The engagement of stakeholders in the value management process, together with visible commitment and leadership by senior management, promotes a value culture which is central to the optimization of benefits across the portfolio.
- The Value Index provides a relatively simple means of tracking and monitoring benefits realization at the initiative level.
- The VfM Ratio may be used to ensure that the full realization of benefits remains worthwhile and that excessive resources are not being used to achieve perfection – an application of the Pareto rule, i.e. it is better to realize 80% of the benefits cost-effectively, than to achieve 100% at greater cost than the benefits are worth.

Use of value management in the Review practice

Value management reviews are recommended at key decision points in the life of an initiative to confirm that the value drivers remain unchanged, that the optimization of value is on track, and to identify and enhance emergent benefits. These reviews can be combined with regular stage/phase gate reviews – including confirming that the solution identified remains the most cost-effective way of achieving the desired investment objectives, outcomes and benefits.

Comprehensive guidance on value management, including the principles, processes, techniques and approach to implementation, are provided in MoV.

6.5 CHAPTER SUMMARY

1. The objective of the Value & Appraise practice is to ensure resources are allocated to those change initiatives that represent the optimum use of limited funds and individually and collectively represent value for money.

2. Benefits may be valued in monetary terms to facilitate options analysis, investment appraisal and portfolio prioritization.

3. Valuing cashable financial benefits is relatively straightforward but the value of non-cashable efficiency savings depends on the use to which the time savings are put.

4. Cost avoidance benefits should be treated carefully – they are often appropriate for consideration at the options appraisal stage, but cease to be relevant once a preferred option is selected.

5. Economists have developed a series of techniques to assist in valuing non-financial benefits where market prices are absent. These include 'willingness to pay' and 'willingness to accept'. Such techniques are, however, not without issue. It is therefore recommended that cost-benefit analyses be prepared on both the economists' basis and the management accountants' basis.

6. Cost-benefit appraisal is the most commonly used form of investment appraisal and is based on DCF approaches. These, however, suffer from a number of limiting assumptions including a failure to recognize the value of flexibility. Real options analysis has been proposed as a solution to this, particularly in highly uncertain environments. However, the approach is reliant on complex mathematics and also suffers from the difficulty of determining robust values for key variables in the model.

7. Other approaches to appraisal include cost-effectiveness analysis, which can be combined with 'willingness to pay' analysis to help determine values in relation to mandatory initiatives, and multi-criteria analysis, which combines consideration of financial and non-financial benefits as well as the likelihood that those benefits will be realized.

8. Benefits and value management are mutually supportive disciplines. Value management techniques can be applied to good effect throughout the Benefits Management Cycle.

Chapter 7

Chapter 7 – Benefits Management Practice 3 – Plan

7.1 OVERVIEW OF THIS CHAPTER

So far we have identified and quantified benefits, and valued and appraised them to confirm the investment rationale and that they represent value for money. We now need to plan for their realization. The objectives of the Plan practice can be summarized as ensuring accountability and transparency for the realization of identified benefits, the changes on which they are dependent, mitigation of dis-benefits (both expected and unexpected), and identification and leveraging of emergent benefits.

The Plan practice includes the following seven main elements:

1. Validating the benefits forecast.

2. Prioritizing benefits.

3. Managing pre-transition activity.

4. Selecting appropriate benefit measures.

5. Managing benefits risks and opportunities.

6. Planning effective stakeholder engagement and communications.

7. Preparing benefits documentation – bringing the above together in the main initiative-level benefits management documentation (portfolio-level documentation is covered in Chapter 10).

These seven elements are considered in turn below – but we first emphasize four themes that underpin the effective operation of the Plan practice.

7.2 THE FOUR THEMES THAT UNDERPIN THE PLAN PRACTICE

The four themes that run across and underpin the effective operation of the Plan practice are:

1. Incorporate iterative feedback loops.

2. Undertake planning as an activity.

3. Planning extends beyond the forecast benefits.

4. Manage to achieve transparency and accountability.

7.2.1 Incorporate Iterative Feedback Loops

As stated in Chapter 4, while the Benefits Management Cycle at an initiative level is a broadly sequential process, there are iterative feedback loops throughout. Thus much of the groundwork for the preparation of the documentation outlined below in Section 7.9 will have already been undertaken. For example, we introduce the Benefits Management Strategy in this chapter, although in practice this may well be completed at the commencement of the initiative as it will include guidance on benefits identification, quantification, mapping and

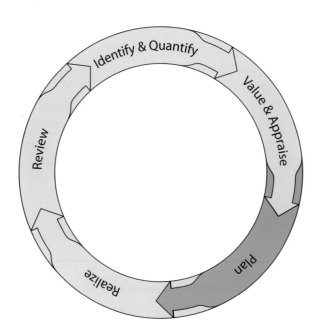

Figure 7.1 – The Plan practice in the Benefits Management Cycle

valuation. So we bring planning-related activity together in this chapter for ease of understanding rather than because the practices occur in a strictly sequential manner. The linked point is that the documents referred to below should also be maintained and updated during the Realize and Review practices. To be clear – the Plan practice extends across the Benefits Management Cycle and the various documents should be updated on a regular basis.

7.2.2 Undertake Planning as an Activity

The focus is more on planning as an activity than plans as documents. As former US president, Dwight D. Eisenhower said, *"In preparing for battle I have always found that plans are useless, but planning is indispensable".* The OGC case study on benefits management at the DVLA (2005) also highlights that *"Benefits Management is not about form filling, it's a mindset that drives benefits accountability and delivery".* Planning should therefore engage stakeholders, so ensuring a reliable basis for investment decisions, and also lay the basis for stakeholder engagement in the benefits realization process. That said, documents are important, and we outline the main initiative-level benefits management documents in Section 7.9.

7.2.3 Planning Extends Beyond the Forecast Benefits

Planning should extend beyond the forecast benefits to encompass identified dis-benefits, and to include provision for activity to identify emergent benefits and dis-benefits:

- Emergent benefits – the challenge is to identify, disseminate and leverage these benefits. But this will only happen if we take dedicated steps to ensure this happens by establishing feedback mechanisms (e.g. appointing local benefits champions), ensuring Business Change Managers actively seek out emergent benefits, and including provision in benefits reports for regular updates on the type and scale of emergent benefits identified.

- Dis-benefits – for example, downsizing initiatives in which a large number of staff are invited to apply for redundancy can deliver

significant savings and also create opportunities to remove organizational layers and empower staff. On the other hand, there is a very real risk of the loss of key skills sets and the increasingly common practice of inviting staff to re-apply for their jobs can seriously affect staff morale. These risks need to be actively managed and mitigated by strategies that include: providing people with time to adjust, active listening to their concerns, being open and recognizing their 'pain', financial compensation etc.

7.2.4 Manage to Achieve Transparency and Accountability

The result of this practice should be:

- Transparency or a 'clear line of sight' – it should be clear what benefits are envisaged, when they will be realized, how they will be measured/evidenced and who is responsible for their realization.

- Clear accountability – for the business changes on which the realization of benefits depends, and for benefits realization at the individual and collective levels. The NAO (2006) reports that one example of success was provided by the Department for Work and Pensions' Payment Modernization Programme, which had been through a successful Gate 5 Gateway review and had developed a Benefits Realization Plan assigning responsibility for promoting and securing benefits to named individuals – Benefit Owners – following implementation. Another example comes from the OGC case study on benefits management at the DVLA (2005) – here the Full Business Case was accompanied by a Benefits Delivery Plan. Senior business managers identified who would be responsible for realizing and measuring benefits after each capability had been delivered. In this way, the end accountability for delivery of benefits remained with the business.

These four themes should underpin all activities undertaken as part of the Plan practice. We now turn our attention to the seven main elements of the Plan practice.

7.3 ELEMENT 1. VALIDATING THE BENEFITS FORECAST

So we've identified and quantified the benefits from an initiative – but there still remains a key step to complete, and that's to validate the forecast benefits. Aspects of this activity will in many cases already have been undertaken as part of the appraisal process. Validation is considered in this section because it should have a specific focus on ensuring benefits are both realistic and realizable – and there are some considerations discussed below that have a direct link to planning for realization.

Validation encompasses the following five aspects:

1. **Checks to ensure benefits claimed are consistent with the organization's benefits eligibility rules** contained within the Portfolio Benefits Management Framework – including whether forecasts have been adjusted for optimism bias, or to reflect the organization's track record in benefits realization ('reference class' forecasting). To be clear, this is more than a test for technical compliance – the objective is to test the assumptions underpinning the benefits forecast by asking whether they are reasonable and reflective of the benefits likely to be realized? This check will normally be undertaken by the Portfolio Office in a *'Management of Portfolios'* (MoP) environment – and specifically, by the Portfolio Benefits Manager. Better than identifying inconsistencies between an initiative's Business Case and the Benefits Management Framework, is a policy of getting it right first time. This calls for clear communication with initiative teams and Business Case Writers to explain the role and content of the framework. This will often be supported by training sessions in the more complex and specialist aspects including benefits modelling. In this way compliance with the benefits eligibility rules can be built into the Business Case development process.

2. **Undertaking a 'dog that didn't bark' test** to avoid what Kahneman (2011a) calls the WYSIATI effect ('What You See Is All There Is'), i.e. assessing not only the identified benefits, but also asking are there any additional benefits that haven't been included? Research shows that up to 25% of potential benefits are ignored or not identified in the Business Case (Simms, 2012). The use of standard approaches to benefits categorization (see Chapter 10) can assist in this regard by prompting questions about whether all potential benefits have been identified.

3. **Checks for overlaps and dependencies with initiatives elsewhere in the organization's change portfolio.** This will usually be undertaken by the Portfolio Benefits Manager or initiative Benefits Manager, to determine:
   - ☐ Whether there are any planned or current initiatives that might impact on the benefits claimed.
   - ☐ Whether there are any anticipated changes to the strategic objectives that would impact on the benefits.

4. **Validation of each benefit with the recipient or owner** – most usually, Operational Managers in the relevant business unit, but also Strategic Planners or Policy Leads in relation to non-financial benefits that contribute to a strategic objective. This step more than any other helps ensure benefits are realizable by ensuring they are agreed with those who will be responsible for their realization in practice, and prior to investment. An example of this is shown in Example 7.1.

5. The technique of, wherever possible and appropriate, **'booking the benefits'**. Jeffery Kaplan (2005) argues, *"A lot of people ask how to track the results of ... investments. Don't track them. Book them! Build the expected benefits into the financial forecast or resource plan."* This technique is linked to the technique of agreeing 'benefits contracts' as illustrated in Example 7.2. 'Booking the benefits' is not restricted to financial benefits, and can be extended to encompass 'booking':
   - ☐ Cashable efficiency savings/improvements from all types of initiative – 'booked' in unit budgets, headcount targets or unit costs. Such savings should be agreed with the finance department and the relevant budget holder.

Example 7.1 – Validating benefits with the recipients

Validating benefits is important, but who to agree the benefits with? Where organizations have a business change function or manager that is clearly a good place to start. The approach adopted by the CJS IT portfolio involved asking each department/agency to nominate a Benefits Realization Manager (BRM). If an initiative wanted to claim benefits in their Business Case they had to agree them with these BRMs and where there was a difference of opinion it was the BRM's view that held sway. There was also a secondary form of validation:

- Efficiency/productivity benefits were agreed with the Finance Director of each relevant organization who took an obvious interest in whether or not these savings were booked in budget cuts or were reflected in lower unit costs.
- Effectiveness/performance benefits were agreed with the strategy planning function to ensure that claims were reasonable and were reflected in planned performance targets.

☐ Non-cashable efficiency improvements – as an OGC case study of benefits management in the DVLA (2005) says, *"Delivery of project headcount reductions must be accompanied by an operational resource planning process that restricts the uncontrolled migration of staff to other work."* So 'book' them in terms of planned performance improvements to be enabled by the time savings released.

☐ Non-financial strategic contributions – 'booked' by updating strategic and business delivery plans (and relevant organizational, business unit and functional performance targets) to reflect the agreed impact of the initiative.

☐ Benefits generally (both intermediate and end) – 'booked' in individuals' personal performance targets. As it says in *'Managing Successful Programmes'* (MSP), *"One way to make this 'ownership' meaningful is to link benefits realisation to personal performance targets".*

While not all benefits can be 'booked', the technique does have a number of advantages. Firstly, we gain greater confidence that benefits will be realized, although this is not without issues as we shall see below. Secondly, there is greater clarity about the benefits that will be realized, where and when. Thirdly, it provides a basis for user engagement. This is illustrated in Example 7.2.

But some words of warning – 'booking the benefits' can result in:

☐ A failure to manage the realization of benefits as it is assumed that, since we have 'booked' them, they'll automatically occur.

☐ Following on from the above, insufficient attention being given to the management of emergent benefits.

☐ Benefits minimization where people only commit to what they are sure they can achieve.

What matters is the context within which benefits are 'booked' – if the organizational culture is one based on backward-looking strict accountability for performance against forecast, then the above is often the result. Alternatively, if applied in a culture based on forward-looking learning and planning for success, then it is possible to both 'book' the benefits and optimize them. There is more on this in Chapter 8.

7.4 ELEMENT 2. PRIORITIZING THE BENEFITS

The reason why benefits may need to be prioritized is that on occasions the Identify & Quantify practice results in a long list (and sometimes a very long list) of potential benefits, and an even longer list of measures to track. Ultimately, resources are constrained and benefits realization activity therefore needs to focus on

---

Example 7.2 – Benefits contracts in Bristol City Council

Bristol City Council has adopted a system of benefits contracts that represent a binding agreement between those responsible for delivering the tools to enable change (programmes/projects) and those service areas responsible for taking the tools and embedding the changes into business as usual (BAU) so that benefits are realized. Benefits contracts can cover financial cashable benefits, financial non-cashable benefits and non-financial benefits, and serve the same purpose in all cases – to hold those responsible for realizing benefits to account. These responsibilities include:

■ The Senior Responsible Owner (SRO)/Project Executive and the Business Change Manager(s) for the programme/project are responsible for the realization of the benefit detailed within the contract.
■ The Business Partners sign to agree that the benefit detailed is realistic and achievable in their professional opinions and that benefits will be included in appropriate corporate plans. This sign-off also helps ensure that there has been no double counting of the benefit.

During the life of a project or programme, the appropriate sign-offs must be updated each time a contract is created or amended, otherwise the contract is not valid; the Project Manager will be held accountable for such an oversight. The format of the contract is shown in Table 7.1.

Table 7.1 – Benefits contract at Bristol City Council

Contract sign-off			
Project Executive sign-off:		Date:	
Benefit Owner sign-off:		Date:	
Business Partner sign-off:		Date:	
Business Change Manager sign-off:		Date:	

Provided with the kind assistance of Paul Arrigoni (Director, Business Change and ICT) and Ken Robinson (Portfolio Accountant /Benefits Realization Manager), Bristol City Council.

---

those benefits that are judged to be most significant. Approaches that can be used to identify the relative importance of each benefit include:

1. Use benefits mapping to relate benefits to the strategic objectives to enable identification of those benefits that make the greatest strategic contribution. In this way we can apply the Pareto or 80:20 rule by focusing on the 20% of benefits that represent 80% of the value.

2. Agree the relative priority of each benefit as part of the benefits discovery or mapping workshops – note, for example, that the Investment Logic Map discussed in Chapter 3 allocates percentage importance ratings to each strategic driver, investment objective and benefit. The Value Profile (Section 6.4) and

Benefits Dependency Map in Chapter 5 can also incorporate percentage ratings for intermediate benefits leading to each end benefit, and from the end benefits to the bounding objective.

3. Consider what the primary investment objective is. Most change initiatives are designed to achieve one of **four generic investment objectives**:
    1. Increase sales turnover/income – in which case the most important benefits will be those that contribute to increased income.
    2. Save costs – in which case the most important benefits will be cashable savings.
    3. Meet a legal or regulatory requirement, or maintain BAU – in which case the most important benefits will be those that relate

to whether the requirement has been met and therefore avoidance of the costs (financial or otherwise) associated with non-compliance or systems failure.

4. Contribute to the achievement of a strategic objective or business priority – in which case the most important benefits will be those that contribute most to the strategic objectives.

4. Use the Analytic Hierarchy Process to determine relative priorities by means of pair-wise comparisons – here the relative merits of benefits are debated in pairs and are ranked by assessing how much more important one is compared to the other on a sliding scale from, for example, extremely more important to extremely less important. The results can be consolidated (usually by a software programme) to provide a prioritized ranking of benefits. Software programmes can also help identify examples of what is termed Condorcet's paradox, for example where B is preferred to A, and C is preferred to B, but A is preferred to C.

7.5 ELEMENT 3. MANAGING PRE-TRANSITION ACTIVITY

MSP identifies three stages to benefits realization: pre-transition, transition and post-transition. The second and third stages are considered in Chapter 8, while pre-transition activities, which encompass the analysis, preparation and planning for business transformation, are considered here. The objective is to ensure appropriate arrangements are made for the business change upon which benefits realization is dependent. According to MSP, managing pre-transition includes the following flow steps:

- **Establish benefits measurements** – this is addressed separately below.

- **Monitor benefits realization** – this is addressed below in Section 7.6 and more fully in Chapter 8 of this Guide.

- **Plan transition** with consideration being given to:
  - ☐ Staff and their working practices.
  - ☐ Information and technology.

- ☐ Temporary facilities for those managing the transition.
- ☐ Levels of stakeholder support and engagement in the areas to be changed.
- ☐ The cultural and infrastructural migration from the old to the new.
- ☐ Integration with the programme plan to be aware that a tranche end approaches.
- ☐ Maintaining business operations during transition.
- ☐ Exit or back-out arrangements should the change fail badly.

- **Communicate the change** – taking the affected business areas, operating units and the individuals themselves through the engagement cycle for the planned changes, to raise awareness and interest, and to get engagement and involvement. MSP emphasizes that change must be carefully communicated well before actual transition.

- **Assess readiness for change** – a critical responsibility of the Business Change Manager(s) and the team involved in change is to be fully engaged with the project teams and the business operations and to immerse them in the change that is coming. This happens at a point where the project outputs have been, or are being, delivered and the Business Change Managers need to make the decision as to whether the capability meets the needs of the business and that the business is ready for transition. The recommendation is made by the Business Change Manager, but the ultimate decision sits with the SRO, who remains accountable for benefits realization. Factors to consider in coming to this recommendation and decision include:
  - ☐ Recent track record and experience of change.
  - ☐ Past experience of implementing this type of change.
  - ☐ Availability of resources to support the change in terms of volume, competency and experience.
  - ☐ How the intended change fits with the organization's culture and values, i.e. whether it goes deeper than a change to ways of working.

□ Effectiveness of the supporting systems that could enable change – for example, communications channels.

□ Skills and mobility of the workforce.

□ Current status of service-level performance to customers and degree of satisfaction.

□ Third-party supplier performance and alignment with change plans.

□ Service management's ability to support the organization through transition and in its new operational state.

Another approach to assessing readiness for change is that outlined in Section 10.3.2.1.

As part of the pre-transition stage, the Benefit Profiles and Benefits Realization Plan should also be updated (these documents are covered in Section 7.9 below).

High-level responsibilities for pre-transition management in an MSP environment are shown in Table 7.2.

The importance of this element of the Plan practice should not be underestimated – insufficient focus is often given to planning the process and the organizational changes on which benefits realization is dependent. The Benefits Dependency Network (see Section 5.2.2.3) can help address this by identifying and recording the enabling and business changes on which benefits realization is dependent – and for which accountabilities can then be assigned.

7.6 ELEMENT 4. SELECTING APPROPRIATE BENEFITS MEASURES

Firstly, it needs to be stressed that measurement starts well before transition with baselining current performance as explained in Chapter 5. The usual approach to identifying benefits measures is via a facilitated workshop including: the Benefit Owners and end-users/customers; the Portfolio Benefits Manager; Business Change Manager; representatives from the performance management function (to advise on what current measures may be appropriate); and those who will be responsible for collecting the data in due course including the Project/Programme Office Benefits Manager.

A number of considerations need to be kept in mind when selecting appropriate measures, and these are discussed below, but first we need to think about why we measure, what are the characteristics of a good measurement system, and what types of measure are available to us.

Table 7.2 – Typical responsibilities for pre-transition management

Flow steps	SRO	Programme Manager	Business Change Managers (and Team)	Programme Office
Manage pre-transition				
Establish benefits measurements	A	C	R	C
Monitor benefits realization	A	C	R	C
Plan transition	A	R	R	C
Communicate the change	A	C	R	C
Assess readiness for change	A	C	R	I
R = responsible (gets the work done); A = accountable (answerable for the programme's success); C = consulted (supports, has the information or capability required); I = informed (notified but not consulted).				

7.6.1 Why Do We Measure?

Agreeing benefits measures serves several purposes:

- Measures can help in forecasting/quantifying the scale of benefit anticipated.
- Agreeing measures helps communicate what is regarded as important and contributes to a collective understanding as to what constitutes success.
- Agreeing measures for each of the benefits with relevant stakeholders provides a basis for tracking and managing benefits realization.
- The use of leading measures can help in providing an early warning where things may not be going according to plan, so enabling timely corrective action to be taken.
- Measures provide a basis for obtaining feedback about what works and so enable more evidence-based benefits management based on insight and learning.
- Measures provide a basis for accountability – if the Business Case Writer and project sponsor know that benefits claimed will be tracked and evaluated, they are more likely to ensure that benefits claimed are reasonable and that appropriate plans are put in place for their realization. This also helps build confidence on the part of stakeholders, particularly those involved in the funding allocation process.
- Measures influence behaviour – and so can support (or conflict with) the desired outcomes and benefits. Appropriately designed, measures can engage stakeholders in the optimization of benefits realization (see Chapter 8), but they can also have the opposite effect as illustrated below in Section 7.6.6.

7.6.2 What Are the Characteristics of a Good Measurement System?

The characteristics of good measurement systems are that they are:

- **Efficient:** the benefits measurements should be linked, wherever possible, to the organization's performance management system and make use of data available from the management information system – this helps minimize the additional costs of new measurement systems. Where additional measures are required, try to make provision for this in the design of the initiative – so measurement data is automatically collected. This requires that consideration be given to benefits measurement during initiative design.

- **Effective:** this means they should:
  - □ Avoid negative unintended consequences.
  - □ Be motivational and drive the required behaviour.
  - □ Be reliable, i.e. changes in the measure should reliably reflect changes in the underlying performance and be reliably attributable to the initiative.

- **Sufficient:** the measures should provide sufficient assurance that the key underlying benefits have been realized. This means that consideration will need to be given to issues such as sample size as well as selecting a suite of measures.

Much of the above is reflected in the extract shown in Example 7.3 from Standard Chartered Bank's Benefits Management guidelines.

7.6.3 What Types of Measure Are Available to Us?

Measures can be categorized into pairs as follows: quantitative or qualitative; financial or non-financial; leading or lagging; and direct or indirect (see Table 7.3).

The approach to measuring and tracking benefits should be recorded in the initiative's Benefits Management Strategy and the specific measures to be used for each benefit should be recorded on the relevant Benefit Profile and in the Benefits Realization Plan (see Section 7.9).

On the other hand, as Einstein is reputed to have said, *"Not everything that can be counted counts, and not everything that counts can be counted"*. Consequently, measurement is not without its issues. Some of the key issues to consider in relation to benefits measurement are outlined below, along with appropriate solutions.

Example 7.3 – Standard Chartered Bank: guidance on selecting KPIs

A key performance indicator (KPI) provides a 'leading' indicator, demonstrating that a change has occurred as forecast by a project. This is particularly useful where non-financially quantifiable benefits are targeted, but is also of value when a number of initiatives contribute to one overall benefit. To measure the varying success and contribution of each initiative, KPIs should be employed to monitor changes in performance at the same time as the realization of the (financial) benefit is tracked.

Where possible, existing KPIs should be used rather than establishing new KPIs. These KPIs should be:

■ Simple to understand and communicate to all involved in producing change.
■ Specific and detailed – if KPIs are too high-level, it becomes difficult to confirm the cause and effect relationship between programme activity and change, as many other influences will come into play.
■ Supported by data that is available on a regular basis with limited resource investment.
■ Available in a meaningful frequency of measurement.
■ Where possible, aligned to individuals' performance objectives.

Source: *'Management of Portfolios'*. Provided with the kind agreement of Tim Carroll.

Table 7.3 – Types of measure

Measure type	Description
Quantitative or qualitative	Quantitative – measures expressed in numerical terms, e.g. hours saved, income generated etc.
	Qualitative – measures expressed in descriptive terms, e.g. satisfaction ratings.
Financial or non-financial	Financial – measures expressed in £/$/€ terms, e.g. increased revenue, reduced cost etc.
	Non-financial – measures expressed in non-financial terms, e.g. increased production, customer satisfaction etc.
Leading or lagging	Leading – measures that 'lead' to attainment of an outcome or lag measure, e.g. completion of a customer training programme, which results in improved customer satisfaction and in turn to improved financial performance via improved customer retention. Referred to by Kaplan & Norton (1996) as 'performance drivers'.
	Lagging – measures that 'lag' the change and which reflect the impact of something that has already occurred, e.g. increased profits from improved customer retention resulting from improved customer service which result from a customer service training programme. Referred to by Kaplan & Norton as 'outcome measures'.
Direct or indirect (proxy)	Direct – measures where there is a direct relationship between the measure and the benefit it is seeking to measure.
	Indirect/proxy – a measurement of one physical quantity that is used as an indicator of the value of another. For example, per capita GDP is often used as a proxy measure for the standard of living.

7.6.4 Don't Confuse the Monetary Value Attributed to a Benefit With the Underlying Benefit

Where non-financial benefits are valued in monetary terms there is a very real risk that managers will confuse such attributed monetary values with the real nature of the benefit – it is therefore emphasized that monetary values used for appraisal and prioritization purposes should be reviewed and amended where required for benefits realization management purposes. What this means is that the measure should be appropriate to the benefit. This can be aided by the adoption of a Benefits Measurement Taxonomy relating the measures selected to the type of benefit – as shown in Table 7.4.

Example 7.4 shows how measures can be related to the various categories of benefit – in this case various types of financial benefit.

7.6.5 Measuring the Wrong Things or Reaching Unreliable Conclusions

As the quote attributed to Einstein above highlights, sometimes what is important is difficult to measure. The risk is therefore that we focus on the easily measured, but unimportant benefits, and/or over-rely on measures that don't actually reflect the underlying reality of benefits realization. The solutions include: prioritizing benefits as discussed above, and developing a suite of leading and lagging measures encompassing quantitative and qualitative data including proxy indicators, evidence events, case studies, surveys and stories. The value of a suite of measures is that they can provide insight into, and a 'rich picture' of, benefits realization by providing feedback from more than one perspective.

A particular problem concerns attribution, i.e. the extent to which we can confidently say that a change in the measure's value reflects a change in the underlying benefit; and the change in the measure can be attributed to the initiative, rather than some other factor. Partial solutions to the attribution issue include: benefits mapping to agree the logical chain of cause and effect, agreeing lead as well as lag/outcome measures, and recognizing the uncertainty that exists by applying confidence ratings to benefits and their measures – see Figure 7.2.

Table 7.4 – A Benefits Measurement Taxonomy

Benefit category	Measures and indicators	Measure/indicator type
Efficiency – cashable	Budget reductions	Quantitative financial
	Lower unit cost	Quantitative financial
Efficiency opportunity value	Time redeployed to other activities	Quantitative non-financial
	Activity measure in the area to which resources have been redeployed, i.e. what differences has the redeployment of resources made?	Quantitative non-financial
	Value of time saved	Quantitative economic
Effectiveness/performance improvement	Leading and lagging indicators relevant to the area of performance impacted	Quantitative and qualitative non-financial
	Value of improved performance	Quantitative economic
Cost avoidance	Money recycled to fund the initiative running costs	Quantitative financial
	Operating budget reductions	Quantitative financial
	Indicators of what the money saved has been used for	Quantitative economic or non-financial or qualitative

Example 7.4 – Financial benefits – example measures in Openreach

Financial classification	Benefits description	Example measures
Cost reduction	**Bankable savings** – year-on-year reductions to the existing cost base for the same (or comparable) volume of work.	Unit costs, people numbers, cost per component, other relevant key performance indicators (KPIs) (e.g. overtime levels), bad debt reduction, specific cost line movements.
	Potential savings – enablers to savings, e.g. processes automated or changed.	Cost per process decreased (through time taken), increase in asset utilization, systems availability increased, Right First Time (RFT) measures improving.
	Released capacity – higher usable time for the same number of people.	Sickness decreased, Lost Time Incidents (LTIs) reduced, ineffective time reduced, training days decreased.
Cost avoidance	Actions which stop the existing cost base increasing for the same (or comparable) volume of work.	Systems availability maintained, RFT measures maintained, other relevant KPIs maintained, legal or regulatory incidents kept to minimum, specific cost lines maintained.
Increased revenue	Sales from new products or services, sales in new markets, higher sales from existing products/services.	Sales made £ and volume, revenue per sale, revenue per customer/market/product, market share.
Revenue assurance	Retaining business otherwise lost.	As above.

Provided with the kind agreement of Jim Runnacles, Openreach (a BT Group company), and Sarah Harries, Head of Business Improvement, BT.

RAG matrix for assessing confidence in benefits realization		Possibility that factors outside the initiative impact on benefit realization			
		High	Medium	Low	Nil
Confidence in attributing benefits realization to the initiative	Score	1	2	3	4
Empirical evidence supporting cause and effect	3	Red 3	Amber 6	Green 9	Green 12
Logical argument for cause and effect supported by some empirical evidence that is testable over time	2	Red 2	Red 4	Amber 6	Amber 8
Logical argument for cause and effect but with little or no empirical evidence and testing the relationship is problematic	1	Red 1	Red 2	Red 3	Red 4

Figure 7.2 – Assessing confidence in benefits using a red/amber/green (RAG) matrix

7.6.6 Measures Can Have Unanticipated Consequences

Measurement is rarely passive and can have unanticipated, and even unintended, consequences. These consequences include:

- A positive benefit that was not forecast or was not forecast in the scale realized, i.e. unplanned or emergent benefits. An example is the largely unforeseen popularity of texting by users of mobile phones.

- Unanticipated dis-benefits that occur as well as the planned and emergent benefits. For example, irrigation schemes provide water for agriculture, but also increase waterborne diseases that can have serious negative effects on the health of the local population.

- 'Gaming' the system, i.e. where people pursue the measure but with little impact on the intended outcome. Meadows (2008) describes this as *"perverse behaviour that gives the appearance of obeying the rules or achieving the goals, but that actually distorts the system"*. For example, it is widely reported that the result of the NHS target that patients should be able to get an appointment with a GP or nurse within 48 hours is that many patients find it difficult to book an appointment more than 48 hours ahead.

- A perverse incentive exists, which means that the outcome is actually the opposite of what was intended. This is illustrated by Example 7.5.

Solutions include making clear to all concerned that the benefit is what matters not appearance manipulation, closely monitoring the impact, monitoring both leading and lagging measures,

and, according to Meadows (2008), *"Design or redesign, rules to release creativity not in the direction of beating the rules, but in the direction of achieving the purpose of the rules"*. This last point highlights the potential that exists to use measures, when appropriately designed, not as a way of tracking against a pre-set forecast, but as a way of engaging stakeholders in the active realization of benefits. So, consider the measures set and ask: do they motivate behaviours that are consistent with, or contrary to, the desired outcomes and benefits? Then review performance to ensure measures have the anticipated effect.

7.6.7 Don't Confuse Forecasts With Targets

Linked to the last point, managers often confuse forecasts with targets, in particular where strict accountability means that benefits are tightly tracked against forecasts. The problem is that this often results in appearance manipulation, particularly where benefits forecasts were overstated in the Business Case as a way of justifying funding for the initiative. This issue of selecting appropriate measures is considered further in the next chapter. For the time being, it is emphasized that:

- Forecasts are prepared to inform the investment decision and should therefore be accurate and realistic.
- Targets should be 'SMART': Specific, Measurable, Achievable, Relevant and Time-bound. But 'achievable' does not have to mean 'easy' – ambitious and aspirational targets can have a motivational effect when used in a forward-looking rather than backward-looking way.

Example 7.5 – Perverse incentives and the 'Cobra effect'

The term 'Cobra effect' is derived from an anecdote from the time of British rule in colonial India. The British government wanted to decrease the population of venomous cobra snakes, and so they offered a reward for every dead snake. At first this policy was successful as the resourceful locals set about killing the snakes. However, in due course, some realized there was an income to be made from breeding cobras. When the government realized this, the reward was cancelled, and many of the breeders set the snakes free. The snakes subsequently multiplied, and increased the cobra population. The result – the situation the policy was designed to address was made worse by that very policy.

What all this means is that, while at least one measure should be identified for each benefit, these measures need to be selected with care, and consideration should be given to selecting a suite of measures. While benefits should belong to one category in the benefits eligibility rules, several measures may be selected for each benefit to provide evidence of realization from multiple perspectives. In this way a 'rich picture' of benefits realization can be obtained from measures that include:

- Leading and lagging measures – selected to evidence benefits realization across the chain identified in the Benefits Map encompassing:
  - Leading measures of enabling changes, business changes and intermediate benefits.
  - Lagging measures of end benefits.
- Proxy indicators – especially where direct measures are difficult to obtain.
- Evidence events – i.e. events that can be observed and which provide evidence that the benefit has been realized. These can be stated in the form of a 'date with destiny'; for example, *"Three months from today, the SRO will visit a front line office and discuss the improvements seen with staff and customers"*.
- Case studies – capturing both good and bad news, as well as lessons learned.

- Surveys – of users, staff and management. This is addressed in the next chapter.
- Stories – to provide a living example of the potential benefits from change. See Example 7.6.

This 'rich picture' approach is further illustrated in Examples 7.7 and 7.8.

7.7 ELEMENT 5. MANAGING BENEFITS RISKS AND OPPORTUNITIES

Our focus here is on providing a high-level overview of benefits risk (and opportunity) management. More detailed guidance on risk management is available in *'Management of Risk'* (M_o_R) and MSP.

MSP defines risk as an uncertain event or set of events that, should it occur, will have an effect on the achievement of objectives. Risk management concerns the identification and assessment of risks, and the planning and implementation of appropriate risk responses.

Risk management extends throughout the Benefits Management Cycle – prior to transition the focus will be on identifying potential risks to benefits realization and appropriate mitigation strategies, while post-transition the focus will be

---

Example 7.6 – Stories – The Crown Prosecution Service Case Management System in action

When a lorry fire on a motorway prevented a Crown Prosecution Service (CPS) file being delivered to the prosecuting lawyer at the Crown Court it looked like a potentially dangerous criminal could go free on bail. The defence counsel made a bail application on the basis that the prosecution could not establish the grounds for opposing bail without any paperwork, therefore compelling the Judge to accept the defence version of events. However, they hadn't counted on the Case Management System (CMS)! The case had initially been logged by a duty lawyer working at a charging centre. Details were sent electronically to the magistrates' court and the case was subsequently referred to the Crown Court, with details being updated on the CMS. The availability of a secure computer terminal at the Crown Court allowed the prosecutor opposing bail to call up the case details and the defence subsequently withdrew their application. The defendant was remanded in custody on charges of possession with intent to supply, grievous bodily harm, kidnap, and intent to kill. The defendant was subsequently convicted of having an offensive weapon, assault occasioning actual bodily harm, common assault and possessing a Class B drug – resulting in a sentence of three and a half years' imprisonment.

Sourced from: http://www.eurim.org.uk/activities/pi/data_sharing_case_studies/dscs9_logicacmg.pdf
[Last accessed 16 June 2012]

Example 7.7 – Tell Us Once: a flexible approach to measurement

The approach adopted by the cross-government Tell Us Once (TUO) programme was tailored to the specific benefits under the following headings:

- **Citizens** – time and cost savings in notifying government of change of circumstances, and improved experience from reduced avoidable contact.
- **Staff** – belief in improved services and job satisfaction.
- **Local government** – improved use of resources, reduced fraud, reduced write-offs of overpayments, and reduced administrative costs.
- **Central government** – more efficient use of resources including reduced overpayments and hence write-offs and administration of recovery costs.

Thus, in relation to savings to central government, the focus was on establishing that planned savings were realistic and actually achieved, and ensuring clear accountability for this. In relation to local government, front-line staff and citizens, the approach was one based less on tracking forecasts and more on learning and feedback. This reflected the primary investment objective of improving the customer experience, while at the same time confirming that forecast efficiencies were realistic and that there was not an unfunded pressure on local authorities. As part of this approach a Benefits Realization Management Toolkit was prepared including Benefits Logic Maps for the Birth and Death service offerings. Local authorities then selected the benefits that were of most importance to them from the relevant Benefits Logic Map, and considered how best to obtain reliable evidence of benefits realization, including indicators, surveys, case studies and evidence events (i.e. pre-scheduled 'dates with destiny' that provide confidence that the forecast impact has transpired – e.g. "on 31st March the Chief Executive will talk to 10 members of the public and front-line staff about what difference the service is making").

These measures were recorded on a Key Benefits Evidence Log, which included sample measures from the early adopter sites. Short surveys were also included – for customers (see Example 8.5), for staff and for management. In this way, the programme sought to obtain feedback on benefits realization from several perspectives, rather than the 'achieved/not achieved' paradigm – and focused not just on forecast benefits but also on emergent/unplanned benefits.

Based on a case study published in ICCPM (2011)

---

more on monitoring risks to ensure that they don't adversely impact benefits realization. Two points should be noted:

1. Here we are concerned with initiative-level benefits realization, both in terms of timing and scale. Chapter 10 addresses portfolio-level benefits risk management.

2. Risk has both a downside and an upside – so we need to consider not only what might go wrong, but also opportunities for increasing benefits realization.

7.7.1 Benefits Risk Management

The Benefits Management Strategy will include the arrangements for managing benefits-related risks at an initiative level. Such risks will vary from initiative to initiative but one way in which their identification can be facilitated is via a benefits risk framework that considers risks to benefits optimization in relation to five sources of failure:

- **Forecasting failure:** for example benefits are not identified or are overestimated.
- **Delivery failure:** i.e. failure to deliver the initiative with the planned functionality and on time, so impacting on the scale and timing of benefits realization.

Example 7.8 – Standard Chartered Bank – selecting a suite of benefit KPIs

The Benefits Management guidelines at Standard Chartered Bank include the following: Assuming that the targeted objective of a fictitious project is 'to increase the number of customers who are highly satisfied by levels of service in all Hong Kong branches by 30% by the end of Q2', the obvious benefit would be increased customer satisfaction. Given this, the targeted improvement to be monitored through KPIs could be:

Performance improvement	Measure	Frequency	Baseline period	Baseline value
Customer satisfaction	Score (out of 10)	Quarterly	Q4	6.34
Queuing time	Average no. of minutes	Monthly	H2 average	2.15 minutes
Customer complaints	Absolute number	Weekly	Q4 average	26
Closed accounts	% per 10,000 customers	Weekly	Q4 average	0.5%

Source: *'Management of Portfolios'*. Provided with the kind agreement of Tim Carroll.

- **Business and behavioural change failure:** i.e. the business and behavioural changes on which benefits realization is dependent don't occur or are poorly scheduled (causing delay in benefits realization).
- **Benefits management failure:** in relation to capturing and leveraging emergent benefits and mitigating dis-benefits.
- **Value for money failure:** the benefits are realized but at excessive cost.

Once identified, risks can usefully be stated in a common format, such as *"Because of (causes), (risk) might occur, which would lead to (effects)"*. For example: *"Because of optimism bias, benefits forecasts might be overstated, which will lead to potentially sub-optimal investment decisions and benefits realization shortfalls"*.

The identified risks can be appraised using the normal Probability x Impact approach and this can be recorded in the initiative risk register along with the risk owner and what mitigating actions are to be taken.

7.7.2 Benefits Opportunity Management – Capturing and Leveraging Emergent Benefits

Risk management concerns exposure to variability in outcomes compared with those forecast. As such it encompasses both downside and upside risk, i.e. outcomes that are both worse and better than those anticipated. Risk management in practice, however, is often more concerned with the mitigation of downside risk than leveraging opportunities to create value and improve benefits realization. But we should not lose sight of the potential for upside variances from forecast – and this is the domain of opportunity management with its focus on capturing and leveraging emergent benefits. How then can organizations ensure that this potential is managed effectively?

The key to opportunity management, as with risk management, is not only to manage what we know, but to also be aware of the limits to our knowledge. To borrow from Donald Rumsfeld: *"There are known knowns; there are things we know we know. We also know there are known unknowns; that is to say we know there are some things we do not know. But there are also unknown unknowns – the ones we don't know we don't know."* This is less about the completion of a written plan, and more about establishing a culture in which opportunities are expected and anticipated. So we are talking about an approach that includes the following five strategies:

1. **Adoption of modular or agile approaches to project design and development** where lessons learned and emergent understandings are captured and applied on a regular, if not continuing, basis. At a minimum, opportunities should be assessed at each stage or phase gate review.

2. Apply what Andrew & Sirkin (2006) refer to as **a 'scout and beacon' approach** in which:
   a. 'Scouts' scan the environment for potential opportunities.
   b. 'Beacons' are 'lit' clearly communicating that ideas are welcomed.

3. **Ongoing participative engagement with users** to capture feedback and provide insight via a suite of measures and 'narrative leadership' (see Section 8.5.6). In such ways, a real and ongoing dialogue with users can help identify emergent benefits and opportunities to create additional value.

4. As with a benefits taxonomy, so there is value in **an opportunities taxonomy** to classify opportunities and assist in their identification. Such a taxonomy includes the following four types of opportunity:
   1. New users/markets for current initiative functionality/components.
   2. New uses/applications for current initiative functionality/components.
   3. Ways in which initiative scope can be changed to meet current user/market needs.
   4. Ways in which initiative scope can be changed to meet unanticipated or emerging user/market needs.

5. Taking **a portfolio approach** – just as portfolio-level risks (as covered in Section 10.3.2.1) can extend beyond the risks of the individual initiatives to encompass both generic and aggregated risks, so too organizations can gain by taking a portfolio-based view of opportunity management. They can ask, on a regular basis (at the portfolio-level reviews for

example), whether opportunities are being identified and leveraged across the organization's portfolio and what lessons can be learned and applied.

7.8 ELEMENT 6. PLANNING EFFECTIVE STAKEHOLDER ENGAGEMENT

In Chapter 5 we considered the technique of 'customer insight' to bring the 'voice of the customer' into the design of an initiative, and in the next chapter we explore techniques that can tap into people's creativity and commitment to optimize benefits realization by winning hearts as well as minds. This highlights that effective stakeholder engagement is so much more than communication – what we are referring to is active participation throughout the business change lifecycle to build commitment to realizing the desired benefits. An enabler for such strategies is an understanding of an initiative's stakeholders and their position in relation to the initiative. This is aided by stakeholder segmentation and analysis:

■ **Segmenting stakeholders** – into relevant groupings which enables messages to be more effectively tailored to the audience. MSP suggests the following four segments:
   □ Users/beneficiaries.
   □ Governance – management boards, steering groups, audit.
   □ Influencers – for example trade unions and the media.
   □ Providers – suppliers, business partners.

   Alternatively, Davies & Davies (2011) suggest three key categories of stakeholder:
   □ Those with an ownership interest – shareholders and government on behalf of taxpayers.
   □ Those who buy, use or are affected by the initiative – e.g. customers.
   □ Those who are involved in the initiative in transforming inputs into outputs and outcomes – e.g. staff and suppliers.

■ **Stakeholder analysis** – for example analysing stakeholders in terms of their interest/ influence. This can then be plotted on an 'influence–interest' matrix as illustrated in

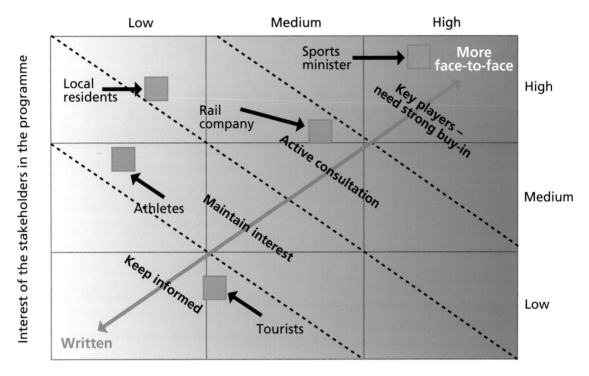

Figure 7.3 – *Example influence–interest matrix of a sports-complex programme*

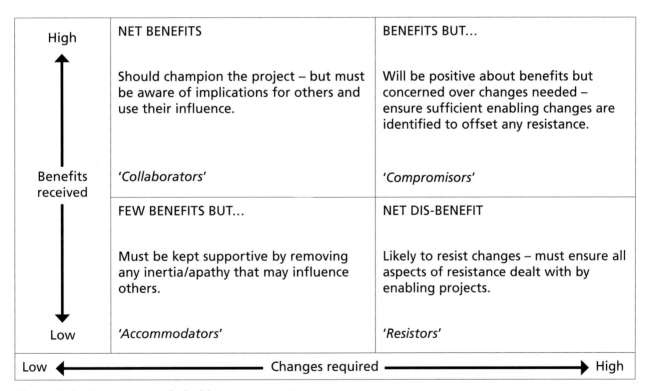

Figure 7.4 – *Summary stakeholder assessment*

Figure 7.3 from MSP. This also enables the identification of appropriate engagement strategies depending on where each stakeholder sits on the matrix.

Another approach to stakeholder analysis is that recommended by Ward & Daniel (2006), which considers stakeholders in terms of the benefits or dis-benefits they will receive and the scale of change the initiative implies for them. This again can be plotted on a matrix, as shown in Figure 7.4.

Whichever approach to stakeholder analysis is used, the purpose of such analyses is to inform the design and delivery of more effective stakeholder engagement strategies. It should also be remembered that an initiative's stakeholders will change over time, as will their relationship to, and views of, the initiative – so stakeholder analysis needs to be refreshed on an ongoing basis. Central to this is effective communications.

7.8.1 Effective Benefits Communications

Effective communications is a theme that runs throughout the Benefits Management Cycle – not least because it can *"excite management buy-in"* (APM, June, 2011) and so contribute to benefits realization. This requires that consideration be given to:

1. **The purpose of the communication,** including:
   - ☐ To inform – in which case ensure the message is succinct and clear. Considerations: augment text with graphical presentation of data (including Benefits Maps) and the use of colour; include both positive and negative information; include an Executive Summary with detailed information in appendices; enable 'drill down' so stakeholders are able to access more detailed information if required.
   - ☐ To act as a catalyst to action – ensure the issue and proposed action is clearly stated, and is addressed to those able to take the required action. Considerations: apply the 'management by exception' technique and highlight those actions that require management attention; consider rating the importance of action using high, medium, low ratings etc.

2. **The audience** – i.e. tailor the message to the audience:
   - ☐ Senior management – high-level, summary data, but broad in scope, i.e. encompassing all types of benefit and the whole organization.
   - ☐ Other stakeholders including operational management – lower-level, more detailed data focusing on specific types of benefit relevant to the specific stakeholder group.

3. **The presentation** – effective communication is aided by:
   - ☐ The use of consistent presentation formats and reporting to an agreed schedule so that the data becomes familiar to the stakeholders.
   - ☐ The use of a common language – the agreement of a Portfolio Benefits Management Framework with agreed definitions for key terms is therefore crucial.
   - ☐ Avoid jargon and use simple English.
   - ☐ Augment text with graphical presentation, and the use of video and audio.
   - ☐ Crucially, ensure data is timely and accurate.

4. **The medium/channel used** – this includes:
   - ☐ Face to face – meetings, conferences, workshops etc.
   - ☐ Paper/text – reports, briefings, plans etc.
   - ☐ Online – intranet repositories holding templates, documents etc.; online magazines and forums; intranet blogs; a multimedia library including video and audio guidance (see Example 9.5); and the use of online discussion groups.

Crucially, there need to be feedback loops that ensure communication is two-way and to ensure communication is effective.

7.9 ELEMENT 7. PREPARING BENEFITS DOCUMENTATION

While the emphasis should be on planning rather than plans, the latter are still important as the embodiment of the former and to ensure a shared understanding by all relevant stakeholders, inform benefits realization activity and act as the baseline against which to assess progress. The output of the Plan practice should therefore be a series of benefits documents that clearly identify what benefits are anticipated from an initiative, how they will be managed and who is responsible for realizing them.

Table 7.5 shows the purposes of the three main initiative-level benefits management planning documents – the Benefits Management Strategy, the Benefits Realization Plan (which will usually

Table 7.5 – Purpose of benefits management planning documentation

Benefits management documentation	Purpose	Approver	Producer	Reviewer
Benefits Management Strategy	Defines the approach to realizing benefits and the framework within which benefits realization will be achieved.	SRO	PgM	BCM
Benefits Realization Plan	Used to track realization of benefits across the programme and set review controls.	SRO	PgM	BCM
Benefit Profile*	Used to define each benefit (and dis-benefit) and provide a detailed understanding of what will be involved and how the benefit will be realized.	SRO	BCM	PgM

* Note – the Benefit Profiles can be combined into a Benefits Register. SRO = Senior Responsible Owner, PgM = Programme Manager, BCM = Business Change Manager.

Table 7.6 – Benefits and the Five-Case Business Case framework

Case – focus	Key benefits perspective
Strategic case – is the initiative supported by a robust case for change?	■ Do the benefits clearly contribute to the strategic objectives? ■ Is the planned strategic contribution quantified?
Economic case – does the preferred way forward optimize value for money?	■ Do the identified benefits exceed the costs and dis-benefits of the initiative and the results of not investing? ■ Does the preferred option optimize value for money? (demonstrated via an options analysis).
Financial case – is the initiative affordable?	■ Are there any cashable benefits that can be recycled to help fund the initiative?
Commercial case – is the initiative commercially viable?	■ Can supplier payments be linked to benefits realization in some form of gain-sharing or reward-sharing arrangement?
Management case – can the initiative be delivered successfully?	■ Have adequate arrangements been made for benefits management and evaluation? ■ Have lessons learned from previous initiatives been applied throughout the Business Case? ■ Has a Benefits Management Strategy been completed and is it consistent with the Portfolio Benefits Management Framework? ■ Has a Benefits Realization Plan, with supporting Benefit Profiles and Map(s), been completed?

include the Benefits Map(s)), and the Benefit Profile – and the relevant roles associated with the production of each.

The typical contents of each of the three documents are shown in Appendix B along with a template for a Benefit Profile.

7.9.1 Benefits and the Business Case

These documents will also be used to inform the preparation, and support the presentation, of the Business Case. Responsibility for producing the Business Case resides with the Programme Manager, although in practice they will be supported by Programme/Project Office staff and in many cases there may be a dedicated Business Case Writer supported by a virtual team.

Different organizations will have varying formats and guidance for the preparation of a Business Case, and those charged with preparing one should always:

1. Check with the Portfolio Office/Programme Office/Centre of Excellence etc. for the template(s) they are expected to follow.

2. Ensure they understand the organization's guidance for identifying, classifying and valuing costs and benefits – contact the finance department for the former and see the Portfolio Benefits Management Framework for the latter.

3. Review the organization's lessons-learned database and/or talk with the Portfolio Office/ Centre of Excellence about lessons learned from previous change initiatives that are of relevance to the initiative at hand.

The OGC recommends (see Flanagan & Nicholls) the use of the Five-Case Business Case framework as shown in Table 7.6.

This format is applied to the development of the Business Case through its various stages – for example, HM Treasury guidance (Flanagan & Nicholls) recommends the three-phase approach shown in Table 7.7.

But less important than the format is the mindset applied in preparing the Business Case. As we saw in Chapter 2, the problems with benefits realization can, in many cases, be tracked back to the Business Case. For this reason it is fundamental that we move beyond 'box-ticking' approaches where the Business Case is used as the vehicle to obtain funding and is then quickly forgotten. The lessons from those who have adopted more effective practices are not that the Business Case can't add value, but rather that the focus should be on answering the following key questions:

1. *"Is it worth spending £x to get the identified benefits?"* rather than *"have we identified sufficient benefits to justify the cost?"*
   - What is the scale of the benefits?
     - Is the strategic contribution clearly identified in measurable terms (and by when it will be achieved)?
     - Have the assumptions underlying the Benefits Map been identified and challenged?
     - Have all potential sources of benefit been identified? Apply the 'dog that didn't bark' test.
   - Does the initiative represent value for money?
     - Do the benefits exceed the costs (all the costs) required to realize those benefits?
     - Is it clear that the option recommended is the most cost-effective way of delivering the desired strategic contribution?
     - Can the costs be reduced without damaging business value?

Table 7.7 – Business Case development

Strategic Outline Case (SOC)	Outline Business Case (OBC)	Full Business Case (FBC)
Phase 1: initial scoping.	Phase 2: planning. Prior to OJEC (pre-procurement).	Phase 3: selection of solution/procurement. Following competition (pre-contract).
Primary purpose:	Primary purpose:	Primary purpose:
1. To establish the case for change and strategic fit with other programmes. 2. To indicate the preferred way forward.	3. To identify a preferred option. 4. To assess potential value for money, affordability and achievability.	5. To select the service solution. 6. To finalize post-procurement arrangements.

OJEC – Official Journal of the European Union

□ Are all parts of the recommended solution necessary to deliver the benefits?

□ Are the implications of not investing clear and reliable?

2. *Will the benefits be realized?*

□ Is there a clear understanding as to how the enabling and business changes will combine to realize the forecast benefits? (e.g. via a Benefits Dependency Map/ Network).

□ Has responsibility for delivering all required enabling and business changes been clearly defined?

□ Has responsibility for realizing each benefit been defined? (the Benefit Owner).

□ Has a suite of measures been identified that will provide sufficient evidence of benefits realization?

□ Are all parts of the solution collectively sufficient to realize the benefits?

□ Have adequate arrangements been made to manage benefits throughout the business change lifecycle (including post-initiative closure) encompassing: planned benefits, known dis-benefits and emergent benefits and dis-benefits?

This last point is crucial – given the emergent nature of many benefits, we need to make provision for their management and the Business Case itself needs to be maintained on an ongoing basis. To borrow from the military analogy – no plan survives contact with the enemy, and the Business Case should therefore be a 'living' document. This extends beyond development from Strategic Outline Case to Outline Business Case to Full Business Case – the last-mentioned should continue to be updated throughout the business change lifecycle, and at a minimum, at each stage/phase gate and end-of-tranche review. As a recent APM thought leadership report (May, 2012b) says – the Business Case is *"the primary tool to monitor and manage the delivery of both required capabilities and the realisation of desired business outcomes. It should be used as a dynamic management tool"*.

One final comment – the Business Case should be accompanied by the Benefits Realization Plan. The DVLA Case Study (2005) for the OGC, for example, concludes that, *"Business case benefits are better understood if a Benefits Delivery Plan is produced at the same time. Projects that plan realisation of benefits at a later date often find that the benefits used to justify the project are not in practice realisable."* So the Business Case approval should be dependent on SRO approval of the Benefits Realization Plan, which in turn should be dependent on agreement of the Benefit Profiles with the Benefit Owners.

7.10 CHAPTER SUMMARY

1. The objective of the Plan practice is to ensure accountability and transparency for the realization of identified benefits, mitigation of dis-benefits (both expected and unexpected), and that emergent benefits are identified and leveraged.

2. Four themes underpin the Plan practice:
   1. The Plan practice extends across the Benefits Management Cycle – although the focus of activity will vary at the different stages.
   2. The focus is more on planning as an activity than plans as documents.
   3. Planning extends beyond laying the basis for tracking forecast benefits to encompass mitigating dis-benefits and leveraging emergent benefits.
   4. The result should be a transparent view on what benefits are envisaged, when they will be realized, how they will be evidenced and who is responsible for their realization; and clear accountability for the business changes on which the realization of benefits depends, and for benefits realization at the individual and collective levels.

3. The main elements in the Plan practice are:
   1. Validation of the benefits forecast.
   2. Prioritization of benefits.
   3. Pre-transition activity to ensure appropriate arrangements are made for the business change upon which benefits realization is dependent.
   4. Selection of appropriate benefit measures to provide a 'rich picture' encompassing evidence from multiple perspectives.

5. Benefits risk and opportunity management.
6. Planning stakeholder engagement.
7. Benefits documentation – completion of the main initiative-level benefits management documentation and the consolidation of benefits data in the Business Case.

Chapter 8

Chapter 8 – Benefits Management Practice 4 – Realize

8.1 OVERVIEW OF THIS CHAPTER

The purpose of this chapter is to describe the Realize practice – the objective of which is to optimize benefits realization by actively managing planned benefits through to their realization; capturing and leveraging emergent benefits; and minimizing and mitigating any dis-benefits.

The Realize practice encompasses the following three main elements:

1. Ensuring that initiative outputs are fit for purpose and can be integrated into business operations. This is considered in Section 8.3 – Transition Management.

2. Tracking and reporting benefits realization at an initiative level – and taking appropriate action where required (see Section 8.4). Consolidating data in a portfolio-level view is addressed in Chapter 10.

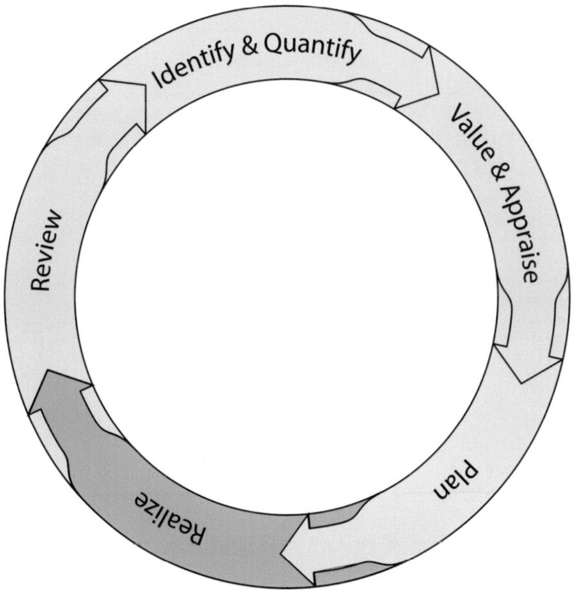

Figure 8.1 – The Realize practice in the Benefits Management Cycle

3. Effective benefits realization also requires that we go beyond processes and practices to consider the softer side of business change, and in particular the people dimension. This requires consideration of how best to achieve the behavioural change on which benefits realization is so often dependent. As David Snowden, former head of Knowledge Management at IBM, said, "*Consider what happens in an organization when a rumour of reorganization surfaces: the complex human system starts to mutate and change in unfathomable ways; new patterns form in anticipation of the event. On the other hand, if you walk up to an aircraft with a box of tools in your hand, nothing changes.*" So we need to consider strategies to achieve the required behavioural change, including ongoing participative stakeholder engagement with 'measures that engage' and 'narrative leadership', so that we win hearts as well as minds.

All of this is discussed in the following pages.

8.2 THEMES THAT RUN ACROSS THE REALIZE PRACTICE

Two themes that run across the Realize practice should be emphasized:

1. While the focus in investment decision-making should be on realism (to overcome the twin risks of strategic misrepresentation and optimism bias) the approach in benefits realization should be based on enthusiasm. As Lovallo & Kahneman (2003) argue, "*Draw a clear distinction between those functions and positions that involve or support decision making and those that promote or guide action. The former should be imbued with a realistic outlook, while the latter will often benefit from a sense of optimism.*" Positive thinking and its motivational effects play a crucial part in overcoming the obstacles that often arise during implementation and delivery.

2. Distinguish between forecasts and targets – the former, as part of the investment appraisal process, should be realistic; the latter should be motivational and aspirational – and that requires that they be used less as a means of backward-looking accountability, and more as a basis of forward-looking insight and learning. What we too often see are situations where benefits management is focused on holding people to account for targets as originally forecast, but which are now out of date. A 'blame culture' emerges in which people's attention shifts to appearance-manipulation to make it seem that the initiative is succeeding even if the opposite is the case – and if people's attention is on appearance-manipulation, there's less focus on optimizing benefits realization.

Fundamental to making this approach work is a culture of planning for success rather than attributing blame, where the emphasis is on learning rather than identifying failure. One myth of leadership is that people are always averse to change. Actually, people can welcome change; what they seek to avoid is the pain of change. So the challenge for leaders is to create an environment where people feel familiar with the change and sufficiently protected to step out of their comfort zones and dare to take risks (Kohlrieser, Goldsworthy & Coombe, 2012). Yes, hold people to account, but the accountability works both ways and is a joint accountability between funders, initiative delivery teams, and the recipients of the new ways of working. Leadership is crucial in this regard – in clearly communicating expected standards of behaviour and in shifting the default mode of thinking from tracking against forecast and justifying variances, to exceeding plan and optimizing benefits realization. Strategies by which this can be achieved are discussed later in this chapter.

We now turn our attention to the main elements of the Realize practice:

1. Transition management.

2. Tracking and reporting benefits realization and taking corrective action.

3. Optimizing benefits realization – winning hearts as well as minds.

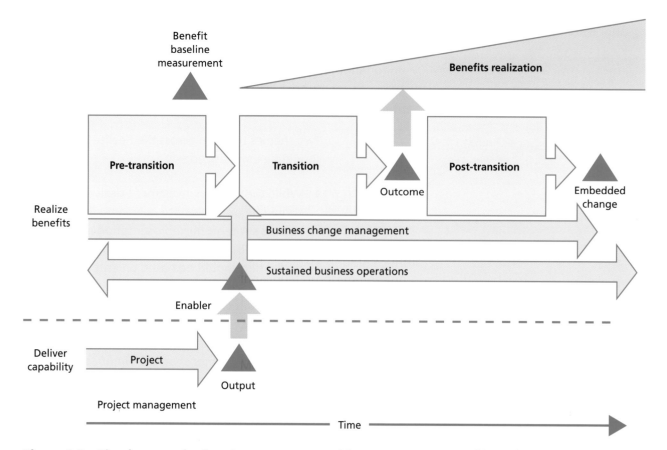

Figure 8.2 – Simple example showing outputs, transition management and benefits realization

8.3 ELEMENT 1 – TRANSITION MANAGEMENT

According to *'Managing Successful Programmes'* (MSP) there are three stages in moving from the old to new ways of working to ensure that capabilities are transitioned into outcomes, legacy working practices are removed and benefits are realized: pre-transition, transition and post-transition (and these activities are repeated as necessary for each tranche of the programme). Pre-transition was covered in the last chapter, so here we address transition and post-transition, which focus on embedding change in the operational business. The relationship of these stages to benefits realization in an MSP environment is shown in Figure 8.2.

8.3.1 Transition – Delivering and Supporting the Changes

Transition is the responsibility of the programme and, as is said in MSP, this includes the following flow steps:

- **Initiate transition** – preparing business operations for implementing the project outputs and take-up of the new capability, while maintaining business as usual (BAU) performance.
- **Establish support arrangements** – for example, from the HR/personnel department to assist with addressing individuals' concerns about the new working environment.
- **Enact transition** – once the outputs are ready for operational use and the programme has verified through quality assurance that they will function correctly together; staff have been trained; business operations are content and contingency arrangements are in place; and the Senior Responsible Owner (SRO), in consultation with the Programme Board, gives approval to start transition.
- **Review transition** – and document lessons learned (more on this in the next chapter).
- **Manage outcome achievement** – but as we have already said, beware of declaring victory too early, and ensure that the change is fully embedded.

8.3.2 Post-transition

Here the focus is on reviewing progress, measuring performance and adapting to change. The flow steps are:

- **Measure benefits** – the measures to be used, baseline performance, targets/expected performance and measurement processes will have been documented in the Benefits Profiles and Benefits Realization Plan in the 'Plan' practice. Now these processes come into operation and data is collected to compare actual performance against plan.
- **Remove access to legacy working practices and systems** – so there is no going back to the old ways of working.
- **Respond to changing requirements** – unanticipated problems and issues should be identified and addressed appropriately.
- **Monitor and report benefits realization** – reports will be made at each end-of-tranche review, at other planned benefits reviews, and on a regular, periodic basis (for example, monthly) for the portfolio benefits reporting.

From a programme perspective, the cycle ends with formal handover of responsibility for monitoring and optimizing benefits realization from the programme to operational management. This includes ensuring the handover of the management of post-transition risks to the operational or corporate risk function. As part of programme closure, the relevant benefits documentation (Profiles, Benefits Realization Plan including Benefits Map, and Benefits Management Strategy) should be updated and the 'reference point' for post-programme benefits activity should be agreed – in an MSP environment this will be the Business Change Manager. While the programme interest in benefits realization ends at this point, from a portfolio perspective, interest in benefits realization continues (see Chapter 10).

8.3.3 Responsibilities for Transition and Post-transition Management

Typical responsibilities for benefits realization as identified in MSP are shown in Table 8.1.

In summary, in an MSP environment:

Table 8.1 – Typical responsibilities for transition and post-transition management

Flow steps	SRO	Programme Manager	Business Change Managers (and business change team)	Programme Office
Manage transition				
Initiate transition	A	C	R	I
Establish support arrangements	A	C	R	I
Enact transition	A	C	R	I
Review transition	A	C	R	C
Manage outcome achievement	A	C	R	I
Manage post-transition				
Measure benefits	A	C	R	C
Remove access to legacy working practices and systems	A	C	R	I
Respond to changing requirements	A	C	R	C
Monitor and report benefits realization	A	C	R	C
R = responsible (gets the work done); A = accountable (answerable for the programme's success); C = consulted (supports, has the information or capability required); I = informed (notified but not consulted).				

- The **SRO** is the single individual who is accountable and responsible for ensuring that a programme meets its objectives and delivers the projected benefits.

- The **Business Change Manager** reports to the SRO and is responsible, on behalf of the SRO and business operations, for:
  - Ensuring that responsibility for realization of each benefit/dis-benefit is clearly assigned to named Benefit Owners.
  - Advising the SRO on readiness for transition.
  - Embedding the capability delivered by the programme in business operations, and facilitating the business changes to leverage that capability.
  - Assessing progress on benefits realization and achievement of outcomes in terms of measured improvements in business performance.

Consequently, the Business Change Manager needs to be 'business-side' to bridge the gap between the initiative and business operations.

The Business Change Manager will need to work closely with the individual **Benefit Owners** who monitor the successful delivery of enabling and business changes and collect and report data to evidence benefits realization.

Note that:

- If more than one part of the business is affected by the initiative, each part may nominate a Business Change Manager.
- Business Change Managers may be supported by a business change team with several Change Managers, or by what Bradley (2010) calls 'Change Champions' who fill an ambassadorial role.
- Some organizations call the Business Change Managers the 'business change authority'.

■ *'Portfolio, Programme and Project Offices'* (P3O) also envisages the establishment of a benefits role within the Portfolio, Programme or Project Office – providing a benefits realization support service to Programme Managers, Business Managers and Business Change Managers. This role is referred to as the **Benefit Manager** in this Guide.

Important note

Organizations do not need to follow the above to the letter – different job titles may exist and the responsibilities may be shared by more than one person. But what is crucial is that someone owns the responsibilities identified here and in Appendix C – and in particular that:

■ Someone is responsible for the required business changes.
■ Benefit Owners are identified for each material benefit.
■ Someone has overall accountability for benefits realization from the initiative.
■ Responsibility extends beyond the life of the initiative.

An example of the benefits realization governance model from one organization is shown in Example 8.1.

8.4 ELEMENT 2 – TRACKING AND REPORTING BENEFITS REALIZATION AND TAKING CORRECTIVE ACTION

8.4.1 Why Track and Report?

We saw in Chapter 3 that one of the principles of effective benefits management is integration of benefits into the performance management system. But this does not represent a complete solution to the task of managing benefits realization. Indeed, some dedicated effort is still required in relation to the following.

The objectives of benefits tracking and reporting

■ Understanding what is actually causing changes in performance and so addressing the attribution issue by benefits mapping, tracking leading as well as lagging measures, and using confidence ratings.

Example 8.1 – Benefits realization governance – Bristol City Council

Bristol City Council has established a Benefits Realization Board to ensure that the Council optimizes the return from its investment in business change. Core membership is as follows:

■ Strategic Director: Corporate Services – primary focus: financial benefits (cashable and non-cashable).
■ Strategic Director: Business Directorate – primary focus: non-financial benefits.
■ Service Director: Business Change and ICT – primary role: Head of Profession and facilitation of the meeting.
■ Portfolio Accountant/Benefits Realization Manager – primary role: Medium-term Financial Plan focus and meeting administration.

The purposes of the Benefits Realization Board as documented in their Terms of Reference are to:

■ Ensure clear ownership and responsibility in relation to benefits realization within the service areas.
■ Track and drive benefits realization throughout the programme and project lifecycles and beyond.
■ Challenge the benefits being delivered to ensure that they are ambitious, but realistic and unambiguous.
■ Receive and agree exceptions to the Business Case, where the benefits are at risk of exceeding tolerances, or have exceeded them.

Example continues

Example 8.1 continued

- Challenge programme and project dis-benefits with a view to mitigating them as far as possible.
- Make recommendations to Projects, Programme and Business Change Managers as to how benefits realization can be strengthened.
- Advise the Strategic Options Delivery Board (SODB) of any significant changes to forecast and actual benefits.
- Make recommendations for action by the SODB to ensure that benefits realization is led at a strategic level.
- Increase confidence in the delivery of savings outlined within the Medium-term Financial Plan.

The Benefits Realization Board meets every six weeks to two months to review up to five programmes/projects on a rolling cycle. This involves review of a Benefits Highlights Report and targeted questions by the Benefits Realization Board members to the SRO/Project Executive and Business Change Manager including:

- The progress of the programme/project in delivering the outcomes/objectives, key milestones and how they relate to the benefits.
- The desired financial and non-financial benefits (from the Business Case), and the targets and measures identified to ensure delivery. It should be clear how they:
  - ☐ Relate back to the baseline measures.
  - ☐ Look forward and forecast the final position.
  - ☐ Give details of any variances and any necessary corrective actions to be taken.
- Any dis-benefits the programme/project has encountered, giving details around whether they were expected, any variances to forecasts and any action being taken to mitigate them.

Note – it is also intended that Programme/Project 'Closure' reports be taken to the Benefits Realization Board. The role of the board in this instance will be to provide a high level of assurance for the authority, and sign off (authorize) the closure of a programme/project. They will review the benefits set out in the closure report and compare them with those detailed in the original Business Case, and ensure that there are realistic plans in place to realize these benefits once the programme or project has closed.

Provided with the kind assistance of Paul Arrigoni (Director, Business Change and ICT) and Ken Robinson (Portfolio Accountant/Benefits Realization Manager), Bristol City Council.

- Ensuring that by 'booking' cashable benefits we have not created an unfunded pressure that results in dis-benefits such as increased overtime or stress-related absences.
- Addressing the *"build it and they will come"* assumption (APM, March 2011) i.e. the too common belief that capability automatically leads to benefits. The reality is that it often depends on management action – and this needs to be monitored to ensure that it occurs and is effective.
- Managing the realization of intermediate benefits as a way of maximizing realization of end benefits.
- Capturing and leveraging emergent benefits.

- Mitigating expected and unexpected dis-benefits.
- Validating the assumptions underpinning the organization's business model.
- Learning about what works, and feeding this back into the design and management of future change initiatives.

For these reasons, even where benefits are integrated into the performance management system, we cannot escape the need to undertake some benefits tracking and reporting. The importance of this should not be underestimated – not least because a recent study of transformational change (Moorhouse, 2012) has found that those *"who track the benefits of their programmes are significantly more successful at achieving their stated objectives"*.

8.4.2 What is the Scope of Benefits Tracking and Reporting?

Tracking and reporting benefits realization encompasses:

- Not just planned benefits but also emergent benefits and dis-benefits. This can be facilitated where the benefits-reporting template includes provision for information on unplanned benefits and dis-benefits.
- Qualitative as well as quantitative feedback – including specific provision for feedback on areas where performance could be improved. Surveys are considered further below.
- Confirmation that benefits 'booked' in, for example, budget baselines have actually been realized. So as well as checking that a budget has been reduced, we also need to check that the savings have had no unanticipated adverse impact on output quantity or service quality.
- While it was emphasized in Chapter 6 that sunk costs should be ignored in investment decision-making, they should not be ignored entirely when monitoring initiatives – if an initiative can only show a positive return by continually shifting the 'starting line', that is a warning sign about the original forecasts contained in the Business Case and, potentially, the initiative's achievability. Transparent reporting of the full-life cost-benefit (value for money or return on investment) position can act as a catalyst to identifying additional benefits to cover any cost escalation.
- And as was said in the last chapter – develop a suite of measures that provide feedback from multiple perspectives and so provide a 'rich picture' on benefits realization. A suite of measures includes:
  - ☐ Leading measures (encompassing enabling changes, business changes and intermediate benefits) and lagging measures (of the end benefits).
  - ☐ Proxy indicators.
  - ☐ Evidence events.
  - ☐ Case studies.
  - ☐ Surveys.
  - ☐ Stories.

8.4.3 How Do We Ensure that Benefits Tracking and Reporting is Effective?

Effective management of benefits realization is aided by the adoption of reports that convey the salient points succinctly. This is facilitated by developing an appropriate format for reporting, identifying when action is required by categorizing benefits status, and adoption of a series of relevant techniques.

8.4.3.1 The Benefits Realization Report

Appropriate formats include:

- **Dashboard reporting** – i.e. developing an initiative-level Benefits Dashboard that reflects the format of the Portfolio Benefits Dashboard (see Section 10.3.5) and adheres to the guidance contained in the Portfolio Benefits Management Framework. The adoption of consistent formats and benefits key performance indicators (KPIs) at portfolio and initiative level aids consolidation of the portfolio picture and 'drill down' from the Portfolio Dashboard Report to initiative/ function/divisional level.

- **Reporting on a normalized scale** – one issue faced regularly is how to present benefits realization information in a succinct form when different types of benefit (financial and non-financial, or a range of non-financials, for example) have different measures. One approach is to apply a points rating system by which a value of 1 is assigned if the actual value matches plan – with values of > 1 where realization exceeds plan and < 1 where it is below plan, and with the values proportionate to the level of realization (for example, if realization is half that planned, a value of 0.5 would be recorded). This is illustrated in Table 8.2.

A complication arises where benefits are realized ahead of schedule – since the planned value is 0, the actual value can't be converted to a points rating. One way around this is to use a proportion of the next planned points value which is greater than zero.

Table 8.2 – Benefits realization ratings

Benefits	Month 1	Month 2	Month 3	Month 4
Benefit 1			–	
Planned value	10	25	40	70
Actual value	10	12.5	50	70
Points allocation	1	0.5	1.25	1
Cumulative planned points	1	2	3	4
Cumulative actual points	1	1.5	2.75	3.75

Source: David Elliott, Director, PBM Consulting and Claire Dellar, Benefits Realization Manager, NSFT

This approach is particularly suited to non-financial benefits, although it can be extended to encompass all categories of benefit. The points allocation can also be expressed as a percentage, which some managers find easier to understand. Either way, this approach enables benefits to be reported on a common scale, the overall position to be consolidated, and reports to be provided in graphical as well as tabular format.

For benefits which are regarded as more significant, weightings can be applied to the points scores to reflect their relative contribution to the initiative's investment objectives. In this way a single figure, the sum of the points, can be used to assess benefits realization progress for the initiative as a whole. This approach can also be taken a step further – by weighting each initiative we are able to calculate a single figure representing progress to date at a portfolio level.

- **Utilize the Benefits Map for reporting** – another option is to combine red/amber/green (RAG) ratings with the Benefits Map completed during the 'Identify & Quantify' practice. Each element or link on the map is RAG-rated so facilitating monitoring of:
  - ☐ Successful delivery of the enabling and business changes upon which benefits realization is dependent.
  - ☐ Achievement of the intermediate benefits identified on the Benefits Map.
  - ☐ Realization of the end benefits that the initiative was designed to achieve.
  Advantages of this approach include early-warning signals are identified that may impact on end-benefit realization; it helps to address the attribution issue because the logic chain is

agreed in advance; it helps to target action where it is required; and where there are issues in realization of the end benefits, the causes can be tracked back through the map.

- **Combine graphical formats with the Pareto rule** – here reporting of progress in terms of benefits realization focuses on the most significant benefits, often utilizing graphical formats and RAG ratings. This approach is illustrated in Example 8.2.

8.4.3.2 Categorizing Benefits Status

Whichever reporting format is used, identifying where corrective action may be required is helped by the categorization of benefits status. Options here include categorization by 'attractiveness' (or scale) and 'achievability' as illustrated in Figure 8.4, use of the traditional RAG ratings (see Example 8.3), and setting 'standards'. Davies & Davies (2011) suggest tracking four plots for each individual measure:

- **Standard** (the level of performance required to be ultimately achieved to sustain the initiative's vision).
- **Planned** (reflecting the trajectory from current performance to standard).
- **Minimum** (standard below which performance is unacceptable).
- **Actual** (which can be compared with plan). This enables worsening performance to be identified (where actual is tracking behind plan) and act as a catalyst for action to be taken before performance falls below minimum standard.

Example 8.2 – Benefits realization reporting at Western Australia Police

The Business Technology Division of Western Australia Police have put in place a quarterly Benefits Reporting Pack to provide increased focus and transparency over benefits realization. This pack includes all live projects as well as those in the development pipeline – to highlight the importance placed on benefits and the ongoing requirement to provide an accurate and balanced picture of the success of the project.

Each quarter, the Senior User of each project provides updated data for their top five benefits to the Portfolio Benefits Realization Manager, who in turn produces a one-page summary for each project in a standardized format. This summary is distributed in a collated reporting pack to the portfolio governance body and the wider project community. Details provided for each individual initiative include:

■ The names of the Project Executive and Senior Users.
■ A summary of the project objectives.
■ Key project dates.
■ A visual representation of the top five benefits, including baselines and targets.
■ RAG status and commentary from Senior Users on the trends visible in the measurement data, particularly where the trend is against expectation and an amber rating has been applied.

The format for benefits reporting is shown in Figure 8.3.

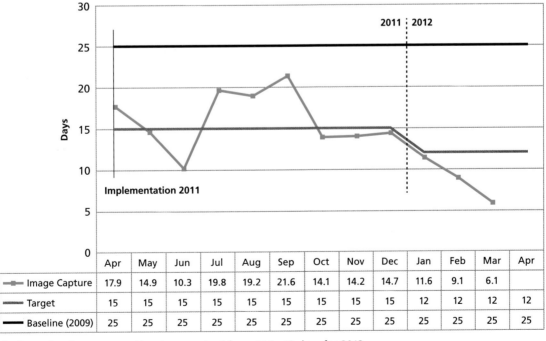

ESE03_01 Speed camera – Time taken to issue infringements

Target: 12 days

ESE03_01 Speed camera – Infringement Image Capture Timeframes

	Apr	May	Jun	Jul	Aug	Sep	Oct	Nov	Dec	Jan	Feb	Mar	Apr
Image Capture	17.9	14.9	10.3	19.8	19.2	21.6	14.1	14.2	14.7	11.6	9.1	6.1	
Target	15	15	15	15	15	15	15	15	15	12	12	12	12
Baseline (2009)	25	25	25	25	25	25	25	25	25	25	25	25	25

The issue timeframes target has been revised from 15 to 12 days for 2012.

Figure 8.3 – Benefits tracking in WA Police

Provided with the kind assistance of Susan Evans (Head of BT Portfolio Office) and Rachel Naisbitt (Exec Manager Benefits & Business Readiness), Western Australia Police

		Low	High
Attractiveness	High	*Action – Address achievability of the benefit*	*Action – Harvest*
	Low	*Action – Ignore unless there is some compelling reason*	*Action – Consider ways to increase the scale/ value of the benefit*
		Low	High
		Achievability	

Figure 8.4 – Categorizing benefits in terms of attractiveness and achievability

---

Example 8.3 – Benefits realization RAG ratings – Bristol City Council

Bristol City Council monitoring of benefits realization is informed by the following RAG ratings:

- Red: No benefit realization plans are in place or plans have been substantially delayed and therefore there is a significant likelihood that the benefit will be diminished or not realized.
- Red/Amber: Benefit realization plans are in place, but progress has been delayed, which is impacting on the original target delivery date and/or reducing the likelihood of delivery of the full benefits.
- Amber/Green: Benefit realization plans slightly delayed but full benefits are still forecast to be realized.
- Green: On target to realize (or have realized) full benefits as planned.

Provided with the kind assistance of Paul Arrigoni (Director, Business Change and ICT) and Ken Robinson (Portfolio Accountant/Benefits Realization Manager), Bristol City Council.

8.4.3.3 Techniques that Aid Benefits Monitoring

Effective benefits monitoring is also helped by the following techniques:

- **'One version of the truth'** – whereby each element of progress reporting (in this case benefits – the position on benefits realized to date and the revised forecast) is derived from an agreed source and reported according to an agreed schedule. This is then recognized as the authoritative source of information used for monitoring, reporting and management decision-making.

- **'Clear line of sight' reporting** – a technique that seeks to ensure a transparent chain from strategic intent through to benefits realization and vice versa. In this case, linking benefits reporting at initiative level to the agreed outcomes or investment objectives. It's harder to 'play games' when the numbers (financial and non-financial) are open for all to see. The Portfolio Office has a key role to play here in ensuring that a consistent view is applied to all change initiatives, and that this is then consolidated into a portfolio-wide view.

- **The Pareto (80:20) rule** – focus on the benefits that deliver the greatest contribution to the initiative's investment objectives and, in turn, the organization's strategic objectives.

- **'Management by exception'** – by which only variances from plan (both in relation to benefits forecast and benefits realization) that exceed a pre-set control limit are escalated for management attention. This helps determine when action is required.

8.4.3.4   Other Issues

Consideration will also need to be given to the questions of when to start measuring and how long benefits should be tracked and reported. Regarding the former, the general guidance is 'as soon as possible' as this helps to:

- Validate baseline data (and provide such data where it is missing).
- Identify early warnings where corrective action might be required.
- Identify early evidence of/potential for emergent benefits.
- Collect evidence of 'quick wins' which can help to build stakeholder commitment.

In practice, this means monitoring the delivery of enabling and business changes, and intermediate benefits as well as the end benefits. This provides enhanced confidence that the initiative has actually resulted in the end benefits.

With regard to the latter question – a 'red flag' indicating that an initiative is on the wrong path is when people ask, *"How long do we have to track benefits for?"* This shows that the focus is on backward tracking against forecast, rather than trying to understand how value is being created and can be further leveraged. No hard-and-fast answer can be given that will apply to all circumstances, but in general, tracking and reporting should continue until it is clear that the new ways of working and business changes are embedded as BAU, that the benefits are being realized, and that ongoing tracking won't add significant additional value.

Beyond the above, effective tracking and reporting depends on three other factors.

1. Firstly, as we saw in Chapters 5 and 6, measures are not without effect. On the one hand, the Hawthorne experiments showed that the act of measurement can influence what is being measured in a positive manner. On the other hand, measurement can have unintended consequences of the negative kind where changes in the indicator are pursued at the expense of overall system performance and people engage in gaming behaviour and appearance manipulation. So monitor performance to ensure that measurement is having the desired effect and that the underlying performance is not being adversely affected.

2. Secondly, recognize that things change – and this means that as Farbey, Land & Targett (1999) say, evaluation *"is always taking place on a moving staircase"*. The point is also made by Thorp: *"Benefits don't just happen, and they rarely happen to plan."* The answer is to adopt a forward-facing perspective that focuses on organizational learning as a basis for benefits realization, rather than a backward-looking tracking approach that is fixated on comparing actuals against an outdated forecast. The importance of this has been highlighted in the recent research study referred to above (Moorhouse, 2012) – which found that having an accurate picture is crucial, and this requires honest reporting, which is dependent on *"Creating an environment where honest progress and potential issues can be reported without fear of reprisal"*.

3. Thirdly, as was stated at the start of this chapter and linked to points 1 and 2 above – don't confuse targets with forecasts. Seddon (2008) argues that *"Targets drive people to use their ingenuity to meet the target, not improve performance"*. Davies & Davies (2011) quote the example of a major defence contracts programme where *"Managers are assessed by their ability to maintain a defined margin. Such is the pressure for and pain of failure in not delivering these margins that monthly reports become smokescreens behind which problems are hidden until much later when a myriad of other circumstances can be blamed."* The ethos should therefore be one of planning for success, rather than attributing blame, and should be based on close engagement with users to identify measures that are meaningful to them; using feedback to inform action aimed at benefits realization rather than blame attribution; and employing a suite of measures to provide a 'rich picture' with different perspectives on performance – including via surveys, which are considered below.

One final note – the Benefit Profiles and Benefits Realization Plan completed as part of the 'Plan' practice should be updated on a regular basis –

Example 8.4 – User surveys – BT and the RiO system

Guidance developed by BT to assess user views and experience of using the RiO electronic patient record system in the NHS included the following key considerations in designing a survey:

- KISS – Keep it Short and Simple (no more than 10 questions).
- Use multiple-choice questions.
- Cover the main functional areas.
- Structure the questions as positive statements and give the user the option to agree or disagree.
- Use a rating scale ranging from 5–1, where 5 = strongly agree, to 1 = strongly disagree; alternatively use a 4-point scale, which eliminates a middle-ground response and forces a positive or negative rating.
- Add a general comment field for those who may want to provide additional comments.
- Keep it anonymous.

Example statements against which ratings were provided included:

1. RiO has improved the time taken to access patient demographic and clinical information.

2. RiO has improved the sharing of patient records across multi-disciplinary services.

3. RiO has improved the time taken to update patient records.

4. RiO has enabled the recording of new assessments and the viewing of existing ones and fewer repeated assessments.

5. RiO improves the management of appointments in diaries and clinics.

6. RiO better supports the CPA process.

7. RiO reduces duplicate records.

8. RiO improves risk management.

9. RiO improves multi-disciplinary caseload management.

10. RiO has helped to move toward a paper-light system.

In terms of channels used to get the survey to the targeted users, the BT guidance included considering the use of online survey providers, such as SurveyMonkey™, which provide templates to facilitate survey design, consolidate responses and analyse the results.

Provided with the kind agreement of BT Group plc and NHS Milton Keynes Community Health Services.

---

and this extends into the benefits tracking phase. The Business Change Manager should therefore monitor the information reported and update the Benefit Profiles and Benefits Realization Plan when required.

8.4.4 Customer and Staff Satisfaction Surveys

We saw in Chapter 5 that 'customer insight' can play a key role in designing change initiatives that meet customer needs, wants and desires. Chapter 7 then referred to the development of a suite of measures to inform our understanding of benefits realization by gathering evidence from multiple perspectives – including the use of surveys to assess customer, staff and management satisfaction. This can then be used, not just for accountability purposes, but also in providing insight and feedback, and so optimizing benefits realization.

In designing a survey, *three key questions* need to be addressed:

1. **What to ask?** Good practice suggests keeping the number of questions to a minimum to aid completion (see Examples 8.4 and 8.5 – both limited the number of questions to ten). Ratings (for example, from very satisfied to very unsatisfied) can be used to measure overall customer satisfaction, but they don't explain what underlies the ratings given. Consequently, we also need service-specific measures such as those shown in the examples below. These questions can then be used as diagnostic measures to improve understanding of the causes of satisfaction or dissatisfaction. In this regard, research by MORI (Cabinet Office, 2007) has identified five common drivers of customer satisfaction: service delivery and how problems are handled; timeliness (waiting times); information (accuracy and being kept informed); professionalism (competent staff and fair treatment); and staff attitudes. These factors were found to explain 67% of the variation in customer satisfaction.

2. **Who to ask?** This includes the sample size and sample selection. If statistically sound conclusions are required, relevant professional advice should be sought from statisticians or operational researchers.

3. **How should the information be collected?** What channels should be used, for example: face-to-face, by telephone, by post, or online?

Examples 8.4 and 8.5 illustrate how these issues were addressed on two programmes.

Of course, just getting surveys completed is of limited value – the results need to be analysed – and here, as with forecasting, we need to be aware of confirmation bias or the tendency to only pay attention to those surveys that confirm

the results we'd like to hear. Solutions include the use of free-text boxes (as above) and key-driver analysis – using regression analysis to identify, within each customer segment, those factors that most influence levels of satisfaction and dissatisfaction.

> **Important note**
>
> Some will argue that the requirement to track and report on benefits realization is an additional and unnecessary form of bureaucracy. They will, however, presumably accept that costs need to be managed with a dedicated finance function, financial and management accounting systems with charts of account, data-capture systems and regular budgetary reports. It's important to remember that, in managing the change portfolio, costs are a constraint while benefits are the rationale for investment. Consequently, benefits should be managed at least as robustly as costs.

8.5 ELEMENT 3 – OPTIMIZING BENEFITS REALIZATION – WINNING HEARTS AS WELL AS MINDS

The adoption of benefits management processes can have a significant impact – for example:

- Payne reports that *"By applying rigorous Benefits Management, expected benefits can increase from 70% to 85%, with an additional project or programme overhead that should not exceed 5%."*
- It is reported that a leading portfolio manager in the USA (Retna) *"demonstrates how his company applied advanced portfolio management techniques to realize in excess of 80% of expected business benefits from its corporate investments"*.

Compared to the statistics quoted in Chapter 2, this scale of achievement is not to be understated since it potentially represents an improvement from 30%–40% to 70%–85%. But it does indicate that KPMG (2005) was right when it concluded, *"Project success appears to equate to achieving an acceptable level of failure or minimising lost benefits."*

Example 8.5 – User surveys – Tell Us Once

The Tell Us Once (TUO) programme included a commitment to seeing the service *"'through the eyes of the citizen and front line staff' – it is their perceptions that count and which will inform our understanding of how to optimise value"*. The Benefits Realization Management Toolkit developed to help local authorities (LAs) manage benefits realization therefore included guidance on surveying customers, staff and management.

The objectives of conducting surveys were identified as including:

- To provide qualitative evidence of the perceptions of citizens, staff and management on the difference that TUO has made/is making.
- To provide insight about how services can be improved and what lessons can be learned for future service design.
- To confirm the assumptions made in the benefits forecast.

The approach to surveying was based on the following high-level principles:

- Keep it simple i.e. restrict the number of questions asked to encourage completion.
- Focus on the key benefits anticipated.
- Include provision for general feedback.
- Welcome all feedback – positive and negative.

The questions asked were designed to provide evidence in relation to the forecast benefits, while also reflecting research about the drivers of customer satisfaction. The proposed surveys/interview questionnaires were also informed by the experience of surveys undertaken at the Pathfinder sites.

Types of Survey

It was decided that separate surveys should be prepared for:

- Customer/citizen surveys for each TUO service.
- A general staff survey to assess satisfaction with the services provided.
- A management survey to provide qualitative evidence on the specific benefits forecast.

As an example, the customer survey for the TUO Birth Service is shown in Table 8.3.

Table 8.3 – Customer survey – TUO Birth Service

Statement	Strongly agree	Agree	Disagree	Strongly disagree
The service was easy to use.				
The service was convenient to use (i.e. it was provided where I wanted it).				
The service was provided promptly when I needed it.				
I was treated with respect and dignity throughout.				
I trust the service provided.				
The service has saved me time in notifying government of the birth.				
The service provided has saved me money in notifying government of the birth.				
I will recommend the service to others.				
Overall I am satisfied with the service provided.				
Please record below any other comments you would wish to make – either positive or negative.				

Provided with the kind agreement of Matthew Briggs, TUO Programme Manager.

But this should not be the limit of our aspirations. Indeed, if we adopt more realistic planning for benefits realization (including more accurate and reliable forecasting as outlined in Chapter 5) – along with a more active approach to benefits realization based on ongoing participative stakeholder engagement, feedback and learning – there is no reason we should not exceed the forecast by:

■ Realizing more of the planned benefits.
■ Better mitigation of dis-benefits.

■ Capturing and leveraging emergent benefits.
■ Exploiting capabilities across the portfolio.

Crucial to this is moving **from optimism in forecasting and passive tracking, to realism in forecasting and enthusiasm in delivery.** Central to this shift of focus is an ongoing participative approach to stakeholder engagement – as Marchand & Peppard (2008) say, *"Business change initiatives are about engaging the minds, hearts and values of people in making change happen and achieving shared business results and* *benefits, and not about possessing new tools, renewing legacy systems or standardizing technology to reduce costs."*

Strategies to achieve this run throughout the Benefits Management Cycle – for example during initiative design (via customer insight); delivery (aided by stakeholder segmentation, analysis and communication); and after implementation. The latter is crucial because the realization of benefits from many change initiatives is dependent upon not only business change, but also behavioural change on the part of:

■ Managers – for example, applying a benefits-led approach to change initiatives.

■ Employees – for example, in adopting more customer/citizen-facing services.

■ Customers – for example, buying goods online rather from the high street, or submitting their tax return online rather than in paper format.

■ Citizens – for example, in adopting healthy eating or saving for retirement.

Marchand & Peppard (2008) make the point with the example of Customer Relationship Management (CRM) systems – *"CRM is not a product that can be purchased. It is a disciplined, integrated approach to managing relationships with customers that requires continuous improvement. It is a strategy to improve customer orientation, not a tactic, and although supported by IT, it involves considerable organizational re-design, including changing the mindsets and behaviours of managers and employees of the organization."*

Effective stakeholder engagement can help to achieve this behavioural change by winning hearts as well as minds – and strategies that enable this include:

1. Align incentives with benefits realization.

2. Recognize the power of conversations.

3. Adopt new routines.

4. Apply insights from the fields of neuroscience and psychology.

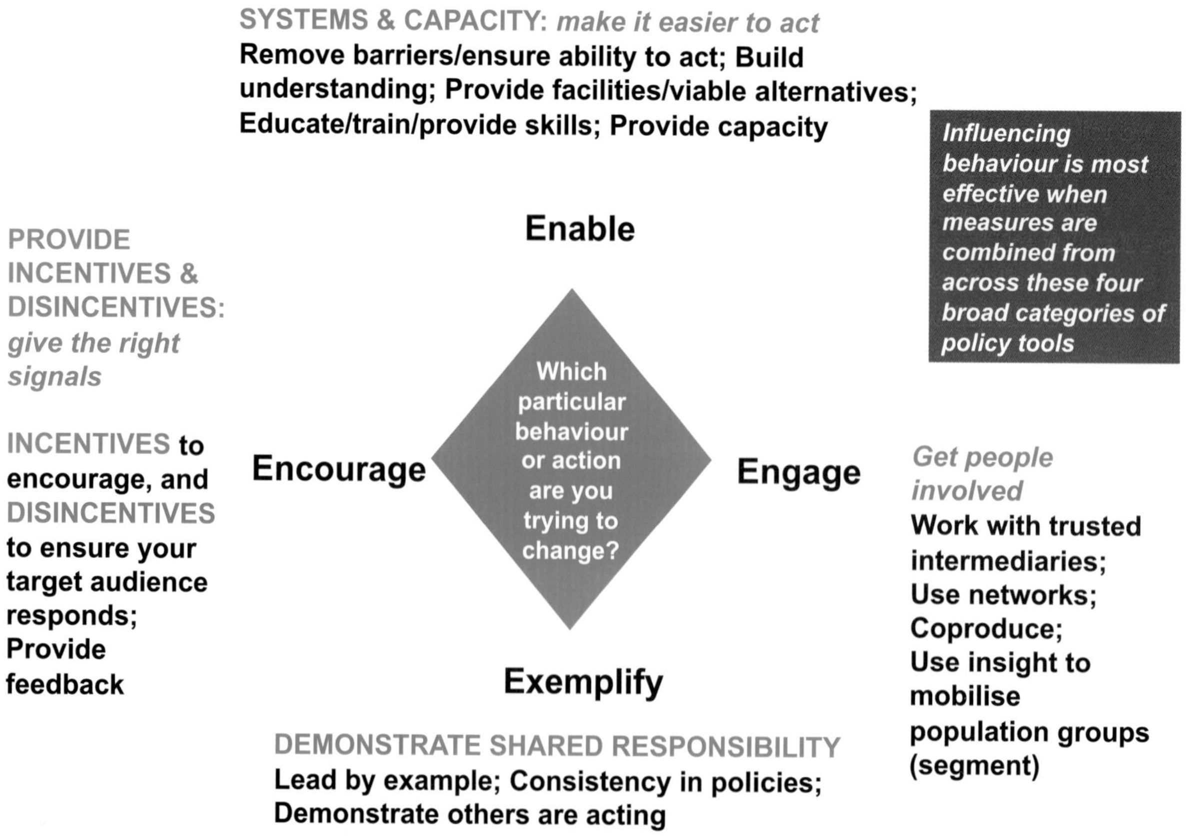

SYSTEMS & CAPACITY: *make it easier to act*
Remove barriers/ensure ability to act; Build understanding; Provide facilities/viable alternatives; Educate/train/provide skills; Provide capacity

Influencing behaviour is most effective when measures are combined from across these four broad categories of policy tools

PROVIDE INCENTIVES & DISINCENTIVES: *give the right signals*

INCENTIVES to encourage, and DISINCENTIVES to ensure your target audience responds; Provide feedback

Enable

Which particular behaviour or action are you trying to change?

Encourage

Engage

Get people involved
Work with trusted intermediaries; Use networks; Coproduce; Use insight to mobilise population groups (segment)

Exemplify

DEMONSTRATE SHARED RESPONSIBILITY
Lead by example; Consistency in policies; Demonstrate others are acting

Figure 8.5 – The Defra 4Es model[1]

1 For more information see http://www.hiveideas.co.uk/attachments/045_4Es%20approach.pdf.

5. Develop measures that engage and influence.

6. Utilize 'narrative leadership' and storytelling.

But to emphasize one point – the above are not alternatives, they work most effectively in combination. This point is illustrated by Figure 8.5 – Defra's 4Es model, in which influencing behaviour is most effective when measures are combined from across the four broad categories of the policy tools identified.

8.5.1 Align Incentives with Benefits Realization

The use of incentives is a common approach to behavioural change – for example:

- A reform paper from the Cabinet Office (2009) included, under the heading 'what drives successful delivery', *"Clear personal accountability ... support people to perform ... **reinforced by incentives and consequences to drive the right behaviour**"*.

- A thought-leadership paper from the APM (2010) refers to *"the importance of incentivising the right behaviours to ensure success"* and *"Wherever possible align the benefits to the individual's performance objectives, especially if there is financial reward or enhanced reputation at stake"*.

This is important because the HR performance management system sends messages about what management regards as important. Misalignment of the performance management system with that required for benefits realization (for example, where the former reinforces internal competition for a limited bonus 'pot', and the latter depends on cooperation) can have serious consequences for benefits realization.

On the other hand, it should also be recognized that purely financial incentives and consequences are often less effective than is commonly thought:

- They can encourage the sorts of game-playing and appearance-manipulation discussed in the last chapter and above.

- Extrinsic rewards can deliver a short-term boost, but the effect often wears off – and worse, it can reduce longer-term commitment. Cialdini (2007) finds that financial rewards *"may motivate compliance, but it is unlikely to produce long-term commitment"*. Deci (2010) concludes, *"Careful consideration of reward effects reported in 128 experiments lead to the conclusion that tangible rewards tend to have a substantially negative effect on intrinsic motivation ... when institutions focus on the short term and opt for controlling people's behaviour, they do considerable long-term damage."*

- Financial incentives do not appear to be particularly high up the list of motivators for most people. For example, one survey (McConnell, 1996) found the top five motivators and incentives were as shown in Table 8.4.

Interestingly, salary came 6th for the general population and 8th among project managers. This mirrors the research of academics like Herzberg (2003) who argue that factors such as salary are 'hygiene' factors, the absence of which can cause dissatisfaction, but which don't create satisfaction. Rather, satisfaction is derived from 'motivators' that are intrinsic to the job such as achievement, recognition, responsibility, and growth or advancement.

Table 8.4 – Motivators and incentives

	Project managers	**Team members**
1	Responsibility	Achievement
2	Achievement	Recognition
3	Work itself	Work itself
4	Recognition	Responsibility
5	Possibility for growth	Advancement

Because of this, we need to look beyond 'the carrot and the stick' paradigm in the pursuit of behavioural change – and in particular to effective strategies for stakeholder engagement, including the power of conversations.

8.5.2 Recognize the Power of Conversations

Ford & Ford (2002) argue that conversations are more than tools to facilitate change – they are the *"medium through which the construction, deconstruction, and reconstruction of realities occurs … change managers work to create and shift networks of conversations to produce intended results. The effectiveness of an organization's change is thereby a function of the change manager's ability to identify the network of conversations that is operative in the organization, and to add, modify, and delete conversations in that network until the desired outcomes are realized."*

Ford & Ford distinguish between two types of conversation – 'committed' and 'uncommitted'. The former are conversations *'for'* something, whereas the latter are *'about'* something. They can also be distinguished as follows – in committed conversations, both the speaker and the listener are engaged in, and accountable for, moving the action forward. In contrast, in uncommitted conversations, they are not accountable for taking an action or producing a result. Understanding this difference is crucial to those engaged in change management because 'committed' conversations *"move things forward, make things happen, and produce breakdowns or breakthroughs. Uncommitted conversations on the other hand, slow things down or even stop the action altogether."* Research indicates that the pace at which change is implemented reflects the ratio of 'committed' to 'uncommitted' conversations. Successful change management is therefore dependent in many cases on achieving this shift in balance between 'committed' and 'uncommitted' conversations.

Ford & Ford identify four types of 'committed' conversation:

1. **Initiative conversations** – these create a call to action via an assertion (*"We need to do something about … "*); a request (*"Will you help us address … ?"*); a promise (*"We will reduce spend by 20%"*) or a declaration (*"We will significantly improve customer satisfaction"*).

2. **Conversations for understanding** – in which people seek to understand the drivers and evidence for the initiative conversations. These are important because they have two by-products that support successful change – the specification of the 'conditions of satisfaction' (i.e. what does success look like and the timeframe for its achievement); and the *"involvement, participation and support"* of those involved as they understand their role in the change. The purpose of these conversations is not action, but understanding – and the latter does not automatically follow from the former. Achieving action therefore depends on the next category of committed conversation.

3. **Conversations for performance** – a network of requests (*"Will you do x by y?"*) and promises (*"I will do x by y"*) spoken to produce a specific action and result. It is argued that increasing the frequency of 'conversations for performance' can significantly improve the pace at which business change is achieved and, hence, benefits realization.

4. **Conversations for closure** – which are characterized by the use of assertions, expressives and declarations to bring closure to the change, and so allowing people to move on. Crucially, they should include acknowledgements – of both accomplishments and failures.

The role of conversations in organizational learning is illustrated in Example 9.5.

8.5.3 Adopt New Routines

We saw in Chapter 3 that many change programmes fail because they are premised on the flawed belief that changing an individual's attitudes will lead to changed behaviour, which when repeated across many people results in organizational change. According to Beer et al (1990), attitudinal change can follow behavioural change, and one way to achieve the desired behavioural change is to ensure that people start playing the roles expected of them – including introducing new job titles, revising job descriptions, implementing new processes and reporting, and changes to the physical environment.

Further evidence for this comes from the field of sociology where Giddens argues that our sense of well-being is heavily dependent on 'ontological security' – which is derived from a sense of continuity in our lives, i.e. a belief that today will be like yesterday. Crucial to this sense of continuity are routines – hence organizations as diverse as schools (starting the day with assembly), the armed forces (drill routines), and the Church (Sunday service) place such a strong emphasis on routines. So it is with private, public and third sector organizations – a new initiative may well disrupt people's 'ontological security', but this can be restored by establishing new roles and routines.

8.5.4 Apply Insights from the Fields of Psychology and Neuroscience

From the field of psychology, Cialdini's extensive, evidence-based research (2007) has provided insights into how behavioural change can be achieved. He argues that much of human behaviour is hard-wired, and he has identified six principles that direct human behaviour – and which change initiatives therefore need to consider wherever behavioural change is required. These are shown in Table 8.5.

Developments in the field of neuroscience are also providing fresh insights into the area of behavioural change – and what works and doesn't work. For example, Rock & Schwartz (2006) argue that the traditional approaches have failed – behaviourism, based on incentives and consequences, rarely succeeds beyond the short term; and humanism, based on connection and persuasion, doesn't engage people sufficiently. The solution lies in recognizing that:

Table 8.5 – Cialdini's Six Principles of Influence

Principle	Description
Consistency	Once we make a commitment, we feel a sense that we need to act in a manner that is consistent with that commitment. This links to our consideration of behavioural change following people's adoption of new roles. As Cialdini (2007) notes – man's *"behaviour tells him about himself; it is a primary source of information about his beliefs and values and attitudes".*
Reciprocation	Providing a small favour results in a sense of obligation to repay – if only because of a feeling of indebtedness.
Social proof	One way we determine what is appropriate is to see what others are doing. Much advertising is based on social proof. This links to the discussion below of the power of hearing the same message on a regular basis. Cialdini (2007) argues, *"The most influential leaders are those who know how to arrange group conditions to allow the principle of social proof to work maximally in their favour."*
Authority	We tend to follow the directions of those perceived to be in authority – as demonstrated by the Milgram experiments (see Cialdini, 2007, pp. 211–14).
Liking	Compliance is aided where we know and like the person making a request of us, or the request is linked to something we like. Active stakeholder engagement seeks to achieve this by using messages that engage people on a personal level.
Scarcity	Cialdini (2007) says, *"People seem to be more motivated by the thought of losing something than by the thought of gaining something of equal value."* Indeed, there is evidence that we value losses avoided twice as much as equivalent gains (see Appendix D).

- **Expectation shapes reality** – we see what we expect to see, so cultivate moments of insight that are generated from within, rather than being presented as conclusions.
- **Focus is power** – repeated attention to something actually leads to changes in the brain, so get people to focus on solutions not problems and create the conditions in which people remain focused on their insights.

This in turn means that behavioural change depends on strategies such as:

- Repeated attention is aided by getting people to adopt new roles and processes – reinforcing the points made in the preceding section.

- Cultivate moments of insight so that attitudes and expectations change more rapidly than they otherwise would – apply 'narrative leadership' (see Section 8.5.6 below).

- Recognize that change and learning are mutually reinforcing – so support training by ongoing coaching which helps people remain focused on the insights gained during training. One study found that productivity improved 28% following a training programme, but with the addition of follow-up coaching the improvement increased to 88%.

- Change is often characterized by 'tipping points' where new behaviours spread exponentially. So recognize the power of familiarity, which, according to psychologist Virginia Satir, is one of most powerful motivators – even more so than comfort. The influence of advertising, for example, is largely based on repetition and social proof. Familiarity, or the lack of it, rather than simple inertia is the reason that change is often so difficult. So in business change initiatives, the task is to communicate the message consistently and continually so that the new ways of working become familiar to those that need to change. Additionally, cultivate advocates or apostles to spread and repeat the message.

8.5.5 Develop Measures that Engage and Influence

We saw in the last chapter that measures are rarely passive and can have unfortunate side-effects and unintended consequences. The good news is that they can, if appropriately designed, influence benefits realization in a more positive manner. But this requires that in selecting measures, consideration is given to what actually influences the user, and that measures are used to inform understanding, rather than to allocate blame – for example, Cabinet Office guidance (2008) on promoting customer satisfaction quotes Tony Hinkley of Dudley Council, *"Feedback provides insight whereas targets distort actions"*.

In Chapter 3 we mentioned the 'backcasting' approach to initiative planning advocated by Fowler & Lock (2006), as an example of benefits-led change. They also have some observations on how appropriate measures can support this benefits-led approach by the use of:

- *Recognition Events®* – a real-life happening that, when it occurs, shows a sponsor and other stakeholders that one particular objective of the initiative has been met. They are thus results-led ends, not milestones on the way to the end. Although they lead to achievement of numerical targets, recognition events are real-life, not quantitative or numerical. They are events that can be recognized at a specified time and place – for example, being shown the first time a new system is used to make a sale. There is no limit to the number of recognition events for each initiative objective, but one is enough and most objectives have no more than three or four. Note: these are similar to the evidence events already discussed.

- *Value Flashpoints®* – these are recognition events at which a particular cash benefit starts to be realized, for example, *"The Q1 budget shows a reduction in staffing spend of £x compared to the previous quarter."*

Organizations that have utilized this approach include one Scottish Council where 40 'Show Me Events' were identified including *"I meet with the Council archivist and she shows me evidence that documents have been destroyed and sites where* documents are no longer stored." *(Available to Scottish Programme and Change Management Group members at http://www.communities.idea.gov.uk.)*

In this way, appropriately designed measurement can tap into people's creativity and commitment and so overcome the unintended consequences referred to in the last chapter. Even better, by expressing such measures in terms of 'a date with destiny' we can positively influence their achievement. This potential for positive behavioural consequences from measurement is illustrated in Examples 8.6 and 8.7.

8.5.6 Utilize Narrative Leadership and Stories

According to MacGregor Burns (1978), *"Much of what commonly passes as leadership … is no more leadership than the behaviour of small boys marching in front of a parade, who continue to strut along Main Street after the procession has turned down a side street … The test of their leadership function is their contribution to change, measured by purpose drawn from collective motives and values."* Effective stakeholder engagement is central to the leadership of change in helping to create these collective motives and values.

Ongoing stakeholder engagement after implementation is important because in many cases benefits are emergent as people find new

---

Example 8.6 – Measures that engage

Once when I was with Mr Carnegie I had a mill manager who was finely educated, thoroughly capable and master of every detail of the business. But he seemed unable to inspire his men to do their best.

"How is it that a man as able as you," I asked him one day, "cannot make this mill turn out what it should?"

"I don't know," he replied; "I have coaxed the men; I have pushed them; I have sworn at them. I have done everything in my power. Yet they will not produce."

It was near the end of the day; in a few minutes the night force would come on duty. I turned to a workman who was standing beside one of the red-mouthed furnaces and asked him for a piece of chalk.

"How many heats has your shift made today?" I queried.

"Six," he replied.

I chalked a big '6' on the floor, and then passed along without another word. When the night shift came in they saw the '6', and asked about it.

"The big boss was in here today," said the day men. "He asked us how many heats we had made, and we told him six. He chalked it down."

The next morning I passed through the same mill. I saw that the '6' had been rubbed out and a big '7' written instead. The night shift had announced itself. That night I went back. The '7' had been erased, and a '10' swaggered in its place. The day force recognized no superiors. Thus a fine competition was started, and it went on until this mill, formerly the poorest producer, was turning out more than any other mill in the plant.

From Schwab (1917).

Example 8.7 – Making measurement real in the WUYJ programme

At a national level, the potential benefits of the Wiring Up Youth Justice (WUYJ) programme were reflected in the improvement targets set for the youth justice system. But how to make this contribution real at a local level? The programme worked with local management to ensure that change happened by making measurement meaningful and by 'keeping it real and keeping it simple'. This meant developing a suite of measures that were meaningful to the users (those who do the change), managers/decision makers (those who make the change happen) and stakeholders (those who fund or have an interest in the change).

Engaging local users was an area of particular focus. Getting local management to agree to cashable benefits can be both problematic and counter-productive – it turns people off the system and so damages the exploitation of capability that creates value. This is particularly so in a cross-agency environment such as the youth justice system. The WUYJ programme recognized this by focusing on articulating and agreeing a set of behaviours that have been shown to produce better outcomes for young people. In this way, the measurement process becomes a catalyst for change. Active measurement was also recognized as bringing important by-products in terms of evidencing early gains and so addressing the 'what's in it for me?' question.

The value of this approach was recognized in an independent review which concluded, *"The process for identifying, agreeing and managing the intended benefits is to be commended. Such an end user focused and inclusive approach means that tangible benefits are being realized and appreciated by the YOTS and wider YJS."*

From Jenner (2011). Provided with the kind agreement of Phil Sutton, WUYJ Head of Business Change and Benefits, and Lisa Stewart, WUYJ Benefits Manager.

---

ways of working that were previously unanticipated. As Benko & McFarlan (2003) say, real breakthroughs take longer than expected because people walk *"into the future backward, viewing the future through the lens of their past experiences"*. Consequently, if we are to optimize benefits realization from our investments in change we need to ensure that this dialogue is ongoing; check that it is forward-looking with an exploration of 'what might be'; and engage users at an emotional level by tapping into their reserves of energy and commitment. As Dearing, Dilts & Russell (2002) say, *"We shy away from forceful demands for loyalty and commitment, but we flock to and swarm round focal points where 'cool stuff' seems either to be happening or about to happen. Good leaders work with our hunger to involve ourselves, with others, in interesting work and exciting projects."*

One way in which this degree of involvement can be encouraged is via narrative leadership – which utilizes the medium of stories and storytelling to engage stakeholders in an exploration of the potential for benefits realization from change. The power of stories to influence behavioural change is highlighted by a wide range of change management experts and academics including:

- Stephen Denning, former Director of Knowledge Management at the World Bank, who says, *"Analysis might excite the mind, but it hardly offers a route to the heart. And that's where you must go to motivate people not only to take action but to do so with energy and enthusiasm."*

- Nassim Nicholas Taleb (2007) Professor in the Sciences of Uncertainty, *"Ideas come and go, stories stay."*

- David Fleming who argues that organizations *"must learn to capitalize on the role of uncertainty and ambiguity. One of the most powerful ways for leaders to make sense of the ambiguity-opportunity cycle is to tap the power of one of humanity's oldest art forms, storytelling."*

- In the *Harvard Business Review*, screenwriting coach Robert McKee states that *"most executives struggle to communicate, let alone inspire. Too often, they get lost in the accoutrements of companyspeak: PowerPoint slides, dry memos, and hyperbolic missives from the corporate communications department"* – and the solution to motivating people is *"engage their emotions, and the key to their hearts is story"*.

- In another *Harvard Business Review* article Warren Bennis (1996), leading academic in the field of leadership, argues that *"Effective leaders put words to the formless longings and deeply felt needs of others. They create communities out of words. They tell stories that capture minds and win hearts."*

Marchand & Peppard (2008) cite an example from New Zealand where the project team wanted to make the vision recognizable and "real" for all staff – this was achieved *"through many change management techniques including storytelling, senior management promotions, videos and even posters and pens. They also placed strong emphasis on stakeholder engagement, working to build and sustain relationships."*

Example 8.8 – Engaging 'hearts and minds' for growth at Tetra Pak

A focus on growth

In 2000, Tetra Pak launched a growth initiative labelled '5005' – to grow the business 50% by 2005. Although the growth did not come entirely from the areas expected, the target was achieved one year ahead of schedule by the end of 2004. The leadership team then wanted another 'Big, Hairy, Audacious Goal' (in the words of Collins & Porras, 2002) to maintain the focus on growth, though this time without a specific time limitation. Other required enhancements were recognized as including:

- Branding – the symbol that had been used for '5005' was a corporate one, relevant for the company in its totality, but not useable at country or unit level.
- Emphasis on market share – '5005' had delivered strong growth in terms of revenue and packages sold, although without also focusing on market share.

The message – creation of *'Triple V'*

The two key challenges facing the team responsible for the launch of the new growth initiative were therefore to agree on a clear message that would encapsulate the wider definition of growth, and to define a communications strategy to make it 'come alive' across the organization. The result was *Triple V* – the three measures that would be used to assess progress on the growth ambition:

- **Value** is the value we provide to our customers expressed as Net Sales.
- **Volume** is what we actually deliver and is expressed as the Number of Packages sold.
- **Voice** relates to a particular market or category, in relation to our competition and is expressed as Market Share.

Although *Triple V* was primarily about a general mindset, corporate targets were set based on aggregate inputs from all countries and units:

- **Value:** Net Sales in billions of euros.
- **Volume:** Number of Packages sold in billions of packages.
- **Voice:** Market Share increased by a set percentage.

Each unit also set its own *Triple V* targets.

Example continues

Example 8.8 continued

The medium – bringing *Triple V* to life

So far so good, but nothing too innovative – but what was new and incredibly effective was the means used to communicate the message and engage staff across the globe in its delivery. The objectives were to find a way of launching *Triple V* that would capture the imagination of people at all levels of the company and drive a change in mindset and behaviour. Key criteria were the need to:

- Be understandable by everyone – 21,000 employees in 165 countries.
- Work at all levels of the company – senior and middle management, factory staff and office workers.
- Work across all cultures – from Scandinavia to Iran.
- Be consistent with and leverage existing organizational culture and values.

In a radical move, the launch team decided to use a cartoon to communicate the challenge. Factors influencing this decision were:

- **Cartoons work across cultures and ages**
  One of the biggest challenges for any organization is to translate strategy into something tangible and meaningful for everyone in the company across the globe. Cartoons work across all cultures and all ages as evidenced by the success and widespread appeal of movies like *Toy Story*.
- **Cartoons are timeless**
  The growth ambition needed to last for a number of years and related more to a general mindset focusing on continuous improvement rather than a fixed target. The imagery used therefore needed to be relatively timeless, and cartoons do not date in the way that other images can.
- **The need to connect hearts and minds**
  The message had to reflect the company's core values and engage people – it therefore needed to have some liveliness and fun.

The characters as symbols

The cartoon characters were designed to reflect the diversity of the population within Tetra Pak in terms of age, gender, nationality and individuality.

The lady represented value, the large man represented volume and the Asian man represented voice. Previously, the company had used the imagery of wolves and the pack to symbolize leadership. The incorporation of 'Spirit' the wolf provided a degree of continuity and familiarity, while maintaining a focus on core value.

Figure 8.6 – Triple V *cartoon characters*

The launch of *Triple V*

The new concept was unveiled at a top management gathering. A *Triple V* video was introduced as a story with a voiceover explaining the challenges facing our *Triple V* super heroes. The characters then flew around the world interviewing people from all levels of the organization about what *Triple V* meant to them – from Argentina to Taiwan. A DVD package was sent to each office around the world containing, amongst other things, the film, a PowerPoint presentation, a screensaver and downloadable files of the characters. Magnetic characters, badges, drinks mats and posters were created and distributed and the images were used widely on all corporate materials. Howling 'Spirit' the Wolf plush toys were also distributed around the world.

The results of the *Triple V* launch

Feedback from staff surveys was exceptionally positive and awareness of the initiative was outstanding – in a global survey six months after the launch, 97.5% of employees were aware of the company's *Triple V* growth ambition. Even more significantly, the cartoon story captured the imaginations of employees from across the globe – within weeks examples were flooding in from local offices showing how the story was being adapted to local conditions. In some countries, management had donned *Triple V* cartoon costumes at kick-off sessions, *Triple V* colouring packs were created and distributed at company family days, and some canteens even created *Triple V* desserts!

Provided with the kind agreement of Jorgen Haglind, Senior Vice President Communications, Tetra Laval. Tetra Pak is the world's leading supplier of food processing and packaging systems.

These themes are illustrated in Example 8.8, which demonstrates how a creative, multimedia approach was applied to engage stakeholders in an initiative with a global reach; and in Example 8.9 that shows how storytelling was used to re-engage employees in a business transformation programme.

What these examples illustrate is the power of storytelling to effectively engage stakeholders in a dialogue about how the organization might adapt to change and how to optimize benefits realization. This is not about transferring information, but about *"catalyzing understanding"* (Denning).

Example 8.9 – Storytelling at Parcelforce

Following a prolonged phase of operational restructuring, employees' enthusiasm for the ongoing change effort was waning. It was recognized that what was needed was a more creative and memorable way of making strategy relevant to the employees. The solution – an engagement campaign called 'Making the Next Big Difference' was designed to re-engage the workforce, communicate the business plan and stimulate a call to action. Central to this was a StoryMap – a simple narrative framework structured into a series of chapters that explained in simple terms the journey the organization was on and the priorities they wanted people to focus on – called 'Focus on Four':

- Improving our service.
- Growing our profitable revenue.
- Working smarter.
- Developing our skills and capabilities.

The StoryMap was brought to life through a comic-book style format and the messages were supported by a series of real-life stories from the business which gave the messages meaning by making them relevant to employees' daily tasks and by explaining what success looked like.

The StoryMap was rolled out across the organization with the help of senior leaders and managers, supported by interactive employee sessions, posters and an employee recognition programme ('The Big Thank You'). Employees were also invited to build their own story by contributing their own experiences and generating new ideas.

Provided with the kind agreement of Alison Esse, The Storytellers, and based on an article available at: http://www.melcrum.com/ presentations/ukbb0508/presentations/13_All_About_Change/Making%20a%20difference.pdf [Last accessed: 16 March 2012]. *Parcelforce* is a trading name of Royal Mail Group Ltd.

Key features of effective stories and storytelling are that they should be:

- **Structured** – with a beginning, a middle and an end, and make clear the consequences of failing to take effective action.

- **Memorable** – this is helped by:
  - ☐ Media – the use of different media helps to convey the message using verbal presentations as well as the written word, so engaging the audience's attention by both sight and hearing.
  - ☐ Message – making the message memorable via creative presentation. In this regard, note how change management books have utilized animal analogies to help make the message memorable ('*Who Moved My Cheese*' (Mice – Spencer Johnson); '*Our Iceberg Is Melting*' (Penguins – Kotter); and '*Squirrel Inc.*' (Denning)).

- **Alive** – making the story 'live' by:
  - ☐ Including a physical component.
  - ☐ Incorporating drama.
  - ☐ Allowing the story to adapt as the initiative progresses.

- **Engaging** – the story should be told from a viewpoint with which the audience can associate; and actively involve stakeholders in the 'story' and its development, encouraging them to adapt it to the local circumstances.

- **Relevant** – the problem needs to be relevant to the stakeholders in creating ownership and a shared experience.

8.6 CHAPTER SUMMARY

1. The objective of the Realize practice is to optimize benefits realization by actively managing planned benefits through to their realization; capturing and leveraging emergent benefits; and minimizing and mitigating any

dis-benefits. This includes ensuring that the business and behavioural changes on which benefits realization is dependent actually take place.

2. While the focus in decision-making should be on realism (to overcome the twin risks of strategic misrepresentation and optimism bias), the approach to benefits realization should be one based on enthusiasm to help overcome the obstacles that can often arise during implementation and delivery.

3. Transition management includes ensuring that the business changes on which benefits realization is dependent actually occur.

4. In monitoring benefits realization we should distinguish between forecasts and targets – the former, as part of the investment appraisal process, should be realistic; the latter should be motivational and aspirational – and this requires that they be used less as a means of backward-looking accountability, and more as a basis of forward-looking insight and learning.

5. Effective monitoring and management of benefits realization is aided by the selection of a suite of measures including leading and lagging measures, proxy indicators, evidence events, case studies, surveys and stories, to create a 'rich picture' providing feedback on benefits realization from multiple perspectives; as well as by techniques including: 'one version of the truth', 'management by exception', and 'clear line of sight' reporting.

6. Benefits realization is often dependent on behavioural change. Strategies that can contribute to this include:
   - Align incentives with benefits realization.
   - Recognize the power of conversations.
   - Adopt new routines, which can lead to behavioural change.
   - Apply insights from the fields of neuroscience and psychology.
   - Develop measures that engage and influence.
   - Utilize narrative leadership and storytelling.

Chapter 9

Chapter 9 – Benefits Management Practice 5 – Review

9.1 OVERVIEW OF THIS CHAPTER

In this chapter we consider the last practice in the Benefits Management Cycle – Review. The objectives of the Review practice are to ensure, and assure, that:

- The benefits to be realized are achievable and continue to represent value for money.
- Appropriate arrangements have been made for benefits monitoring, management and evaluation.
- Benefits realization is being effectively managed.
- Lessons are learned for both the current initiative and as a basis for more effective benefits management practices generally.

The scope of this practice encompasses reviews undertaken:

- At the commencement of an initiative – for example, start gates and pre-mortems.

- During the lifetime of an initiative – 'in-flight' reviews including those undertaken at the end of a tranche within a programme, and those at mandated stage/phase gates.
- After implementation – post-implementation and post-investment reviews.

No matter when they occur, benefit reviews include consideration of:

- Planned benefits, i.e. are the forecast benefits still realizable/being realized?
- Emergent benefits, i.e. are unplanned benefits identified and leveraged?
- Dis-benefits (both anticipated and unanticipated), i.e. are dis-benefits mitigated effectively?
- Is value for money being maximized?
- Are the practices used to manage benefits efficient and effective?

Important note

The scope of the Review practice runs throughout the business change lifecycle from start-up, through 'in-flight' (i.e. change initiatives included in the change portfolio at the design, development or implementation stage), to after initiative closure and integration into business as usual (BAU). It also includes reviews undertaken internal to the initiative, as well as independent reviews such as the OGC Gateway™ reviews, and stage/phase gate reviews.

'Review' is an active practice going beyond passive, desk-based assessment of performance against plan. The focus is on identifying and applying lessons learned and planning for success by taking appropriate action.

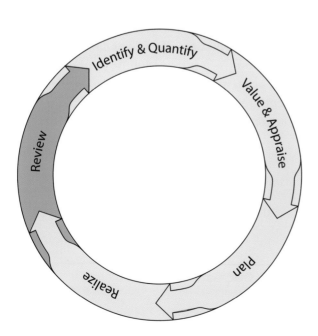

Figure 9.1 – The Review practice in the Benefits Management Cycle

9.2 INITIATIVE-LED AND INDEPENDENT REVIEWS

Reviews encompass those undertaken as part of the initiative governance process on behalf of the Senior Responsible Owner (SRO)/Sponsor (to *ensure* that benefits are efficiently and effectively managed and provide confidence that benefits realization will be, or is being, optimized) and those undertaken independently (to *assure* that benefits are efficiently and effectively managed and benefits are realized) to provide confidence to the portfolio governance body, external funding agencies etc. – see Table 9.1.

9.3 BENEFIT REVIEWS AT START-UP

Here we are concerned with consideration of benefits at start gates and the technique of pre-mortems.

9.3.1 Independent Review at Start Gate

Analysis of successful IT-enabled business change programmes and projects by the NAO (2006) identified that success depends on having a clear understanding from the outset of the potential benefits of the business change, and putting mechanisms in place to determine whether these benefits have been achieved and optimized. Start gate is crucial in this regard, i.e. an early stage review to ensure that the transition from strategy/policy to formally established change initiative is justified.

Key issues to address at the start of an initiative include, from a benefits perspective:

- Is it clear what the problem is that the initiative is designed to solve or what the opportunity is that the initiative is designed to exploit?
- Is the solution that has been identified the most cost-effective way of achieving the desired investment objectives and benefits?
- Are all elements of the solution **necessary and sufficient** to realize the required benefits? This is fundamental – see Example 9.1.
- Are benefits forecasts informed by 'an outside' view?
- Is there a clear understanding of the full scope of the change effort required to realize the benefits?
- Can the scale of the change be absorbed when other planned initiatives are taken into consideration?
- Is there clear evidence that the Benefits Management Strategy has taken on board lessons from recent post-implementation and post-investment reviews on how best to ensure benefits realization?
- Have appropriate arrangements been made for monitoring and evaluation throughout the business change lifecycle?

Experience shows that it is particularly important that the start gate review is undertaken independently of the initiative to overcome the biases discussed in Chapters 4 and 5. For example Nobel Prize-winner Daniel Kahneman (2011b) argues that management decisions can be improved by what he refers to as *"adversarial collaboration"* – a form of robust scrutiny based not on academic point scoring but on a real and in-depth review of the investment rationale. Similar arguments are made by:

Table 9.1 – Initiative and independent reviews

Initiative stage	Initiative benefit reviews	Independent reviews
Start-up	Pre-mortems.	Start gate.
'In-flight'	End-of-tranche reviews and other reviews (time- or event-driven) undertaken by the initiative.	Stage/phase gate reviews. OGC Gateway reviews.
At closure	Post-implementation review undertaken as part of initiative closure.	Post-investment reviews. OGC Gate 5 review. Closing gate.

Example 9.1 – A cautionary tale about initiative funding

One day, not so long ago, a company was expanding its network to gain more access to potential customers. They prided themselves on having a good handle on cost management, especially capital expenditure (Capex). Each department knew exactly how much they could spend each year and expenditure was tracked weekly. They held weekly Capital Approval Board meetings to control the release of the funds.

The Business Case

So, along came the project team and asked for a lot of money to buy a telecoms switch so that they could handle the traffic from their five million additional potential customers. The revenue projections were good and the return enormous . . . and the wise men on the Capital Approval Board approved the project.

The following week, another project team came along and said, *"You know that lovely new switch you approved last week? It doesn't like getting wet, so here is a submission to construct the building around it to keep it dry."* The revenue figure was the same as before, as, without this building, the switch wouldn't work and no customer revenue would flow . . . and the wise men on the Capital Approval Board approved the project.

A week later, another team arrived. *"You know that lovely building and switch? Well, it won't work without electricity, so here is the submission for the uninterrupted power supply systems for it."* . . . and the wise men on the Capital Approval Board approved the project.

Yet another week or two later, yet another team arrived. *"You know that switch, and powered building you approved? Well, switches don't like getting hot, so we need you to approve this cooling system. If you don't you won't get any revenue."* . . . the wise men on the Capital Approval Board were getting a little annoyed, but approved it as they really wanted all that lovely revenue.

The final straw came a month later. *"You know that lovely switch in its cool, dry environment with lots of power? Well, it's useless unless it is connected to the core network; the calls and data will have nowhere to go. If you really want the revenue (which we have attributed to this project's business case), you have to approve this business case as well."* The CEO (who chaired the CAB that day) exploded.

Lessons learned

This is a true story. The result was that from then on, projects and programmes were not bounded by departmental budgets (Opex or Capex) but by the work needed to get the revenue or other benefit. Initiatives became bigger as they included all the work needed, across any departments needed, and only **one** Business Case was developed to cover the lot. There were also far fewer initiatives, so it was easier to see what was going on, and the multiple counting of revenue and benefits decreased dramatically. Individual departments contributing to an initiative could no longer veto or reprioritize their 'portion', as they no longer owned the initiative.

Look in the mirror – what do you see?

Are all your change initiatives 'complete'? Is the scope **sufficient** to realize the benefits and are all elements of the initiative **necessary** to realize those benefits? Or has the initiative been 'salami sliced' into smaller 'enabling initiatives', each of which, in isolation, contributes little or nothing, and just consumes resources?

Provided with kind agreement of Robert Buttrick, Project Workout Limited.

- Ayres (2007) – who has suggested that boards should have an "'Advocatus Diaboli' ... *whose job it is to poke holes in pet projects. These professional 'No' men could be an antidote to overconfidence bias.*"

- Davidson Frame (1994) – who proposes the use of *"murder boards"* – a cross-departmental panel charged with pulling a proposal apart to *"make sure that arguments in support of project ideas do not have built into them the seeds of their own destruction"*.

An interesting example of this independent scrutiny at the start of an initiative is shown in Example 9.2.

Other options for independent scrutiny via a start gate include the organization's non-executive directors, the Internal Audit function, and in a *'Management of Portfolios'* (MoP) environment, the Portfolio Direction Group/Investment Committee.

9.3.2 Pre-mortems

This approach was developed by Gary Klein (1998) and in turn is based on work by Russo & Schoemaker (1990) on what they termed 'prospective hindsight'. The pre-mortem (which should be differentiated from post-mortem reviews that are undertaken after an initiative *has* failed) is a facilitated workshop undertaken at the start of an initiative. The initiative team is invited to imagine that the initiative *has* failed and the benefits haven't been realized. This is important – we are not concerned with what might go wrong; rather, the focus is on what '*has*' gone wrong. The causes of the failure are explored using techniques such as brainstorming, and may include factors such as: optimistic forecasts, inadequate resources, technical failure, absence of business change, failure to achieve behavioural change etc. In this way we can tap into people's creativity, not in defending their plan, but in identifying potential causes of failure. This can be an extremely effective way of mitigating against optimism bias and the planning fallacy.

Example 9.2 – Robust scrutiny of the Business Case by a 'Dragons' Den'

One practitioner advocates the concept of exposing investment propositions to rigorous and robust challenge at a 'Dragons' Den' – the concept is derived from the BBC's TV series in which budding entrepreneurs get three minutes to pitch their business ideas to five multi-millionaires willing to invest their own cash. In this case, the initiative sponsor is required to present the Business Case to a panel of experts from the business – including those with a strategic, finance and operational perspective. The panel scrutinize the proposition in terms of:

- What are the specific outputs, outcomes and benefits?
- Does the scale of benefits represent an adequate return for the funds required and are the estimated costs realistic?
- Are the benefits realizable? In particular – what business and behavioural change is required?

Such exercises can be used to test the veracity of a particular proposition or Business Case, or compare a number of propositions or Business Cases to enable an organization to choose those that represent and deliver most value. Indeed, the technique has been found to be of particular value when funding is tight and the number of competing change initiatives exceed those that can be funded. Scoring can be achieved via:

- Traditional ratings for 'attractiveness' and 'achievability' – with the results being recorded on a portfolio map.
- Pair-wise comparisons – where competing initiatives are compared in pairs.
- Or even by allocating 'Monopoly' money to the panel – which helps to illustrate the point that once the available funds have been allocated, there's no more available.

Provided with the kind agreement of Nick Wensley, Director, Farthing Consulting Ltd.

9.4 BENEFIT REVIEWS 'IN-FLIGHT'

'Managing Successful Programmes' (MSP) states that benefits reviews can be time- or event-driven, and at a minimum will occur at the end of each tranche in a programme. The objectives of a benefits review identified in MSP are to:

- Assess and update the individual Benefit Profiles and the Benefits Realization Plan to ensure that the planned benefits remain achievable and have not changed in scope or value.
- Check that the overall set of benefits included within the Benefits Map and Benefits Register remain aligned to the programme's objectives and to reprioritize or realign them as necessary.
- Inform stakeholders and senior management of progress in benefits realization and help to identify any further potential for benefits.
- Assess the performance of the changed business operations against their original (baseline) performance levels.
- Assess the level of benefits achieved against the Benefits Realization Plan.
- Review the effectiveness of the way in which benefits management is being handled, so that lessons can be learned and improved processes can be developed and implemented. If there are fundamental concerns about the effectiveness of benefits management, the Benefits Management Strategy may also need to be revised.

With regard to the last point, one issue that should be closely monitored is whether benefits measures are having the desired influence on behaviour, or whether they are encouraging appearance manipulation and perverse outcomes. Where required the Benefits Map, Profiles and Benefits Realization Plan will be updated by the Business Change Manager.

While these end-of-tranche reviews will be undertaken on behalf of the SRO, independent reviews are also carried out in many organizations as part of the formal portfolio stage/phase gate process, where continued funding for 'in-flight' initiatives is related to successful progression

through each gate, and confirmation that the initiative remains justified. This is addressed in the next chapter.

9.5 POST-IMPLEMENTATION REVIEW

The importance of post-implementation review cannot be overestimated – as a basis for building a reference class of data to inform forecasting, organizational learning and continuous improvement in benefits management. Indeed, number one in the top ten differentiating practices between higher- and lower-performing organizations in one academic study (Ward et al, 2007) was "Transferral of lessons learned". Yet it appears that these reviews are often far from effective. For example:

- A study by Mott McDonald (2002) for HM Treasury found: *"Moreover most projects did not have any post project appraisal that could provide an indication of how successful the delivery of benefits had been."*
- The NAO (2009) report that 80% of government departments don't use Gateway 5 (Benefits Evaluation) and *"OGC is also aware that Government departments are not systematic enough in completing post-implementation reviews on projects or programmes that have gone particularly well or badly"*.

The problem is not one that is restricted to the public sector – Ward et al (2008) note that in one European survey 80% of respondents reported that the review and evaluation of completed projects was inadequate. Recent research in Ireland by the APM and CIMA (2012) has reported that only 4% of respondents stated that the formal post-implementation reviews always provide value. The study concludes that there is a *"need for a fundamental re-evaluation of how organisations approach post-implementation reviews with the focus on a more effective form of assurance for post-implementation benefits realisation"*.

Why might this be? Part of the explanation lies in a series of cognitive biases that affect our ability to learn from experience, or to learn the appropriate lessons. These biases include:

- **Self-serving bias** – the belief that our successes are due to our efforts and abilities, whereas failures are due to external events and bad luck. As the Duke of Wellington said, *"Victory has a thousand fathers; defeat is an orphan."* Consequently, there is nothing to learn because any failure is perceived as just bad luck or due to some external, uncontrollable factor.

- **Hindsight bias** – the tendency to see past events as being more predictable than they actually were. So the outcome is seen as inevitable.

- **Outcome bias** – the belief that the outcome determines whether a decision was correct, rather than whether it was the right decision given the information available at the time.

- **The Texas Sharpshooter fallacy** – the tendency to assess the success of an initiative (and the appropriateness of the original investment decision) in terms of the actual outcome rather than asking whether the benefits the initiative was designed to deliver were actually realized and whether the outcome represents value for money, i.e. drawing the target after performance has been measured, and calling that success.

The consequences are seen in the following comment from a Director at the NAO in a feature interview in *Project Magazine* (May, 2011), *"The fact that we see the same issues coming up time and again on projects suggests lessons are not being learned when investment decisions are being made. If people acted on the lessons you would hope they would become less prevalent over time. But the truth is we're not seeing much change."*

The failure to undertake effective post-implementation/investment reviews and learn from experience is another example of the 'knowing–doing' gap discussed in Chapter 4. Addressing this requires that we:

- Make specific provision for evaluation in the Business Case, which should clearly identify when reviews will take place, by whom, and that provision for the costs of monitoring and evaluation has been included in the initiative budget.
- Ensure that the Portfolio Benefits Management Framework includes guidance on evaluation that encompasses both summative (did the benefits' 'performance' match the 'promise') and formative (learning) aspects.
- Expect and monitor learning – even if the management adage 'what gets measured gets done' is only partly true, then it is crucial that organizations measure learning. For example, via tracking performance at a portfolio level in terms of:
  - ☐ Benefits realization compared to forecast – what is our organization's track record and is it improving?
  - ☐ Improvements in the benefits management practices – in what ways are they more efficient and effective than 12 months ago?

9.5.1 Post-implementation and Post-investment Reviews

It is helpful to distinguish between:

- **Post-implementation reviews** undertaken as part of initiative closure on behalf of the SRO (although in an MoP environment the conclusions will also be reported to the Portfolio Direction Group/Investment Committee, as it is the governance body that authorized the initial investment); and then undertaken by operational management post-initiative closure to ensure that benefits realization is optimized. In an MSP environment, responsibility for benefits reviews after initiative closure lies with the Business Change Manager. It is emphasized that post-implementation reviews should be undertaken for *all* change initiatives, although, if the 'in-flight' reviews have been undertaken appropriately, then this should not be particularly resource-intensive.

- **Post-investment reviews** are undertaken independently of the initiative and report (in an MoP environment) to the Portfolio Direction Group/Investment Committee, i.e.

the board that authorized the initial investment. They will be undertaken on a more select basis (based on potential learnings) and include:

- □ In-depth reviews that examine an initiative from start to finish, with a focus on identifying and applying lessons more widely. They include both successful and failed initiatives.
- □ 'Deep-dive' reviews that examine a thematic subject (for example, forecasting, reporting etc.) across a number of completed initiatives to identify how efficient and effective benefits management is, and how it can be improved.

Post-investment reviews may be undertaken by a team established for the purpose (including Internal Audit), by External Audit (reporting to the Audit Committee for example), by the Portfolio Office, or by a dedicated unit – see Example 9.3.

The timing of such reviews will clearly depend on the initiative, but won't normally be undertaken until some time after initiative closure so that definitive conclusions can be reached.

Example 9.3 – Independent post-project appraisal at BP

Gulliver has reported in the *Harvard Business Review* on the effectiveness of post-project appraisals at BP. Key features of the Post-Project Appraisal Unit were identified as including:

- Reviews were limited to six per annum, with the subjects of each review being carefully selected – focusing on the largest initiatives and specifically those where the most valuable results were anticipated. For example, the unit would not review initiatives where the results were likely to duplicate those from a previous review or where a similar initiative was unlikely to be undertaken.
- The review team were independent of the initiatives reviewed and so they could evaluate them objectively.
- The scope encompassed the causes of success and failure – and so learning from the latter and repeating the former.
- The conclusions were consolidated into guidance on lessons learned from previous reviews – and this was widely disseminated to BP's managers. In this way, guidance on lessons learned was kept up to date.
- The unit was also part of the investment appraisal procedure – which helped ensure that mistakes were not repeated.

Russo & Schoemaker (1990) note that the Post-Project Appraisal Unit reported to the board and was charged with communicating lessons learned across the organization. The result – savings in the "tens of millions of dollars".

Pfeffer & Sutton (2000) also note that BP adopted, as part of their approach to post-project appraisal, four mechanisms to ensure that lessons were not only identified, but more importantly, shared and applied:

1. Peer assists – whereby staff were loaned temporarily to another business unit to help resolve an issue. This helped to transfer knowledge via people with the required explicit and tacit knowledge and skills.

2. Peer groups – of business units facing similar problems were established and met quarterly.

3. Federal groups – were established to review common issues that cut across the peer groups.

4. Personnel transfers – to facilitate knowledge development and transfer.

9.5.2 Questions to Ask

The scope of both post-implementation and post-investment reviews will encompass:

Outcomes

- Analysis to determine whether the forecast benefits have been realized and represent value for money (and if not whether any action is appropriate).
- How additional value has been/can be created and what lessons can be learned to improve delivery and benefits realization in the future.

This analysis can also be informed by a comparative assessment of the outturn position against one or more counterfactuals, i.e. alternative outcomes based on different states of the world. For example, the impact of an initiative in Area 1 could be compared with performance in Area 2 where the initiative was not implemented. The analysis will also be informed by the views of the SRO/Sponsor on how successful or not the initiative was, and what went well/not so well.

Decision-making

- Whether the original decision to invest was the right one given the information available at the time and what can be learned for future decision-making. In particular, we need to distinguish decision outcomes from the process used to make the decision – for example, was success 'deserved' or just 'dumb luck'? (See Figure 9.2.)

- Review to confirm or disconfirm the business model – the elements in the model, their drivers and the linkages between them.

Benefits management

- Updated data to inform 'reference class' forecasting.

- How efficient and effective was the Benefits Management Cycle and are any changes to the Portfolio Benefits Management Framework required? This includes assessing to what extent success or failure in realizing benefits was due to the initiative, the benefits management practices, compliance with those practices, or some other factor – and if the result was a failure to realize benefits, whether such factors could have been avoided.

9.5.3 From Lessons Learned to Lessons Applied

It is crucially important that we go beyond capturing and recording lessons learned to actually applying them. Strategies that can play a part in achieving this are illustrated in Examples 9.4 and 9.5.

Key themes from these examples include:

- A focus on applying lessons learned widely via networks of people, rather than storing the knowledge gained, and establishing mechanisms to facilitate collaborative working by bringing people together.
- The use of multimedia solutions to share and disseminate lessons learned.
- The application of dialogue/conversational formats and storytelling to more effectively communicate key messages – building on our discussion of conversations and storytelling in the last chapter.

9.6 OGC GATEWAY REVIEWS

Project assurance within the Major Projects Authority incudes: Gateway review, major project assessment reviews, starting gate and closing gate. The best known, and longest established, of these are the Gateway reviews applied to initiatives that procure services, construction/

Process used to make decision	Outcome	
	Good	Poor
Good	'Deserved success'	'Bad break'
Poor	'Dumb luck'	'Poetic justice'

Figure 9.2 – Outcomes and the decision process

Source: Russo & Schoemaker, 1990.

Example 9.4 – Applying lessons learned at Openreach

Openreach recognizes the importance of not just learning lessons, but also applying them. To help ensure this happens it has instigated a process whereby, as part of submitting a Business Case to the board, the writer needs to get a template with a unique reference number. In order to get this template, they must first visit the lessons learned database, where lessons learned are categorized to aid identification of the most relevant ones. The Business Case writer is also expected to name the lessons learned that have been taken note of, in the Business Case submission.

Table 9.2 – Openreach lessons-learned database extract

Type of Case	Type of Lesson	Applies to	Display?	Key message	Contact	Case title	Case approval date	Type of review	Review date	Title
Other	Requirements Capture	All cases	Yes	Working alongside the designers and developers results in them understanding the requirement better and leads to faster delivery, better solutions and far less re-work			11/02/2011	IFR	29/11/2011	Co-location
Other	System Testing	All cases	Yes	Leave 3 months from deployment to actual go live so that live data can be used for User Acceptance Testing.			11/02/2011	IFR	29/11/2011	Testing - use live data
Other	Cost Assumptions	All cases	Yes	Post deployment fixes as a result of poor specification or user requirements are chargeable, so ensure a little contingency in the funding to cover these.			11/02/2011	IFR	29/11/2011	Post delivery fixes
Other	Benefit Assumptions	All cases	Yes	A proof of concept phase is essential for large complex deliveries (especially when it can utilise live data); it gives confidence in the design, early visibility of additional complexity and is invaluable in communicating the objectives of the programme.			11/02/2011	IFR	29/11/2011	Proof of Concept
Infrastructure	System Design	All cases	Yes	Ensure solution designs are vetted by the Openreach systems architecture forum for compliance to minimum standards and cost			30/06/2010	IFR	28/02/2011	Architecture Forum
Product New	Benefit Assumptions	All cases	Yes	Make sure that sufficient benefits time lag is allowed, for example between the release date and the CP ability to consume the product.			25/09/2010	IFR	24/09/2011	Revenue Timing 2

Provided with the kind agreement of Jim Runnacles, Openreach (a BT Group company).

Example 9.5 – Knowledge management in NASA

Exploration Systems Mission Directorate (ESMD) Integrated Risk and Knowledge Management System

Lengyel (2011) reports that knowledge capture and transfer activities are designed to document project execution lessons learned and best practices in a contextual manner using a conversation-based format. This is an abrupt departure from the notion of lessons-learned databases that often have been hard to use, typically fragment 'the story' and, most regrettably, lack context. Knowledge capture and transfer also rejects the notion of asking participants to fill out questionnaires. Rather, knowledge capture and transfer uses the most natural method, conversation, but carefully structured and controlled conversation. Individual issues are summarized, aggregated, and a composite analysis is provided. Results are rapidly provided to stakeholders using a variety of communication modes including briefings, design review check-lists, peer assists, knowledge cafes (small group 'brainstorming') and video interviews. An edited report is also developed as an archive and made available electronically to management.

NASA's Knowledge Sharing Initiative in the Academy of Program and Project Leadership (APPL)

Hoffman (2011) reports that the Knowledge Sharing Initiative (KSI) gathers and shares knowledge and emphasizes informal first-person storytelling by NASA project managers. It promotes cross-centre collaboration across the agency via annual conferences; an online magazine; forums; publications; and a multimedia library of presentations providing managers, scientists and engineers with concrete examples of obstacles overcome, successes achieved and failures analysed. By employing the power of storytelling to gather, store and share insights, and telling anecdotes from experienced programme, project and engineering professionals, it continues to create and maintain communities of practice across NASA's decentralized project-based organization.

From: ICCPM (2011).

property, IT-related business change projects and procurements utilizing framework contracts. They are undertaken at key decision points in the business change lifecycle by a team of experienced reviewers who are independent of the project or programme team but report to the SRO. These key decision points are:

- Gateway 0 – Strategic assessment – applied at the start of a programme and major projects.
- Gateway 1 – Business justification.
- Gateway 2 – Procurement strategy.
- Gateway 3 – Investment decision.
- Gateway 4 – Readiness for service.
- Gateway 5 – Operations review and benefits realization.

Reviewer guidance includes suggested 'areas to probe' and the sorts of evidence expected in relation to benefits and benefits management at each of the above reviews. A summary of this guidance in relation to benefits management is shown at Appendix G.

> **Important note**
>
> The guidance for OGC Gateway reviewers provides a useful *aide-mémoire* to those involved in other benefits reviews – particularly in relation to the changing benefits management emphasis as the initiative progresses through the business change lifecycle.

9.7 CHAPTER SUMMARY

1. The Review practice extends throughout the business change lifecycle and is an active process designed to optimize benefits realization and identify and apply lessons learned.

2. Benefits review at initiation includes start gate review, with a focus on ensuring that the initiative is designed with the end in mind, and the technique of pre-mortems to overcome the issues of optimism bias and the planning fallacy.

3. In-flight reviews focus on both a backward look (does benefits realization to date match the forecast?) and a forward look (what action is required to optimize benefits realization?). They also include reviews undertaken directly for the SRO and those undertaken independently as part of the portfolio stage/ phase gate process.

4. Research indicates that post-implementation reviews are generally poorly done, which is in part due to cognitive biases such as the self-serving bias, hindsight bias, outcome bias and Texas Sharpshooter fallacy. Overcoming these biases and the 'knowing–doing' gap requires more disciplined approaches to 'Review', with a focus on applying lessons learned going forward.

5. Post-implementation reviews should be undertaken on all initiatives. Independent post-investment reviews are undertaken on a more select basis and represent an in-depth review of an initiative from start to finish, or a deep-dive thematic review across several initiatives. They may be undertaken by the Portfolio Office, and report to the governance body that authorized the original investment.

6. OGC Gateway review guidance provides a useful list of areas to probe and the evidence expected at various stages throughout the business change lifecycle.

Chapter 10

Chapter 10 – Portfolio-based Benefits Management

10.1 OVERVIEW OF THIS CHAPTER

So far we have focused on the Benefits Management Cycle as it applies to individual change initiatives. The most effective organizations also ensure that these initiatives are appraised in terms of their strategic contribution, subject to an acceptable level of risk, and remain aligned to their strategic objectives. This is where the portfolio approach to benefits management – why and how benefits can be managed at the collective level – comes in. This includes:

- Determining a consistent approach to benefits management that applies to all initiatives included within the change portfolio.
- Applying benefits-led approaches to investment appraisal and portfolio prioritization – ensuring that we invest, and continue to invest, in the 'right' things.
- Managing benefits realization at the portfolio level by, for example, effective management of dependencies, tracking benefits realization and taking corrective action where required – including after initiative closure.

We consider the six main elements identified by 'Management of Portfolios' (MoP), along with the portfolio-level benefits management roles and documentation. As with the other chapters in this Guide, we include examples of how organizations have applied the main elements in practice.

A common theme identified by many researchers is that organizations undertake too much change, with new initiatives being started without considering the existing portfolio and the change capacity of the organization. The results are seen in delivery delays and failure – and so sub-optimal benefits realization. Portfolio management can help address this and other causes of sub-optimal benefits realization such as double counting and ineffective dependency management. Portfolio management is therefore a foundation for effective benefits management, but at the same time, effective portfolio management should be benefits-led. In short:

- Benefits management is most efficient and effective when it is managed consistently across the change portfolio.
- Portfolio management is most effective when it is managed to optimize benefits realization from the change portfolio, within the constraints of available resources and with an acceptable overall level of risk.

The Portfolio Management Cycles used by MoP are shown in Figure 10.1.

Example 10.1 – Benefits-led portfolio prioritization in HMRC

In order to make a measured and balanced judgement on the correct portfolio content, HMRC determined a set of benefit categories and prioritized them according to Treasury priorities. These categories included tax yield, staffing headcount reductions, customer benefits and cost savings. By taking these elements into account across the portfolio options, and by mapping the time and cost of delivering these benefits from a range of possible programmes and projects, HMRC arrived at an optimum affordable portfolio.

Simple tools were developed to allow the implications of each portfolio option to be clearly understood and avoid too much complexity and automation that could mask real-world issues and decision implications from the portfolio governance committees.

Source: 'Management of Portfolios'. Provided with the kind agreement of Paul Hirst, HMRC.

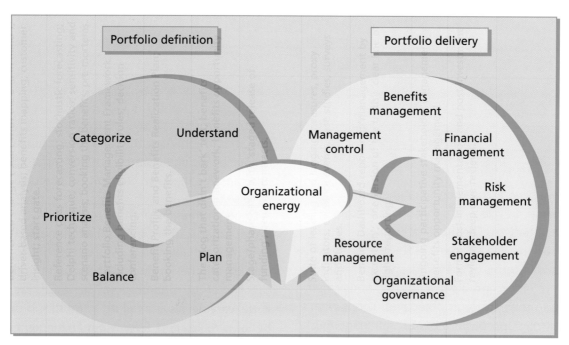

Figure 10.1 – The Portfolio Management Cycles

Note that:

- Benefits considerations run through the Portfolio Definition Cycle including ensuring that assessments of 'attractiveness' and 'achievability', undertaken as part of the 'Prioritize' practice, are benefits-led, and that the Portfolio Strategy and Delivery Plan clearly identify the benefits to be realized and their contribution to the strategic objectives.

- Benefits management is one of the seven practices in the Portfolio Delivery Cycle – but benefits-related issues also apply to other practices including: consideration of benefits (scale and achievability) at stage/phase gates and portfolio-level reviews (part of the management control practice); portfolio-level risks and dependencies (part of the risk management practice); and valuing efficiency benefits and recycling cashable savings (part of the financial management practice).

10.2 WHAT IS THE OBJECTIVE OF PORTFOLIO-BASED BENEFITS MANAGEMENT?

Chapter 3 identified a portfolio-based approach as being one of the seven principles that lay the foundation for effective benefits management. The objectives of portfolio-based benefits management are to ensure the best use of available resources and that the contribution to operational performance and strategic objectives is optimized, i.e. the strategic contribution is maximized subject to constraints such as costs and other limited resources. It achieves this by ensuring that:

- Change initiatives are consistently aligned with the organization's strategic objectives and performance management system.
- Good practice is applied to all initiatives within the change portfolio – with consequent efficiency savings and enhanced effectiveness in terms of benefits realization.
- Double counting is minimized.
- Lessons are learned and applied more widely.
- Benefits realization and value for money from available resources are optimized.

Research by Ward & Daniel (2012) finds that a portfolio management approach is associated with success – "*The more successful organisations select projects on the basis of desirability and their capability to deliver them, not just desirability.*" Whether it is 'desirability' and 'deliverability', or 'return' and 'risk', or 'attractiveness' and 'achievability', it is clear that change initiatives should be appraised on these twin dimensions – and 'achievability' extends beyond consideration as to whether the initiative can be delivered on time and to budget, to an assessment of how likely it is that the benefits included under the 'attractiveness' heading will actually be realized. A common way of presenting this information is in a Portfolio Map/Bubble Chart where the size of the bubbles usually reflects the size of the investment required (note that the production of such graphics is facilitated by standard chart options in spreadsheet programmes such as Excel). A Portfolio Map/Bubble Chart is illustrated in Figure 10.2.

Unfortunately, often things aren't quite this simple – for example, there may well be initiatives that are not particularly attractive or achievable but which enable others with a more compelling risk:return profile; i.e. there is a 'logical' dependency (as discussed at 10.3.2 below). This is illustrated in Figure 10.3 where initiatives A and G are dependent upon initiative F. The key question of course is whether there is a compelling case for investment in A, F and G as a whole.

10.3 THE SCOPE OF PORTFOLIO-BASED BENEFITS MANAGEMENT

Just as 'Managing Successful Programmes' (MSP) recommends that a programme should have a Benefits Management Strategy, so a Benefits Management Framework should be prepared for the portfolio as a whole – and initiative-level Benefits Management Strategies should be consistent with it. A Benefits Management Framework (which represents the rules and guidelines by which benefits will be managed across the portfolio and the document where these rules and guidelines are recorded) encompasses guidance covering six main elements:

1. Benefits eligibility rules, including a consistent approach to benefits categorization.

2. A portfolio-level Benefits Realization Plan.

Achievability and Attractiveness Chart

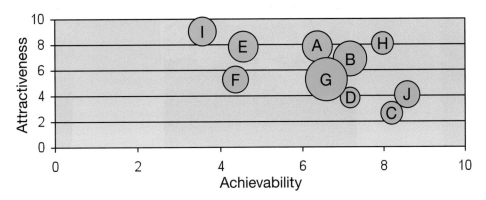

Figure 10.2 – Portfolio Map/Bubble Chart

Achievability and Attractiveness Chart

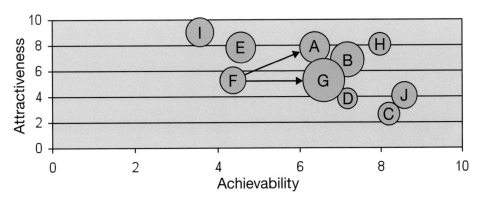

Figure 10.3 – Logical dependencies

3. Inclusion of re-appraisal of benefits at stage/ phase gates and portfolio-level reviews.

4. Effective arrangements to manage benefits post-project/programme closure.

5. Clear arrangements for benefits tracking and reporting at a portfolio level, including via the Portfolio Dashboard Report.

6. Regular and robust post-implementation reviews and feeding lessons learned back into forecasting and the benefits management practices.

These six elements are considered in turn before we examine portfolio-level benefits documentation and roles.

10.3.1 Element 1 – Benefits Eligibility Rules

Benefits eligibility rules define how benefits should be categorized, quantified, valued and validated in the preparation of change initiative documentation, including Business Cases. Benefits eligibility rules serve several purposes – they:

- Allow change initiatives to be appraised on a consistent basis.
- Assist in assessing the contribution of benefits to strategic objectives and business priorities.
- Can also help to prevent double counting – by ensuring a consistent approach to categorization and quantification, and then by validating these benefits with the relevant business representatives.
- Assist in determining the impact on operational performance – including the capacity of different parts of the organization to absorb business change, and so help in the effective scheduling of implementation.
- Help to consolidate benefits data for the purpose of benefits realization tracking and reporting.

Important note

In one portfolio the value of an hour saved for a member of staff being paid £30,000 pa varied from £15 in one department to over £33 in another, due to differing assumptions about how much productive time is worked in a day and how many productive days there are in a year (with no other difference in terms and conditions). This severely undermined portfolio prioritization, as the value of staff time savings from different initiatives was not compiled on a consistent basis. So just as costs in Business Cases should be prepared on a consistent basis, so too with benefits – benefits eligibility rules therefore underpin effective investment appraisal and portfolio prioritization.

Central to portfolio-wide benefits eligibility rules is a consistent approach to benefits categorization. This also helps in the identification of benefits and facilitates a 'level playing field' for investment appraisal and portfolio prioritization. Common approaches to categorization include allocating benefits to one or more of the following categories:

- Financial and non-financial benefits.
- Cashable and non-cashable benefits.
- Economy, efficiency and effectiveness benefits.
- Strategic objective.
- Balanced scorecard category – financial, customer, internal business process, and learning and growth.
- Risk level reflecting the likelihood of benefits realization.
- Stakeholder group.

Example 10.2 illustrates a benefits categorization framework which includes specific consideration of dis-benefits and distinguishes between cash-releasing and non-cash-releasing benefits and dis-benefits.

The appropriate form of benefits categorization will vary depending on the circumstances, but in selecting benefit categories, organizations should consider the following **features of an appropriate benefits categorization system**:

Example 10.2 – Benefits categorization in Bristol City Council

Bristol City Council has adopted the following benefits categorization framework:

- Financial cashable: refers to a benefit that can be measured in monetary terms and will result in actual cashable savings to the organization, i.e. the reduction of a service budget.

- Financial non-cashable: refers to a benefit that can be measured in monetary terms, but cannot actually be cashed by the organization. For example, an efficiency saving resulting from redesigned processes that equates to one full-time equivalent (FTE). However, this saving is split across a number of staff, as the saving is made up of a small portion of multiple people's day jobs. Therefore, it is not possible to release an actual individual from the organization to cash the saving, but the benefit can be realized through reinvesting the time saved in other areas.

- Non-financial: this refers to a benefit that is not measured in monetary terms, but rather an improvement such as increased customer satisfaction, staff morale, reputation etc. While such benefits are not measured in monetary terms, there must still be a mechanism to measure the benefit in order to prove whether it has been realized (or not). Therefore, a baseline needs to be established and measures taken at intervals to monitor progress.

- Dis-benefit – cashable: this refers to a dis-benefit resulting directly from a project that can be measured in monetary terms, i.e. resulting in an actual cost to the organization.

- Dis-benefit – non-financial: this refers to a dis-benefit resulting directly from a project that is not measured in monetary terms, such as a reduction in staff morale.

Provided with the kind assistance of Paul Arrigoni (Director, Business Change and ICT) and Ken Robinson (Portfolio Accountant/Benefits Realization Manager), Bristol City Council.

- *Complete/fully inclusive* – the system should be flexible enough to accommodate all relevant benefits.
- *Mutually exclusive/unambiguous* – the categories used should be sufficiently different to minimize confusion as to what category individual benefits best fit.
- *Wide applicability* – the categorization should apply to all types of initiative facilitating comparisons between investments and over time.
- *Simple* – the categorization used should be easy to understand.
- *Self-checking* – ideally, the system should support the validation of claimed benefits and help deter and detect double counting. See the coverage of dual dimension categorization below.

Note: the Benefit Profile should specify which category each benefit belongs to.

10.3.1.1 Dual-dimension benefits categorization

Of particular value are approaches that combine more than one dimension in the categorization of benefits (for example, by allocating benefits (and dis-benefits) firstly into financial cashable and non-financial categories, and then analysing them by stakeholder group). This can be shown on a simple matrix with rows for each stakeholder group and columns for the benefit types (what Bradley, 2010, refers to as a Benefit Distribution Matrix). See Example 10.3.

Two other examples of such 'dual-dimension' benefits categorization are those suggested by Ward & Daniel (2006) and Bradley (2010).

Ward & Daniel recommend categorizing benefits by:

- Firstly – the cause of the benefit: 'do new things', 'do things better' or 'stop doing things'. This highlights that benefits are often only realized when people do something

---

Example 10.3 – Benefits categorization in the CJS IT portfolio

The UK Criminal Justice System (CJS) IT portfolio used an efficiency/effectiveness categorization framework (with sub-categories for cashable and opportunity value benefits) but also enhanced this by analysing which Department or Criminal Justice Organization (CJO) would receive the benefit. This can be particularly effective in portfolios that cross organizational boundaries, as the process of identifying benefit recipients can help to validate forecasts, and also lays the basis for their subsequent realization (see Table 10.1).

Table 10.1 – CJS IT portfolio benefits categorization

Benefit recipient	Benefit type			
	Efficiency		**Effectiveness**	
	Cashable	**Opportunity value**	**Cashable**	**Opportunity value**
	Financial value	**Economic value**	**Financial value**	**Economic value**
	£	**£**	**£**	**£**
Sponsoring CJO				
Other CJOs				
Other parts of the CJS				
Cross-CJS				
Beyond the CJS				

From: Jenner, S. (2011).

---

differently. Thus, faster access to more accurate information from a new management information system is not a benefit but an enabler. The benefits are realized when people use that information with more confidence and earlier than before. An added advantage of this approach is that it can help assess whether the change portfolio is appropriately balanced between, for example: cost cutting, efficiency improvements, and initiatives that expand the organization's service offerings. Note – similar analysis can be undertaken using the economy, efficiency, effectiveness dimensions of value for money discussed in Chapter 2.

- Secondly – level of 'explicitness': financial; quantifiable; measurable; or observable. It is emphasized that the assessment of degree of explicitness may well change over time as more analysis is undertaken.

Bradley (2010) suggests a similar approach – see Table 10.2.

Note: The advice in MSP is that generic terms such as 'better' and 'improved' should be avoided in favour of terms such as 'increased', 'faster', 'lower', 'cheaper' and 'bigger' with the scale of improvement being identified. This also reflects functional thinking – as expressed in value management by the use of an active verb and measurable noun (often qualified by an adjective) to express the improvement. In a similar vein, Thorp recommends the use of the following terms – using the acronym 'MEDIC':

- Maintain, e.g. a level of service Maintained.
- Eliminate, e.g. a function Eliminated.
- Decrease, e.g. turnaround time Decreased.
- Increase, e.g. revenue Increased.
- Create, e.g. a new capability Created.

Table 10.2 – Sigma value types

Value type		Definition	Example	
			Financial/cashable	Non-financial/non-cashable
Tangible	Definite	Value may be predicted with confidence or certainty – not affected by external factors	Reduced costs	Fewer steps in a process
	Expected	Value may be predicted on the basis of someone else's experience or based on historic trends	Increased sales	Quicker performance of tasks
	Logical	Logically, a benefit may be anticipated whose value may be measured but not predicted	Improved management of insurance risk	Greater customer satisfaction
Intangible		May be anticipated, but difficult to substantiate	Improved image	

10.3.2 Element 2 – Portfolio Benefits Realization Plan

Just as individual change initiatives should have a Benefits Realization Plan (BRP), so should the portfolio as a whole; and just as forecast spend on the portfolio should be clearly defined, so too should the combined impact of current and completed change initiatives on operational performance and strategic objectives be clearly stated – profiled over the forthcoming period, analysed by the main benefit categories used, along with the measures that will be used to assess this impact, and an assessment of the risks to benefits realization. This should be recorded in the Portfolio Benefits Realization Plan. The relevant portfolio governance body (the Portfolio Direction Group/Investment Committee in an MoP environment) can then come to a view as to whether, in the light of the organization's accumulated investment in change and the benefits realized to date, the benefits forecast is sufficiently ambitious.

One particular aspect is worthy of special consideration – there will often be staff time savings arising from initiatives, but such savings can be difficult to realize (hence our discussion of conversion ratios in Section 6.2.2.2). This should be monitored at the portfolio level – an initiative may only save an hour or so of each person's time, but when this is combined with the impact of

other initiatives, there may well be greater scope for redeploying staff and realizing savings in overhead costs. This role can be performed by the Portfolio Office.

10.3.2.1 Portfolio-level Benefits Risks and Opportunities

In drawing up the Portfolio Benefits Realization Plan, consideration will also need to be given to portfolio-level risks in relation to benefits management. These encompass:

■ **Generic risks** – that apply across the change portfolio such as inaccurate forecasting resulting in sub-optimal investment decisions and non-realization of forecast benefits. Solutions are covered in Chapter 5.

■ **Aggregated initiative-level risks** – for example double counting, ineffective dependency management and the negative impact on operational performance, and benefits realization of poorly scheduled business change. Considering each of these risks in turn:

Double counting – this occurs when more than one initiative claims to deliver a benefit. Such claims may be reasonable from the perspective of the initiative, but are less so when seen in combination – for example, where three initiatives claim to deliver a 10% improvement, but where a 30% combined improvement is unlikely. Mechanisms that help to address double counting include use of common benefits eligibility rules and categorization; validation of benefits with the recipients; review of individual initiative Business Cases by the Portfolio Office or Portfolio Benefits Manager; and maintenance of an overall portfolio picture of the combined impacts anticipated – which can then be included in the Portfolio Benefits Realization Plan.

Ineffective dependency management – as MoP says, it can be problematic to identify, track and manage dependencies effectively in a portfolio environment. This should be a major focus for the Portfolio Office as it can significantly impact benefits realization and the required contribution to strategic objectives. Dependencies include:

- **Logical dependencies** – where progress on one initiative is dependent on a deliverable from another initiative.
- **Logistical dependencies** – where more than one initiative requires access to a limited resource at the same time.
- **Where benefits realization is dependent on actions beyond the scope of the initiative** (for example, making staff redundant). Techniques such as benefits dependency networking can be helpful here to ensure that all required business and enabling changes are identified and the initiative is appropriately bounded.

Poorly scheduled business change – Benko & McFarlan (2003) argue for the management of business change at a portfolio level to ensure the effective use of the *"finite resource of change capacity"*. In short, there is only so much change the stakeholders impacted can absorb in a given period. Benko & McFarlan suggest estimating how much change capacity initiatives use by assessing four variables:

1. The magnitude of the change required.
2. The ability of the constituency affected to change, including the ease of implementation and whether new skills are required.
3. The willingness of the constituency to change, ranging from 'resistant' to 'welcome'.
4. Timing compared with other simultaneous requests.

Project and programme managers often fail to adequately consider what other initiatives might affect the same parts of the business at the same time – but avoiding change fatigue is crucial to benefits realization. One major telco (with a large and geographically dispersed field-engineering workforce) tackled this by using 'engineer training days' as a currency, with an allowance of X days per quarter for each team, to limit the number of new ways of working (e.g. new processes, new kit, new targets) that each engineer was expected to cope with in each quarter. Rudimentary yes, but it worked because it made initiatives plan the timing of change in a way that was visible to the users. Treating capacity for change as a constrained resource also forced the various initiative Sponsors/Senior Responsible Owners (SROs) to discuss and agree priorities where demands exceeded agreed capacity.

The focus at a portfolio level also extends to opportunity management, including regularly asking: have adequate arrangements been made to identify emergent benefits; what proportion of change initiatives are identifying emergent benefits; what types of emergent benefit are identified; and is there scope for increasing benefits realization by exploiting the capability created? This should be monitored via the Portfolio Dashboard Report.

Once agreed, the portfolio Benefits Realization Plan, or a summary of it, should be included in the Portfolio Delivery Plan and progress against the plan should be monitored by the Portfolio Progress Group/Change Delivery Committee via the Portfolio Dashboard Report. This includes monitoring the impact on the benefits forecast of any changes to initiative schedule or scope. The typical contents of the Portfolio Benefits Realization Plan are shown in Appendix B.

10.3.3 Element 3 – Regular Review of Benefits

The Benefits Management Framework should include a clear commitment to consideration of the updated benefits forecast at each stage/phase gate within the business change lifecycle, and at regular portfolio-level reviews. In this way the investment rationale is reconfirmed on a regular basis in the context of initiative performance, changes in organizational priorities and the wider environment.

10.3.3.1 Stage/Phase Gate Reviews

These gate reviews can be organized around relevant initiative phases (for example, scoping, development, testing and implementation) or, for example, around the main Business Case approval stages – i.e. Strategic Outline Case, Outline Business Case and Full Business Case. Whichever model is adopted, the stage/phase gate review should represent a re-appraisal of the Business Case and should encompass the following questions from a benefits perspective:

- Have the required actions arising from the last review been successfully completed?
- Have all significant benefits been identified from the initiative?
- Is treatment of benefits consistent with the Portfolio Benefits Management Framework and, in particular, the benefits eligibility rules?
- Is it clear that the benefits are not being double counted with those from other initiatives?
- Are the benefits consistent with organizational strategy and initiatives elsewhere in the change portfolio? For example, where one initiative might be focused on consolidating production away from site A, while another seeks to improve productivity at the same site.
- What change in benefits forecast has occurred since the last review?
- What change in the achievability of the forecast benefits has occurred since the last review?
- Does the initiative still represent value for money and a compelling case for continued investment?
- Have benefits been reviewed for value improvement opportunities?
- Are the scale and trajectory for benefits realization still realistic in the light of initiative progress and environmental changes since the last review?
- Have adequate arrangements for benefits management been made including:

  - ☐ Have appropriate measures for each benefit been identified?
  - ☐ Is accountability for realization of all significant benefits (and the business changes upon which realization of those benefits is dependent) clearly assigned?
  - ☐ Has provision for post-implementation review been made including when, by whom; and has provision for the costs of evaluation been included in the initiative's budget?
- What progress has been made in realizing forecast benefits to date?
- Have emergent or unplanned benefits been identified?
- Are dis-benefits being effectively mitigated?
- Are the Benefits Realization Plan and Benefit Profiles up to date?
- What lessons have been learned since the last review in relation to the scale and achievability of the benefits?
- What actions are now required?

In an MoP environment these reviews will be undertaken by, or on behalf of, the Portfolio Direction Group/Investment Committee (start gate and post-investment review) and Portfolio Progress Group/Change Delivery Committee ('in-flight' reviews linked to the portfolio-wide business change lifecycle).

Stage/phase gates should also be linked with the technique of 'staged release of funding', i.e. funding for change initiatives should be released only on passing each stage/phase gate, and should be limited to the funds required to take the initiative through to the next review. In this way initiative funding can be linked to regular reconfirmation that the benefits will be realized and that they continue to represent value for money. All stage/phase gate and portfolio-level reviews should include formal recommitment to realization of the benefits forecast by the relevant SRO and Benefit Owners with updated 'benefits contracts' – so that there are no 'orphan' initiatives.

10.3.3.2 Portfolio-level Reviews

While stage/phase gates occur at the initiative level, there should also be regular portfolio-level reviews every quarter, six months or at least annually. In an MoP environment these will be undertaken by the Portfolio Direction Group/ Investment Committee. The objectives of these reviews are to assess portfolio performance as a whole, the continued balance of the organization's change portfolio, and to ensure that the allocation of resources continues to represent the optimum return from available funds and other constrained resources, in the context of current strategic objectives and business priorities. From a benefits perspective they include:

- Has there been any change in the strategic objectives to which benefits from initiatives in the portfolio contribute?
- Are the forecasts used to support investment appraisal and portfolio prioritization accurate?
- Review of benefits realization across the portfolio and by each benefits category – does performance match the Portfolio Benefits Realization Plan?
- What emergent benefits have been identified, and can they be further leveraged?
- Are dis-benefits being effectively mitigated?
- Does performance confirm or disconfirm the business model – the elements in the model, their drivers, and the linkages between them?
- What lessons have been learned, and is any action required?

Any required actions should be clearly recorded (for example in the investment committee minutes), assigned to the person with the requisite authority to address the issue, and with a timescale for action (including reporting back on progress).

10.3.4 Element 4 – How Benefits will be Managed Post-initiative Closure

As we have already seen, one of the common causes of the failure to realize the full potential benefits from change investments is the premature closure of projects and programmes. This is often a real issue in practice, and one that a portfolio approach can help to address by ensuring continued transparency about benefits beyond formal closure of the initiative and disbanding of the project/programme team.

- The **Portfolio Benefits Management Framework** should include a commitment to, and the governance arrangements for, managing benefits post-completion that apply across the change portfolio, including what should be reported, by whom, how often and to where.

- The individual initiative **Benefits Management Strategy** should specify how the benefits from that initiative will be managed post-initiative completion, and specifically who is responsible for tracking and reporting their realization to the Portfolio Office. In an MSP environment this will fall to the Business Change Manager.

- Including benefits forecasts post-initiative closure in the **Portfolio Benefits Realization Plan.**

- Including benefits realized post-initiative closure in the consolidated data reported in the **Portfolio Dashboard Report**.

- Integrating risks to benefits management post-initiative closure into portfolio, operational or corporate risk registers across the organization.

Ensuring a portfolio-wide, post-initiative focus on benefits realization can be aided by the nomination of a Portfolio Benefits Manager. In an MoP environment this position sits within the Portfolio Office. See Example 10.4 opposite.

10.3.5 Element 5 – Tracking and Reporting Benefits Realization at a Portfolio Level

Consolidated benefits information should be included in the Portfolio Dashboard Report. This includes the revised forecast by benefits category, and benefits realization to date compared with the forecast included in the Portfolio Benefits Realization Plan – again analysed by each category of benefit. This assists with decision-making, particularly where delivery slippage occurs on individual initiatives, as senior management will be able to see the impact on the anticipated contribution to strategic targets. Management control is also aided by the application of the techniques of:

> ## Example 10.4 – Portfolio-based benefits management at DVLA
>
> As noted above, ensuring a portfolio-wide, post-initiative focus on benefits realization is aided by the nomination of a Benefits Manager in a corporate rather than programme or project position. Within the Driver and Vehicle Licensing Agency (DVLA), a centralized change management team has been established with a remit to:
>
> - Support projects and operational change teams in ensuring that change is relevant and fit for purpose.
> - Ensure consistency of business change approaches across the agency.
> - Ensure business readiness for agency change.
> - Ensure that benefits forecasting and realization are accurate and actually happen.
> - Provide an integrated view of change across the agency.
> - Help, support, understand, advise, represent and make life easier for the business areas.
>
> Significantly, the Head of Business Change Management (akin to the Business Change/Portfolio Director role in an MoP environment) monitors and reports on benefits realization and has a seat on all change programme boards.
>
> Source: *'Management of Portfolios'*.

- **'Management by exception'** – where only variances that exceed a pre-set control limit (for benefits forecast and realization) are flagged for management attention.

- **'One version of the truth'** – whereby each element of portfolio progress reporting, including benefits forecast and realization, is derived from an agreed source and to an agreed schedule, managed by the Portfolio Office. Individual change initiatives and business functions provide data inputs in relation to the latest benefits forecast and reports on benefits realized, to the agreed schedule. The resulting data is recognized as the authoritative source of information used for monitoring, reporting and management decision-making.

- **'Clear line of sight' reporting** – a technique that seeks to ensure a transparent chain from strategic intent through to benefits realization and vice versa. In this case, linking benefits reporting at initiative level to the portfolio view.

- **The Pareto (80:20) rule** – focus on the benefits that deliver the greatest contribution to the organization's strategic objectives.

An example of a Portfolio Dashboard Report, including benefit indicators, is shown at Figure 10.4 (from MoP).

Another approach is to complete a separate Portfolio Benefits Dashboard Report to go along with separate reports on spend and progress against key milestones etc. Whether a single Dashboard Report or separate report for benefits is used, indicative portfolio benefits key performance indicators (KPIs) include:

- Benefits realization progress against profiled plan (trajectory) for each category of benefit in the organization's Benefits Management Framework.
- Changes to the total forecast for each category of benefit in the organization's Benefits Management Framework since the last report.
- Percentage of change initiatives with benefits realization ahead, on track, behind plan (alternatively shown using red/amber/green (RAG) ratings).
- Scale of emergent benefits identified and by type.
- Scale of dis-benefits and analysis by stakeholder group.
- Overall cost-benefit position and Value Ratio.

Portfolio indicators

(R) ⇔	**Benefits realization** – 20/130 projects' benefits at risk ($20m)
(R) ⇧	**Budget** – 20/130 projects over budget ($10m at risk)
(A) ⇧	**Risk** – 20/130 projects not managing risks effectively
(A) ⇩	**Resource** – 10/130 projects are short of critical resources
(A) ⇩	**Time** – 90/130 projects behind schedule
(G) ⇔	**Embedding change** – 30/130 projects are following the project mgmt standards

Consolidated and analysed

Project indicators

1 Management and control (i.e. how well the project is being managed, project health)

2 Actual performance/delivery (i.e. how well the project is delivering benefits)

Name	ID	Type	Priority	Project owner	Business unit owner	Stage gate	Management and control		Delivery		Notes	Finish date	R
							This mth	Last mth	This mth	Last mth			
Project 1	11	Efficiency	1	B Wilson	Div C	Deploy	○R ⇩	○A	○A ⇩	○G	PM not allocated since last month's request	Feb-11	✔
Project 2	21	Compliance	3	F Petrou	Div B	PIR	○A ⇧	○R	○G ⇧	○A	Critical systems issue addressed	Jun-09	✔
Project 3	35	Revenue	2	P Ternouth	Div A	Initiate	○A ⇔	○A	○A ⇔	○A	Reporting not improved since last month, review scheduled	Mar-10	✘

- The project's alignment to agreed strategic drivers
- Force ranking of project priority against strategic drivers, complexity (risk) and planned benefits
- Key project ownership information
- Summary of how well the project complies with embedded project management standards e.g. schedule, risk, quality etc.
- Summary of the actual status of the project compared to its approved plans as at the reporting date. For example:
  - actual progress against planned schedule
  - actual spend against planned budget (and use of contingency)
  - benefits realization progress
  - level of risk
- Has reporting been submitted on time and to the required quality?

Figure 10.4 – Example of a Portfolio Dashboard Report

10.3.6 Element 6 – Post-implementation (and Post-investment) Reviews

This was addressed in Chapter 9, but from a portfolio perspective we are concerned with ensuring that:

- All change initiatives are subject to appropriate evaluation after implementation, with independent evaluation occurring where justified.
- Evaluation assesses both summative aspects (looking backwards to compare what actually happened against forecast) and formative aspects (assessing what can be learned to improve change initiatives in the future):
  - Were the initial benefits forecasts accurate?
  - Were the forecast benefits realized?
  - Were dis-benefits effectively and efficiently mitigated?
  - What unplanned/emergent benefits were realized and is there scope to leverage additional benefits?
  - Did the initiative represent value for money (i.e. actual costs compared with benefits realized)?
  - What lessons can be learned for future change initiatives and to improve the way in which benefits realization is managed?
  - Have adequate arrangements been made for managing benefits through to business as usual (BAU)?
- Lessons learned are captured and disseminated effectively.
- Where required, the benefits management practices are revised and the Benefits Management Framework is updated.
- Data on initiative performance is captured and fed into the database of reference class data to guide benefits forecasting.

10.4 PORTFOLIO-LEVEL BENEFITS MANAGEMENT DOCUMENTATION AND ROLES

10.4.1 Portfolio Benefits Documentation

The key benefits management documentation in an MoP environment, and the purpose of each item, are as follows:

■ **Portfolio Benefits Management Framework –** Purpose:
  ☐ To provide a framework within which consistent approaches to benefits management can be applied across the portfolio.

■ **Portfolio Benefits Realization Plan** – Purpose:
  ☐ To summarize the benefits forecast to be realized in the year ahead and so provide a clear view of the planned returns from the organization's accumulated investment in change.
  ☐ To provide a baseline against which to assess the benefits actually realized.

■ **Portfolio Dashboard Report** – Purpose:
  ☐ To provide the portfolio governance bodies with an overview of progress against plan, including benefits realization.
  ☐ To identify areas where action is required to address issues impacting, or potentially impacting, on portfolio delivery.

The typical contents of these documents are shown in Appendix B.

10.4.2 Portfolio Benefits Roles

The key roles with a responsibility for portfolio benefits management in an MoP environment are as follows:

■ **Portfolio Direction Group/Investment Committee** – the governance body where decisions about inclusion of initiatives in the change portfolio are made. Also responsible for approving the Portfolio Benefits Management Framework.

■ **Portfolio Delivery Group/Change Delivery Committee** – the governance body responsible for monitoring portfolio progress and resolving issues that may compromise delivery and benefits realization.

■ **Business Change Director/Portfolio Director** – the Management Board member responsible for the Portfolio Strategy and providing clear leadership through its life.

■ **Portfolio Benefits Manager** (reporting to the Portfolio Manager/Head of the Portfolio Office) – ensures that a consistent 'fit for purpose' approach to benefits management is applied across the portfolio, and that benefits realization is optimized from the organization's investment in change. Alternative names include: Benefits Realization Manager (MSP), Benefits Facilitator (Bradley, 2010) and Benefits role ('*Portfolio, Programme and Project Offices*': P3O).

Typical responsibilities for each role are included in Appendix C.

> **Important note**
>
> These roles may have different titles in practice – the key is not that the above roles exist exactly as defined here, but that responsibility for the identified activities is clearly assigned to someone.

10.5 CHAPTER SUMMARY

1. A portfolio-based approach to benefits management is crucial because it helps to ensure that:
   ☐ Change initiatives are aligned consistently with the organization's strategic objectives and performance management system.
   ☐ Good practice is repeatable across all initiatives within the change portfolio.
   ☐ Double counting is minimized.
   ☐ Lessons are learned and applied more widely.
   ☐ Benefits realization and value for money from available resources are optimized.

2. A portfolio-based approach to benefits management encompasses six main elements:
   ☐ Benefits eligibility rules, including a consistent approach to benefits categorization.
   ☐ A portfolio-level Benefits Realization Plan (and consideration of relevant benefits-related risks, dependencies and opportunities).
   ☐ Inclusion of re-appraisal of benefits at stage/phase gate reviews and regular portfolio-level reviews.

☐ Effective arrangements to manage benefits after initiative closure.

☐ Clear arrangements for benefits tracking and reporting at a portfolio level, including via the Portfolio Dashboard Report.

☐ Regular and robust post-implementation reviews and feeding lessons learned back into forecasting and the benefits management practices.

3. Portfolio-based benefits management is aided by the nomination/appointment of a Portfolio Benefits Manager.

4. Key portfolio-level benefits management documentation are: the Portfolio Benefits Management Framework; the Portfolio Benefits Realization Plan; and the Portfolio Dashboard Report (which can be a single report including benefits data, or a separate Benefits Dashboard report).

Chapter 11

Chapter 11 – Implementing and Sustaining Progress

11.1 OVERVIEW OF THIS CHAPTER

This chapter provides guidance on:

- The three main approaches to implementing benefits management.
- Where to start – the first 10 steps that organizations should consider in implementing benefits management.
- How to sustain progress and achieve continuous improvement in benefits management.

11.2 IMPLEMENTING BENEFITS MANAGEMENT

There are three main approaches to implementing benefits management – these mirror the approaches identified in 'Management of Portfolios' (MoP), and are illustrated in Table 11.1.

It is important to emphasize that there is no single right way to implement benefits management – it all depends on the circumstances – for example:

- The big bang approach is most appropriate where strong and widespread senior management commitment is present, top-down approaches to strategy formulation are applied, the environment is relatively stable, and where project and programme management (PPM) is already relatively mature.

- The evolutionary approach will be more appropriate where senior management commitment is mixed, with some enthusiastic supporters but a significant minority remain to be convinced; the environment is dynamic and where strategy is itself emergent; and where improvements in initiative delivery are required. Here progress can be made by starting on areas of greatest priority, building on developments in one part of the organization, or by focusing on specific practices to demonstrate the value of a

Table 11.1 – Approaches to implementing benefits management

Big bang	Implementing benefits management is viewed as a business change programme in its own right and is planned with:
	- A Business Case.
	- A compelling vision for the future state.
	- A blueprint or target operating model.
	- An implementation plan agreed by the Management Board.
	Here a time-bound implementation phase is followed by live running encompassing *all* benefits management practices.
Evolutionary	As above, implementation is treated as a business change programme, but here a staged or incremental approach is taken, starting with areas of greatest need or those where rapid progress can be made. The organization's approach to benefits management then evolves to reflect its needs, opportunities and lessons learned. The end state is kept in mind although the journey to get there will evolve in the light of experience.
Ad hoc	Here there is no expectation that the approach will develop and no commitment to capturing lessons learned to inform development. Instead, implementation is more opportunistic.

benefits management approach. Bradley (2010) for example, recommends that the approach be piloted on a small number of initiatives – this in turn aids evaluation of impact, as the results can be compared to initiatives where the approach is not applied. See Example 11.1.

- An ad hoc approach will be appropriate where little senior management commitment to benefits management currently exists. One option is to start with a new initiative, or one that is in trouble, to demonstrate the value of the approach. The ambition should be to move as soon as possible to an incremental approach which is aided by demonstrating quick wins. This approach is often initiated by individuals who have become 'apostles' of benefits management and who introduce it into the parts of the business or on change initiatives that they can influence. When these forces are multiple and dotted around the organization, joining forces to consolidate efforts and ideas and standardize cross-functional processes can

---

Example 11.1 – Portfolio-based benefits in Transport for London

Transport for London's (TfL) Surface Transport manages London's surface transport network, including one of the largest bus networks in the world, London's busiest roads and the river Thames. It also manages the congestion-charging and low-emission zones, the taxi and private hire trade, and Victoria Coach Station. It delivers policing across the network and is responsible for implementing strategies to effect the Mayor's Transport Strategy to ensure that the transport system is safe, accessible and reduces its impact on the environment.

The Surface Transport portfolio of operational activities and projects is thus vast, varied and complex – ranging from providing bus stops and shelters; building and maintaining the road network, bridges and tunnels; operating traffic signals; encouraging cycling and walking; implementing a cycle hire scheme; to managing the performance of the bus contracts.

In order to be able to manage delivery more effectively and prioritize resources in the context of decreasing budgets, Surface Transport joined up these often disparate activities into a single strategically aligned portfolio, consisting of a number of sub-portfolios (such as Cycling, Smoothing Traffic Flow, Air Quality etc.), each made up of a number of capital programmes and projects delivering benefits which, together with business as usual (BAU), contribute to the achievement of those strategic objectives.

The key prerequisite for structuring the portfolio has been to agree a set of strategic objectives, clearly linked to the Mayor's Transport Strategy, expressed in measurable terms and tested against the degree of control that Surface Transport has over achieving the given objective – for example, ensuring reliable operation of London's road network while reducing congestion, measured through Journey Time Reliability. Wherever possible, the metrics chosen to measure progress towards achieving each strategic objective have been aligned to the existing performance management system metrics. For example, progress in supporting an increase in cycling is measured through the Cycling Index.

The next task has been to align the programmes, projects and activities to the strategic objectives via the benefits expected to be delivered, to understand the strategic contribution to the objectives, and so enable prioritization and decisions about the most effective way of delivering each objective.

The approach Surface Transport took was to pilot the measuring, tracking and portfolio-balancing on a number of sub-portfolios, learn from the pilot and then apply the approach to the whole of the portfolio.

Lessons learned included:

- The need to look beyond the portfolio to BAU in determining the benefits to be derived and their contribution to strategic objectives.
- The value of aligning the metrics used to measure strategic objective progress to the organization's performance management system.
- Benefits at the portfolio level are optimized through facilitating collaborative working across the organization.
- Stakeholder commitment is aided by taking an incremental, evidence-based approach based on a pilot study.

Provided with the kind agreement of Tanya Durlen, TfL Surface Transport Portfolio Benefits Manager.

help to promote more widespread adoption and win support to move to an evolutionary approach.

As MoP says, planned approaches, whether big bang or evolutionary, do have several advantages:

- Planned approaches to the implementation of business change including benefits management are supported by 'Best Management Practice' guidance.
- Experience shows that the use of structured, systematic processes improves the likelihood of success.
- A planned approach, with confirmed senior management buy-in, will significantly reduce the risk of failure. Ideally, a board-level member should fill the role of Senior Responsible Owner for the implementation of benefits management, whether implemented using big bang or in a more evolutionary manner.
- Planned approaches can be quicker, so the potential benefits are realized earlier.
- And as we say below – sustaining progress is aided where implementation is managed as a business and behavioural change programme.

The roles and relevant responsibilities for implementing benefits management will vary depending on which approach to implementation is adopted, but key roles in an MoP/'*Managing Successful Programmes*' (MSP) environment will include:

- The Senior Responsible Owner (SRO) – a board-level champion for benefits management. Will usually be the Business Change Director/Portfolio Director in an MoP environment.
- The Portfolio Direction Group (PDG) – responsible for ensuring benefits-driven investment decisions.
- The Portfolio Progress Group (PPG) – responsible for ensuring a benefits-focus on portfolio delivery.
- The Business Change Manager – i.e. the Portfolio Benefits Manager, who leads on the design of the benefits management practices and consolidates progress reports for the PDG and PPG.

Additionally, it is recommended that a Benefits Management Forum be established with practitioners from all relevant disciplines, to share and disseminate lessons learned across the organization.

11.2.1 Where to Start

Guidance on where to start in implementing benefits management will vary depending on the local circumstances, including current delivery maturity; strategic objectives; resources available etc. That said, experience indicates that early consideration should be given to the following 10 key steps:

1. Undertake driver-based analysis to ensure that the organization's strategic objectives are measurable and so facilitate consistent appraisal of strategic contribution.

2. Implement benefits-led, rather than activity-centred, change initiatives.

3. Compile a Portfolio Benefits Management Framework, including benefits eligibility rules, so that benefits are expressed in a consistent format (so facilitating a 'level playing field' for investment appraisal and portfolio prioritization) demonstrating strategic contribution and utilizing measures from the existing performance management system.

4. Implement consistent approaches to benefits mapping to identify the enabling and business changes upon which benefits realization is dependent and to link benefits to the strategic objectives.

5. Adopt the technique of 'staged release of funding' where continued funding for initiatives is dependent upon incremental benefits exceeding the costs required to realize them, and continuing stakeholder commitment to benefits realization.

6. Ensure clarity about the key benefits of the major initiatives in the organization's change portfolio – starting with the top five benefits from each initiative: what they are, how they will be measured, who's responsible for ensuring they are realized and when they will be realized.

Example 11.2 – The Value Experience Plan

A Value Experience Plan (a form of journey mapping) can be used to identify and communicate in clear terms what difference senior management will see from the implementation of benefits management. This helps to engage senior management and also provides a basis for monitoring progress. An example is shown below in Figure 11.1.

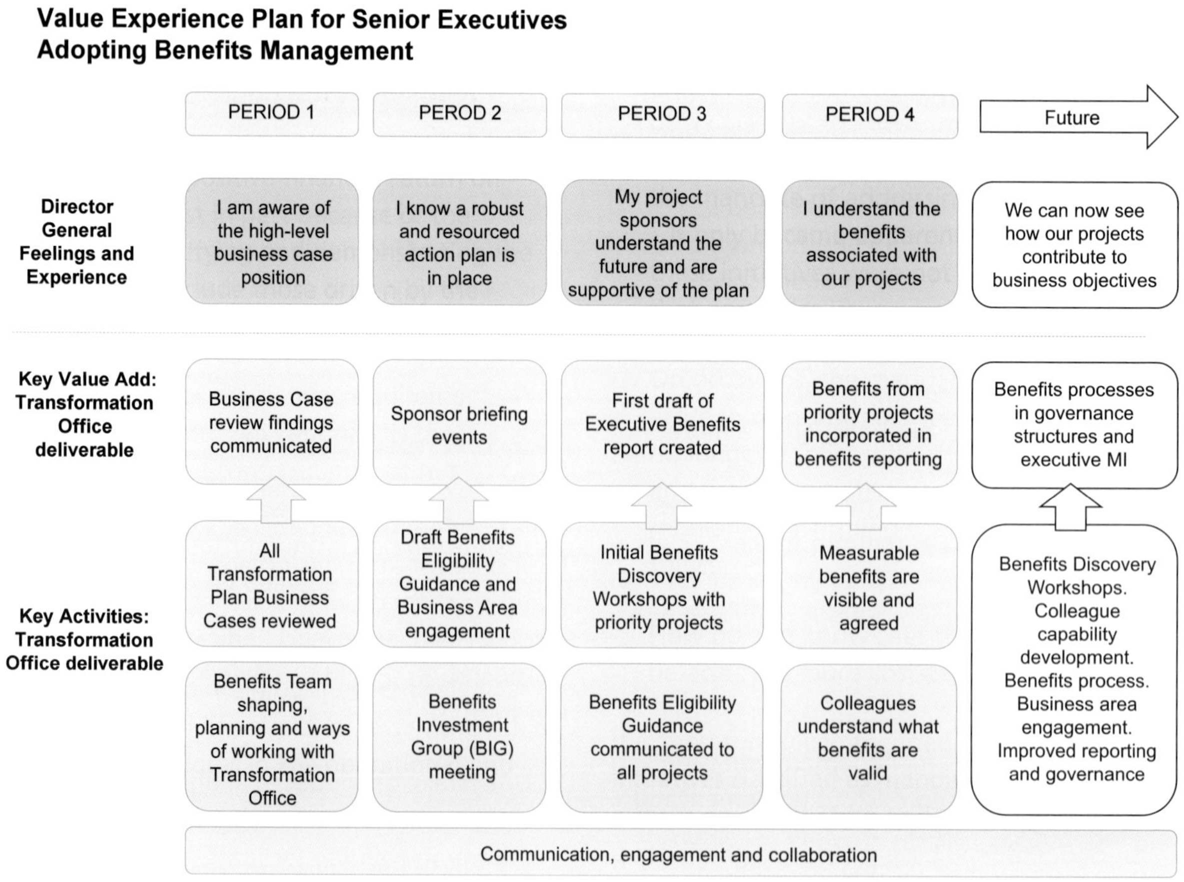

Figure 11.1 – Value Experience Plan

Provided with the kind agreement of Craig Kilford, Cansoti

7. Consolidate the information collected above into a Portfolio Benefits Realization Plan so that it is clear what benefits will be realized in the forthcoming period. This then enables the questions to be asked – is this scale of benefits sufficient and can anything be done to improve the position?

8. Track and report progress against the Portfolio Benefits Realization Plan on a regular basis (at least quarterly) to ensure that performance matches the promise – and apply the techniques of:
   - □ 'Management by exception' to focus attention on the most material variances from plan.
   - □ 'One version of the truth' to ensure reliability of management information on the benefits forecast and realized.

9. Implement post-implementation review on all change initiatives, with independent post-investment review for those initiatives that warrant it. This provides a basis for identifying improvements to the benefits management practices and the collection of a reference class of benefits data to inform future forecasting.

10. Organize a series of briefing sessions to raise awareness of the importance of benefits management, explain what is required, and what forms of assistance will be available. This should encompass all stakeholders, but with a particular focus on senior management. One technique that can facilitate senior management engagement is journey mapping, where activities and events are mapped to a schedule so senior managers are clear about what will be seen, by when and what difference it will make. See Example 11.2.

Example 11.3 – Implementing benefits management in Hackney

The London Borough of Hackney created a Benefits Management Framework combining elements of good practice from MSP and the Capital Ambition-funded Public Sector Programme Management Approach. An understanding of outcomes has formed part of standard PPM documentation for more than five years, so the concept of understanding a project's outputs in relation to outcomes was well ingrained. The framework placed increased focus on benefits and outcomes and aimed to drive the approach that outputs should be seen in the context of benefits and outcomes. The framework explains the 'golden thread' from project outputs through capability, which combines with business changes, to deliver outcomes and benefits, themselves delivering programme or strategic objectives. It focuses on roles and responsibilities for Business Change Sponsors and Project/ Programme Sponsors. Benefit categories were reviewed and revised into:

- Measurable financial (split into cashable and non-cashable).
- Measurable non-financial.
- Not measurable.

A set of principles were agreed, based on lessons learned and good practice, including: undertaking baselining, consideration of payback periods, avoidance of double counting, and clear benefits ownership. Benefits Maps have been used on new programmes and have also been used on some larger projects serving several purposes – making complex information simpler and more accessible, identifying additional benefits, better understanding of responsibilities for project outputs, implementation and adoption.

In Hackney's experience, while frameworks are useful in defining key elements, the biggest impact is felt by making benefits part of key business processes such as project and programme management and procurement. This has had a strong impact in getting the principles and concepts embedded.

Provided with the kind agreement of Richard Caton, London Borough of Hackney.

One issue faced is whether to apply new processes to all 'in-flight' initiatives in the change portfolio, or from a set date. In reality, the world does not stop and requiring all existing initiatives to adapt to suit the new regime is unlikely to be feasible or cost-effective. Consequently, it is recommended that revised practices are implemented by applying them to all new change initiatives from an agreed date.

The approach adopted by one organization is illustrated in Example 11.3.

11.3 SUSTAINING PROGRESS IN BENEFITS MANAGEMENT

Practical experience indicates that implementation is often less an issue than sustaining progress – and establishing a value culture (principle 7 in Chapter 3) where benefits management becomes BAU is rarely easy. Despite the investment of resources and effort, progress can become embroiled in political issues, and further development stalls. The lessons learned from those that have avoided or overcome these obstacles are that continued progress, and overcoming the barriers outlined in Section 4.3, is facilitated by addressing the following six factors:

- Effective governance.
- Treating the development of benefits management as a (benefits-led) business and behavioural change programme.
- Ongoing stakeholder engagement in the development of benefits management.
- Measuring progress.
- Appropriate use of software.
- Relevant training and development.

These factors are considered in turn below.

11.3.1 Effective Governance

Sustaining progress in the development of benefits management is aided considerably by effective governance to maintain focus and demonstrate that the new ways of working are now BAU. Consideration should be given to the elements of effective governance identified in Chapter 3 – clear, aligned, consistent and active – as well as having a senior board-level sponsor, or champion, to maintain focus at the highest level,

and to continually promote benefits management across the organization. This champion should (APM, June 11):

- Have strong leadership skills with the credibility to influence the executive board and the entire management team.
- Have a strong understanding of the dependencies between strategy, change management, operational performance management and benefits realization.
- Have the necessary time and commitment to actively lead the building of organizational capability.
- Be politically savvy and have the courage to successfully address necessary issues.
- Be prepared to challenge (across the organization) negative behaviours that could impact success.

Crucially, the championing of benefits management needs to extend beyond a single person, otherwise progress will be at risk should that person move on. So, look to create 'apostles' for the approach across the organization, bring them together in a Benefits Management Forum to share experiences, insights and lessons learned, and build cross-board commitment – influential non-executive directors can play an important role in this regard.

Progress can also be aided by expansion of the role of the Portfolio Office to form a Value Management Office (VMO) that provides a portfolio-wide and full business change lifecycle focus on benefits and value management. Of course, this is in many ways what the Portfolio Office provides, but the change of title signifies that benefits realization, not initiative delivery, is what really matters. Reporting to the Portfolio or Business Change Director in an MoP environment, the VMO represents a centre of excellence in benefits and value management, and as Thorp (2003) says, it *"acts as an advocate of change in the organization in the way people think about value"*. Lin, Pervan & McDermid (2005) for example, cite a VMO being established in an Australian organization to educate users about the benefits realization methodology and to minimize resistance to its implementation.

Table 11.2 – Value Management Office typical responsibilities

- Developing and maintaining the organization's Benefits Management Framework.
- Developing a standard set of benefits management document templates – Benefits Management Strategy, Benefits Realization Plan, Benefit Profiles and Benefits Dashboard Report.
- Undertaking driver-based analysis to articulate the organization's strategy in measurable terms – with agreed measures for the drivers of each of the elements in the organization's business model.
- Assisting project and programme staff in preparing investment proposals and Business Cases.
- Facilitating benefits discovery workshops and completing Benefits Maps.
- Providing an independent challenge to the assumptions that underpin benefits forecasts; checking benefits forecasts for double counting, for compliance with the benefits eligibility rules, and for consistency of purpose with other initiatives across the change portfolio.
- Ensuring that value management techniques are used to maximize value for money throughout the business change lifecycle.
- Drawing up the portfolio-level Benefits Realization Plan.
- Monitoring benefits realization over time; monitoring the conversion of time savings into benefits; compiling benefits reports including the Portfolio Benefits Dashboard Report; and advising the governance bodies on appropriate actions.
- Participating in post-implementation and post-investment reviews, and developing and maintaining a reference class of data to inform benefits forecasting.
- Monitoring and evaluating the effectiveness of the benefits management regime, and developing proposals for its enhancement.
- Coordinating a cross-organization Benefits Management Forum to share experiences and disseminate lessons learned.
- Monitoring professional developments so that the benefits management regime continues to reflect good practice.

Building on the role of the Portfolio Benefits Manager in the Portfolio Office, the typical responsibilities of a VMO are shown in Table 11.2.

The VMO role is consequently an active one that combines robust scrutiny with a proactive search for value across the organization. If it is to fulfil these roles effectively, the VMO needs to be independent of any initiative delivery responsibility (to demonstrate its objectivity); to have access to the requisite skills in benefits and value management to ensure that its appraisals and evaluations are credible; and to have sufficient status (it will report to the Portfolio/ Business Change Director in an MoP environment) to demonstrate that benefits realization is taken with the seriousness it deserves.

11.3.2 A Business and Behavioural Change Programme

Progress is more likely to be sustained when the implementation of benefits management is treated as an ongoing business and behavioural change programme including:

- Aligning the reward and recognition processes with appropriate behaviours – and applying them through objective-setting and personal reviews. This is especially important for senior management, programme managers and budget holders.

- Following the guidance in Chapters 3 and 8 by recognizing that behavioural change can follow the adoption of new roles and practices – so, for example, ensure consideration of benefits management is a regular item on the board agenda and apply the technique of decision conferencing whereby senior managers actively debate the merits of individual initiatives.

Apply the guidance in Chapter 3 regarding benefits-led rather than activity-centred change. This means that the focus should be less on what benefits management processes introduce and more on the improvements required, which will therefore drive the selection of appropriate solutions. A useful step in this regard is to apply the techniques outlined in Chapter 5 regarding benefits mapping to identify the benefits anticipated from the application of benefits management itself. An example of a generic Benefits Logic Map for benefits management is shown in Appendix F – completing such a map helps to identify the planned benefits, which should then be augmented by a suite of relevant measures and indicators. Regular assessment of progress is also key – and progress that encompasses both process/practice maturity (see Section 11.3.4 below) and impact (using the measures selected in relation to both the end and intermediate benefits on the organization's Benefits Map).

11.3.3 Effective Ongoing Stakeholder Engagement

Stakeholder engagement in the development of benefits management is crucial – as evidenced in a recent study of transformational change (Moorhouse, 2012) which found that programmes where stakeholders have bought into the aims of the programme are better at achieving their stated objectives. Main elements in building such engagement for benefits management are:

■ Application of the champion-challenger model whereby processes are open to challenge and improvement – but until successfully challenged, all participants agree to adhere to the current process. This helps to ensure that stakeholders are actively involved in the development of benefits management practices rather than perceiving them as something that is imposed on them.

■ Focus on the following four core stakeholder groups (APM, June 2011): senior management including the board; Operational Managers responsible for benefits realization; Project and Programme Managers responsible for delivery; and those responsible for business change.

■ It's important that people know what is expected of them – so the agreed processes should be documented, accessible (and people should know where they are), and under change control. Other issues worth considering include making benefits management guidance freely available via the organization's intranet or even the internet – for example the Public Sector Programme Management Approach (PSPMA) used by the London Councils includes information and guidance on benefits realization management. This is available in house as a WIKI and can also be downloaded from the internet.

■ Demonstrate the benefits of benefits management with some quick wins and *"Consolidate early results into a compelling story – continue to enhance and communicate the story widely to reinforce awareness, understanding and commitment across the organisation."* (APM, May 2012b).

■ Deliver a programme of ongoing benefits management workshops, seminars and masterclasses – too often these are run during implementation and are then forgotten. There is real value to be had in providing these on an ongoing basis to train newcomers and to capture and disseminate lessons learned. This is a responsibility that comes within the remit of the Portfolio Benefits Manager.

11.3.4 Measuring Progress

Progress should be monitored in terms of both impact (does the application of benefits management have the desired impact and represent value for money?) and practice maturity (how do practices compare against recognized good practice?).

11.3.4.1 Impact Measurement

As mentioned above, it is important that benefits management is itself managed as a benefits-led initiative – and progress against desired results should be monitored on a regular basis. A Benefits Map should be completed with the intended benefits clearly identified (see Appendix F). A suite of measures should then be agreed to evidence the realization of the intended intermediate and end benefits, including reference class data for each benefits category and business unit, comparing benefits realized against original forecast and the percentage of change initiatives ahead/on track/behind plan in terms of benefits realization. These measures should be monitored and reviewed on a regular basis.

11.3.4.2 Practice Maturity

Many maturity frameworks originate from the Capability Maturity Models developed by the Software Engineering Institute at Carnegie Mellon University. These models provide a repeatable, criteria-based evaluation process that facilitates comparisons over time and provides an incentive to, and a road map for, improvement. In relation to benefits management, regular assessment of maturity can play a role in sustaining progress by assessing progress made to date and identifying areas where action is required.

The Portfolio, Programme and Project Management Maturity Model (P3M3) contains three individual models:

■ Portfolio Management Model (PfM3).
■ Programme Management Model (PgM3).
■ Project Management Model (PjM3).

Each model uses a five-level maturity framework as follows:

■ Level 1 – Awareness of process.
■ Level 2 – Repeatable process.
■ Level 3 – Defined process.
■ Level 4 – Managed process.
■ Level 5 – Optimized process.

P3M3 focuses on seven process perspectives, which exist in all three models and can be assessed against the five levels of maturity. These process perspectives are management control; benefits management; financial management; risk management; stakeholder engagement; organizational governance; and resource management.

Advantages of P3M3 include:

■ The emphasis it places on integration of benefits realization into the organizational performance management framework.
■ Its flexibility – P3M3 allows organizations to review all seven process perspectives across all three models, or they can review just one of the process perspectives (in our case benefits management), whether across all three models or across only one or two of them.
■ Organizations can benchmark themselves against others via the APMG-International Maturity Index and also receive a report on the right level of maturity for their

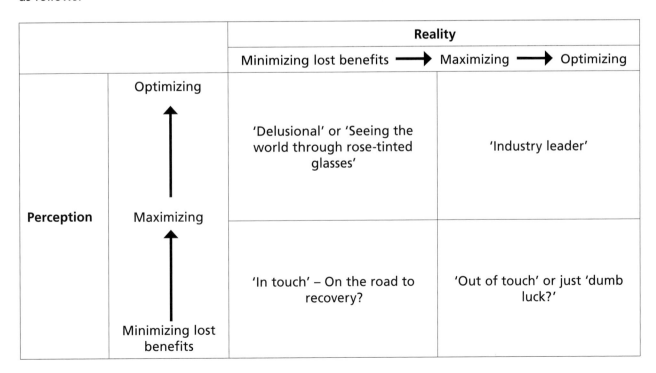

Figure 11.2 – Benefits realization – perception and reality analysis

organization based on the complexity of projects and programmes being undertaken (see http://www.p3m3-officialsite.com/).

Note – it is not necessary for all organizations to attain the highest level of maturity across all seven process perspectives and at each of the project, programme and portfolio levels. In each case progression to the next level should be justified in cost-benefit (financial and non-financial) terms. The full P3M3 coverage of benefits management within all three models is shown in Appendix H.

While there is often no replacement for an in-depth independent maturity assessment, an insight into an organization's current position can be obtained from a health-check assessment – for example, via the short Managing Benefits Health-check Assessment shown at Appendix I. It is also worth comparing perceptions with the organization's actual **demonstrable** performance in realizing benefits – and classifying the position as shown in Figure 11.2.

11.3.5 Appropriate Use of Software

Software solutions can help to embed benefits management and save time and resources. This includes adaption of existing portfolio, programme and project management software in use in the organization (such as Microsoft Project Portfolio Server); generic tools (such as Visio and PowerPoint); and bespoke benefits management software solutions. Areas where software solutions can be of value include:

- Benefits mapping
  - To capture benefits discovery workshop outputs (experience shows that trying to use software tools during the workshop rarely works well).
  - Visualization of the chain from enabling and business changes to intermediate and end benefits.
- Automatic generation of consistent documentation
  - Integration of relevant documentation including Benefit Profiles, Benefits Realization Plans, and relevant sections of the Business Case.

- Automatic updating of the suite of benefits documentation.
- Data collation and analysis
  - Sensitivity and scenario ('what if?') analysis, and pair-wise comparisons to inform options analysis, investment appraisal and portfolio prioritization.
  - Analysis of the impacts of changes in initiative scope on benefits realization.
  - Weighting and scoring to prioritize benefits.
  - Benefits tracking and reporting – consolidation and analysis of initiative data. One lesson learned: red/amber/green (RAG) ratings for individual benefits should be made by the relevant Benefit Owner, not the project team.
- Data storage and information sharing:
  - Document templates and guidance on their completion – with standing data fields automatically completed, including on the Benefit Profiles and Benefits Realization Plans.
  - Lessons learned repositories with downloadable audio and video summaries.
  - Library of past documents and reports.

Appropriately applied, software solutions can add value and save time and money. But remember – the software is there to enable and support an effective benefits management regime; it is not an end in itself. Effective practices and governance come first.

11.3.6 Staff Training and Development

Individual training is of value, but extending this to all those involved in the Benefits Management Cycle (for instance, the PPM community, Benefits and Business Change Managers, finance teams, SROs/Sponsors etc), including via team-based training, can leverage the impact significantly via shared understanding of good practices. Similarly, it is important that the organization's management development programmes encompass realizing benefits from change initiatives.

Benefits management training and development opportunities include:

- Membership of appropriate professional groups and online Communities of Interest (see Chapter 12 for some examples) – research confirms that social networks, including online communities, can be powerful agents for change by providing access to new ideas and support.

- Establishment of a Benefits Management Forum to share experiences and disseminate learning across, and even beyond, the organization. An example of this comes from the Swedish public sector, where a Special Interest Group has been established that is responsible for maintaining and developing the guidance, as well as implementing it within individual organizations. In another case, it has been found that establishing a 'BIG' group (Benefits Improvement Group), helped to get people excited about benefits – the organizer comments, *"Benefits of the BIG are … you get lots of people from key departments like finance and business areas wanting to come just because of the name etc., plus from a comms perspective those people all go and tell their people and so it grows. From a PR and energising perspective … people just love going to the BIG meeting."*

- A commitment to continuous improvement and regular review. This applies at the individual level as well as at the organizational level. A Skills and Competencies Log is attached at Appendix E – this can be used to identify any gaps in current skills/ competencies, as well as the strategies to be used to close these gaps.

- Undertaking Foundation and Practitioner training in '*Managing Benefits*', based on this guide, with APMG-International's Accredited Training Organizations (ATOs). Further guidance is available from http://www.apmg-international.com/. Also remember the discussion in Section 8.5.4 – ensure that lessons learned are applied in practice, and consider ways to enhance this by ongoing coaching and participating in relevant professional Communities of Interest.

11.4 CHAPTER SUMMARY

1. The three approaches to implementation of benefits management are big bang, evolutionary and ad hoc.

2. The suitability of each approach depends on factors such as breadth and depth of senior management commitment; whether top-down or emergent approaches to strategy formulation are applied; whether the environment is stable or dynamic; and the degree of existing maturity in PPM.

3. Whichever approach is adopted, most organizations will need to consider the following 10 first steps:

    1. Undertake driver-based analysis to ensure that the organization's strategic objectives are measurable.

    2. Adopt guidance on benefits-led rather than activity-centred change initiatives.

    3. Compile a Benefits Management Framework including benefits eligibility rules to apply to all initiatives in the organization's change portfolio.

    4. Implement consistent approaches to benefits mapping.

    5. Adopt the technique of 'staged release of funding'.

    6. Ensure clarity about the key benefits of the major initiatives in the organization's change portfolio.

    7. Consolidate the information collected above into a portfolio-level Benefits Realization Plan (BRP).

    8. Track and report progress against the portfolio BRP on a regular basis.

    9. Implement post-implementation and post-investment reviews.

10. Organize a programme of ongoing benefits management workshops and masterclasses.

4. Sustaining progress can be a challenge, but is aided by:

1. Effective governance – including considering expanding the Portfolio Office into a Value Management Office.

2. Treating the development of benefits management as a benefits-led business and behavioural change programme.

3. Ongoing stakeholder engagement in the development of benefits management, including adoption of the champion-challenger model.

4. Measuring progress on a regular basis, including impact and process/practice maturity – for example, via P3M3.

5. Appropriate use of software solutions.

6. Relevant training and development – including accredited training in *'Managing Benefits'* and participation in relevant Communities of Interest.

Chapter 12

Chapter 12 – The Next Steps

So you've read the Guide – what next?

1. Apply what you've learned – and record your experience on the Skills and Competencies Log at Appendix E.

2. Undertake a health-check assessment of your portfolio or change initiative – see the short 'Managing Benefits' assessment at Appendix I.

3. Attend an accredited training course – see http://www.apmg-international.com.

4. Read further, and more widely too – recommended materials are shown below.

5. Join a Community of Interest (CoI)– again, some relevant online groups are shown below, including the 'Managing Benefits' CoI on LinkedIn (http://www.linkedin.com/groups/Managing-Benefits-Community-Interest-4493501.

6. If you have any comments on this Guide, including suggestions for future editions, please contact managing.benefits@apmg-international.com

12.1 RECOMMENDED READING

Benefits Management Books

- Bradley, G. (2006) *Benefits Realisation Management*, Gower. ISBN 9780566086878.

- Bradley, G. (2010) *Fundamentals of Benefits Realisation,* TSO. ISBN 9780113312597.

- Jenner, S. (2011) *Realising Benefits from Government ICT Investment – A Fool's Errand?* Academic Publishing. ISBN 9781906638269.

- Remenyi, D., Bannister, F. & Money, A. (2007) *The Effective Measurement and Management of ICT Costs and Benefits*, 3rd edition, Elsevier. ISBN 9780750644204.

- Simms, J. (2008) *Solving the Benefits Puzzle.* Available as a Kindle edition (2011).

- Thorp, J. & Fujitsu Consulting's Center for Strategic Leadership (2003) *The Information Paradox – Realizing the Business Benefits of Information Technology*, McGraw-Hill, Canada. ISBN 9780071342650.

- Ward, J. & Daniel, E. (2006) *Benefits Management – Delivering Value from IS & IT Investments,* Wiley. ISBN 9780470094631.

Other related books

- Cameron, E. & Green, M. (2009) *Making Sense of Change Management*, Kogan Page. ISBN 9780749453107.

- Davies H.D. & Davies A.J. (2011) *Value Management – Translating Aspirations into Performance,* Gower. ISBN 9781409409557.

- EPMC (2009) *Project Portfolio Management – A View from the Management Trenches*, Wiley. ISBN 9780470505366.

- Fowler, A. & Lock, D. (2006) *Accelerating Business and IT Change: Transforming Project Delivery,* Gower. ISBN 9780566086045.

- Jenner, S. (2010) *Transforming Government and Public Services: Realising Benefits through Project Portfolio Management*, Gower. ISBN 9781409401636.

- Kahneman, D. (2011) *Thinking, Fast and Slow*, Allen Lane. ISBN 9781846140556.

- Kohlrieser, G., Goldsworthy, S. & Coombe, D. (2012) *Care to Dare: Unleashing Astonishing Potential Through Secure Base Leadership*, John Wiley & Sons. ISBN 9781119961574.

- Kotter, J.P. (1996) *Leading Change,* Harvard Business School Press. ISBN 9780875847474.

Cabinet Office 'Best Management Practice' Guides/Manuals

- *Management of Portfolios* (2011) TSO, London. ISBN 9780113312948.

- *Management of Value* (2010) TSO, London. ISBN 9780113312764.

- *Managing Successful Programmes* (2011) TSO, London. ISBN 9780113313273.

- *Portfolio, Programme and Project Offices* (2008) TSO, London. ISBN 9780113311248.

Free Benefits Management Materials

- APM (March, 2011) *Delivering Benefits from Investments in Change: Winning Hearts and Minds.* Available at: http://www.apm.org.uk/news/delivering-benefits-investments-change.

- APM (June, 2011) *Delivering Benefits from Investments in Change: Creating Organisational Capability.* Available at: http://www.apm.org.uk/news/delivering-benefits-investment-change-creating-organisational-capability.

- APM (May, 2012a). *Delivering Benefits from Investment in Change – An essential part of everyday business.* Available at: http://www.apm.org.uk/news/apm-benefit-management-sig-release-two-new-thought-leadership-reports.

- APM (May, 2012b), *Delivering Benefits from Investment in Change – Beyond 'Business as Usual' to 'Value as Usual'.* Available at: http://www.apm.org.uk/news/apm-benefit-management-sig-release-two-new-thought-leadership-reports.

- APM & CIMA (May, 2012). *Delivering the Prize – A Joint All-Ireland Study on Change Leadership and Benefits Realisation.* Available at: www.apm.org.uk.

- OGC (2005b) *Managing Benefits: An Overview*, v1.0. Available at: http://webarchive.nationalarchives.gov.uk/20070205125401/http://www.ogc.gov.uk/documents/ManagingBenefitsV101.pdf.

- *HM Treasury Green Book: Appraisal and Evaluation in Central Government*, http://www.hm-treasury.gov.uk/data_greenbook_index.htm.

- Cabinet Office, Office of the Third Sector, *A Guide to Social Return on Investment.* Available at: http://www.socialevaluator.eu/ip/uploads/tblDownload/SROI%20Guide.pdf.

12.2 COMMUNITIES OF INTEREST

- A *'Managing Benefits'* CoI now exists on LinkedIn and is open to all – http://www.linkedin.com/groups/Managing-Benefits-Community-Interest-4493501.

- APM Benefits Management SIG – http://www.apm.org.uk/group/apm-benefits-management-specific-interest-group. Note – membership is open to non-APM members.

- Benefits Realization Experts forum on LinkedIn – http://www.linkedin.com/groups/Benefits-Realisation-Experts-Forum-3569453.

- Local Government Project and Programme Management Community of Practice – https://knowledgehub.local.gov.uk.

12.3 USEFUL WEBSITES

- APMG-International – http://www.apmg-international.com.

- *'Best Management Practice'* – http://www.best-management-practice.com.

Appendix A

Appendix A – Quantifying and Valuing Benefits – Public-sector Considerations

This appendix includes guidance on quantifying, valuing and managing benefits in relation to:

- Cross-organizational programmes.
- Social value.
- Customers/citizens – the 'time savings' method.

Each of the above is illustrated with examples of how organizations have tackled the issue of quantifying and valuing benefits in practice.

A.1 CROSS-ORGANIZATIONAL PROGRAMME BENEFITS

The realization of benefits in a cross-organizational setting is problematic, in that benefits to one organization may well depend on business change elsewhere in the system. This is a particular feature of the public sector. A report from the Cabinet Office to the Organisation for Economic Co-operation and Development (OECD) in 2006 noted that, in respect of e-government, *"Business cases were found to be particularly strong on the assessment of costs and benefits to the lead department; however the identification and quantification of external benefits i.e. to users or other departments, was less strong, resulting in business cases that often understated benefits and provided an incomplete base for tracking future third-party benefits through to realisation."*

The challenges we face here are firstly to articulate these benefits that run across departmental boundaries, and then to lay the basis for their realization. This requires a joint benefits planning and realization process based on:

- Active participation by subject-matter experts from all organizations affected.

- Workshops to articulate, agree and quantify the forecast benefits and the logic underpinning them.

- Detailed analysis to explore the business changes required to realize the forecast benefits.

- Integration of the forecast benefits into the benefits management regime to ensure that agreements on forecasts are carried through to the benefits tracking process. This in turn requires accountability arrangements that cross departmental boundaries to address the issue where investment in one organization is required to realize benefits in another part of the overall system.

- Trust – ultimately, the realization of cross-organizational benefits depends on trust, based on a shared commitment to improving the system as a whole, even if this is at the short-term expense of one part of the system.

The exact mechanisms used will vary with the situation but are illustrated in Example A1 by the approach adopted in the UK criminal justice system (CJS) IT portfolio.

A.2 SOCIAL VALUE BENEFITS

Investments in the public and third sectors differ from those in the private sector in many ways. For example:

- The investment rationale is often to meet some social objective (public safety, environmental sustainability, public health etc.), rather than to achieve a financial return.

- These social objectives can be difficult to measure reliably. This is complicated by the issue of attribution – even if we can measure an outcome, it is often difficult in practice to attribute any change to a specific initiative given the multitude of factors affecting these outcomes.

Example A.1 – The 'combined effectiveness impact' benefits

The CJS IT portfolio encompassed three government departments (the Home Office, Ministry of Justice and Attorney General's Department) and seven criminal justice organizations (the Police, Crown Prosecution Service, Crown and Magistrates Courts, Prison and Probation Services, and Youth Justice). Because these organizations operate as part of a wider criminal justice system, changes in one organization have effects (both intended and unintended) elsewhere in the system. The Business Cases for the individual projects and programmes, which had in several cases been prepared prior to the formation of the portfolio, were found to be relatively strong in terms of the efficiency benefits forecast to be realized by the sponsoring organizations, but they were less robust in terms of their impact on the effectiveness of the system as a whole – to the extent that, where such benefits were recognized in the Business Cases, the scale of impact was generally unquantified or unsupported by any reliable or consistent form of empirical research or logical analysis. There was consequently no way in which this impact could be reliably assessed to determine whether it had been realized, or any basis for determining whether additional action was required. This was a major shortcoming and failed to reflect the reality that implementing ICT-enabled business change had massive potential – not only in saving money and time but, more significantly, in improving the effectiveness of the system as a whole by bringing more offenders to justice, improving services to witnesses and victims, and reducing re-offending.

The approach adopted was to complete a Root Cause Model to articulate, quantify and value the impact of the portfolio as a whole on the major problems and issues within the CJS – and because these benefits resulted from the combined contribution of several initiatives, they were termed 'combined effectiveness impact' benefits.

The approach consisted of the following six stages:

1. The key problems and issues in the system (or what were termed 'consequences' in the model) were identified and agreed. These included: re-offending; ineffective trials; inappropriate time in custody after trial; offences committed on bail; inappropriate prosecution decisions; unnecessary witness attendance at court; offender self-harm and harm to others; unpaid fines; detections; victim and witness care; and enforcement of arrest warrants.

2. Research was undertaken to ascertain the root causes of these consequences and this analysis was agreed with subject-matter experts from the respective departments and agencies.

3. Interactive workshops were then held with the subject-matter experts, practitioners and initiative representatives, to consider the impact of the portfolio on the root causes of the identified consequences. This analysis was documented graphically (originally in Visio but later using a specialist software package) in a series of cause-and-effect maps for each consequence. The Root Cause Model thus represented a detailed cause-and-effect chain from initiative functionality through to contribution to organizational targets. This analysis was agreed with the Benefits Realization Managers from each organization.

4. The Root Cause Model was also underpinned by cost and measurement data that enabled the performance impacts forecast by the model to be quantified in case or percentage terms, and also to be valued in economic terms using standard costs where available.

5. Consequences were allocated to the agency representative agreed as having the greatest influence over that part of the system, and the Portfolio Office then worked with these representatives to track and analyse the realization of benefits. Relevant benefits were thus included in the standard benefits planning and reporting regime of each agency and as part of the overall portfolio-level benefits reporting – and the Benefit Profiles agreed were in turn validated by the departmental efficiency and strategy planners. In this way, the 'combined effectiveness impact' benefits were subject to validation and tracking mechanisms similar to those for the benefits delivered through sponsor-organization initiatives.

6. Forecasts were reviewed and revised on a quarterly basis to reflect the latest data on system performance and initiative delivery. The model was also refreshed as new initiatives joined the portfolio and as new learning about the impact of initiatives was identified.

Beyond providing a basis for forecasting the quantified impact of the CJS IT portfolio on the effectiveness of the CJS as a whole, the approach was found to have a number of additional advantages, in providing:

- An effective method of mapping from initiative through to Public Service Agreement (PSA) targets and communicating this impact to stakeholders.
- A consistent method for forecasting effectiveness and efficiency benefits at an initiative level that was consistent with the portfolio-level view.
- An adaptable approach to benefits identification – as new initiatives joined the portfolio, the model was revised to reflect their forecast impact on system performance.
- An effective check against double counting – where several initiatives were forecast to impact on system performance, the model enabled the validation of claimed benefits and allowed double counting to be stripped out at the portfolio level.
- A means to improve cross-system understanding by promoting discussion and consideration of the consequences of changes in one part of the system on other parts of the system.
- An improved understanding of how initiatives can impact on performance and what business changes were necessary to realize those benefits.
- A basis for articulating and quantifying the social value attributable to the portfolio – expressing the economic value to UK society from reductions in crime.

Adapted from Jenner, S. (2011). Provided with the kind agreement of the publisher.

- Conversely, interventions can have unanticipated benefits. For example, an experiment in New York (Friedman, 1997) aimed at reintegrating offenders and drug addicts into the community found little impact on arrest rates (the intended objective of the programme), but the treatment group did achieve higher employment earnings and reduced reliance on social services, which justified the economic investment in the programme.

- The beneficiaries (citizens) often do not pay directly for the service received and the absence of a pricing mechanism makes valuing benefits problematic.

- In many cases, the beneficiaries of initiatives include not only those directly 'served' but also wider society – for example, an effective education system is of benefit to those beyond the classroom.

- The public sector generally cannot choose which market segments to target – services such as health, education and justice are generally universal in provision.

- The timespan for evaluating the full impact of change initiatives such as improvements in education and public health, and investments in defence, can extend over many years, if not decades.

- The scope for media and public scrutiny is often greater in the public sector as the funds involved are taxpayers' money and audit reports are in the public domain.

Despite these issues, it is important that we identify the anticipated benefits – as a basis for determining whether investment is justified, selecting between options and prioritizing investments, and as a basis for managing benefits realization, capturing learning and feeding this back into the investment appraisal process. But how should we do this?

Mark Moore's work on the concept of public value provides a useful starting point and has influenced thinking on both sides of the Atlantic, as well as in Australia. Moore (1995) identified three forms of public value:

- **Outcomes** – such as a sustainable environment, public safety, low unemployment, public health and reduced poverty.

- **Services** – such as education, health and justice. Importantly, value is seen as deriving not only from the quality of the service itself, but also from the citizen's experience of the service. Research by Kearns (2004) for the Institute for Public Policy Research (IPPR) in the UK found that perceptions of service quality are driven by five underlying factors: availability (not just to the person but also to others, particularly the most vulnerable members of society); user satisfaction (in turn driven by factors such as quality of customer service experience, level of information available, the degree of choice and convenience, and staff advocacy); the perceived importance of the service; fairness in provision; and cost.

- **Trust** – or public confidence in, and participation in, the democratic process.

While these forms of value are independent, they can also be linked. For example, as Kelly, Mulgan and Muers (2002) note, reports of reductions in crime can improve trust in government and satisfaction with the police, whether or not the police were primarily responsible for the reduction in crime in the first place.

Moore (1995) does not argue that economic or financial investment appraisal (cost-benefit and cost-effectiveness analysis) is inappropriate; indeed, there is an obligation on government to provide services as cost-effectively as possible. Rather, financial and economic appraisal needs to be augmented by appraisal that takes into consideration wider aspects of public value and citizens' needs, wants and desires. Examples of frameworks that take account of these wider perspectives on social value include the WiBe approach discussed in Chapter 6. Two further examples of the practical application of multi-criteria analysis frameworks encompassing the consideration of social value in the e-government context are outlined in the following sub-sections. We then conclude our review of social value by considering the recent Social Return on Investment (SROI) methodology from the Cabinet Office, Office of the Third Sector.

A.2.1 USA – the Value Measuring Methodology

Booz Allen Hamilton, in association with Harvard University's Kennedy School of Government, undertook a study sponsored by the Social Security Administration and the General Services Administration. The objective was to identify a methodology for measuring the value of e-government initiatives unaccounted for by traditional cost-benefit and return-on-investment methodologies. The findings, which were published in 2002, concluded, *"The full value of an e-service must be measured from multiple perspectives … it cannot be captured in a single internal financial metric (i.e. ROI)."* The Federal Government developed the approach further and published revised guidelines, incorporating the lessons learned from applying the approach in practice, in a *'Highlights'* document and *'How-To Guide'*. The resulting Value Measuring Methodology (VMM) is based on consideration of five value factors, encompassing both tangible and intangible benefits, cost and risk. The five value factors are:

1. **Direct user (customer) value** – benefits directly realized by users or multiple user groups: for example, time saved, more convenient service delivery/access etc.

2. **Social (non-direct user/public) value** – benefits related not to direct users but to society as a whole: for example, improved trust in government, participation, and inclusiveness. Measures for aspects of social value were identified and prioritized based on consultation with representative groups.

3. **Government operational/foundational value** – improvements realized in current government operations and processes, or those that lay the groundwork for future change initiatives: for example, enterprise architecture and improved infrastructure.

4. **Government financial value** – financial benefits that have a direct impact on organizational (government service provider) and other federal government budgets via increased revenue, reduced costs or costs avoided.

5. **Strategic/political value** – benefits that move an organization, and government as a whole, closer to achieving its strategic goals and mission.

The value factors were prioritized by allocating weightings, reflecting senior management's priorities and the relative importance of each factor to the organization. In each case, sub-criteria and quantifiable performance measures were identified and prioritized. Normalized scales were used, allowing objective and subjective measures of value to be combined into a single decision metric. It should also be noted that a 'bang for your buck' assessment was accommodated by dividing the resulting value score by the cost, so enabling the value for money of different options to be appraised.

A.2.2 Australia – the Demand and Value Assessment Methodology

The Demand and Value Assessment Methodology (D&VAM) was developed for the Australian Government Information Management Office. It distinguished between benefits (which it defined as *"an outcome whose nature and value … are considered advantageous to an organisation"*) and value (which was seen as *"the broader, collective term for the longer term contribution to*

the business goals and strategies"). The methodology started with an assessment of demand in which the service was assessed from the viewpoint of the end-user. It then moved on to the value assessment, encompassing, as with the VMM, five forms of value:

1. **Agency benefits/value** – operating-cost reductions, increased revenue, improved efficiency and productivity savings, improved effectiveness, and improved service or cycle times.

2. **Strategic value** – how well the initiative was aligned with the most important outcomes (and political objectives) for the organization.

3. **Consumer financial benefits** – time and cost savings, faster payments and revenue generation opportunities for users of a service.

4. **Social benefits** – including improved quality of life, improved decision-making and more integrated delivery, so increasing business opportunities.

5. **Governance value** – contribution to broader whole-of-government objectives, including more open and inclusive government (citizen participation), accountability and improved information availability (transparency).

Social benefits from an initiative were assessed in terms of their:

- 'Reach' in the context of the target group – scores of 1 to 5 were used, where 1 represented less than 5% reach and 5 meant more than 50% reach.
- 'Consequence' or the expected impact on the target social group – again, scores ranged from 1 to 5, where 1 represented 'minimal impact' and 5 meant 'significant impact'.

This was combined with assessments of risk to programme delivery and to the achievement of benefits, to provide a simple but comprehensive assessment of value that could be presented graphically in the form of a radar chart or spider diagram.

A.2.3 Social Return on Investment

SROI is an approach developed in the UK for use in the third sector, but it is one that has real potential for wider use. It includes consideration of economic values and engagement with stakeholders to identify relevant outcome measures representing a *"story about change"*, encompassing quantitative, qualitative and financial information. It can be applied ex ante and ex post, to inform investment appraisals and as a basis for learning and improving

understanding of 'what works'. Most significantly, it encourages a rigorous and consistent approach to the problematic area of calculating social value, with specific consideration of the thorny issue of attribution.

A further example of SROI, this time from Australia, is shown in Example A.4.

Example A.2 – Social Return on Investment

To help address the issue of valuing costs and benefits where no market prices are readily available, the Office of the Third Sector in the UK Cabinet Office has published guidance on calculating SROI. This is based on seven principles:

1. Involve stakeholders.

2. Understand what changes.

3. Value the things that matter.

4. Only include what is material.

5. Do not over-claim.

6. Be transparent.

7. Verify the result.

The process to calculate SROI is based on the following six stages:

1. **Establishing scope and identifying key stakeholders affected by the initiative**. This includes potentially segmenting stakeholders and identifying intended and unintended outcomes for each group (both positive and negative) – for example, via facilitated focus groups. Examining previous case studies can also help to identify unintended consequences.

2. **Mapping outcomes** via an impact map or 'theory of change' demonstrating the logical relationship between inputs, outputs and outcomes for stakeholders – in short, how the intervention will make a difference in the world.

3. **Evidencing outcomes and giving them a value**. This includes developing outcome indicators and outcomes data, establishing how long outcomes will last and valuing them in monetary form. Once again, stakeholder engagement is key in identifying relevant, measurable outcome indicators – for example, through surveys, interviews and focus groups. A crucial factor here is 'knowing the numbers', i.e. you need to understand the current level of performance in order to assess whether the desired improvement has occurred.

In relation to how long the outcome will last, it is recognized that the longer the duration, the more likely it is that the outcome will be affected by other factors. Once the outcome has been quantified, financial proxy values are calculated using techniques such as contingent valuation (willingness to pay or willingness to accept), revealed preference and the travel-cost method (see Section A.3).

4. **Establishing impact**, i.e. whether changes can be attributed to the initiative and eliminating the changes that would have happened without the intervention. This involves considering:

    a. Deadweight – what would have happened anyway, as ascertained via comparison groups and trend analysis.

    b. Displacement – how much of the outcome displaced other outcomes: for example, a crime-prevention initiative in one area results in increased crime in neighbouring areas.

    c. Attribution – how much of the outcome can be attributed to the initiative.

    d. Drop-off – as time passes, the outcome is likely to be affected by other factors and so the impact attributable to the current initiative will be reduced.

    The economic value is then adjusted for factors a to c, which are expressed as percentages. Factor d is considered in Stage 5.

5. **Calculating the SROI and undertaking sensitivity analysis**. The Net Present Value (NPV) is calculated and adjusted for drop-off in future years. Once this is completed, the SROI ratio can be calculated by dividing the Present Value by the Value of Inputs (or alternatively the Net SROI ratio is calculated by dividing the NPV by the Value of Inputs). We can then say £x of value is created for every £y of investment. We may also calculate the payback period, i.e. how long it takes for the social return to exceed the investment required to generate that return.

6. **Reporting, using and embedding the use of SROI within the organization**. This includes communicating the results back to stakeholders and independently verifying the impacts.

Based on material published by the Cabinet Office (2009).

Example A.3 – The SROI in use

An example of the application of SROI in practice relates to the return on investment from user-experience audits for adults with learning disabilities who are in receipt of Independent Living Allowance. Recipients use this allowance to employ personal assistants (care workers) to help them live full and active lives. Many of these recipients, however, have communication difficulties and may get frustrated when they believe that their wishes aren't heard. Additionally, this can mean that more staff are required to ensure everyone's safety, and/or a person's independence may be taken away from them.

We explore elsewhere in this Guide the impact of effective stakeholder engagement techniques in driving behavioural change, but these user-experience audits also led to changes in behaviour. Research found that the benefits included:

Example continues

Example A.3 continued

> - Changes in behaviour among the recipients of allowances, because they feel that they have been listened to, reduced the cost of providing support by £5.78 for each £1 spent on user-experience auditing.
> - Changes in staff attitudes had a positive impact on sickness and turnover, which equated to £1.17 saved for each £1 spent on user-experience auditing.
>
> Organizations met more of the quality standards they are required to meet, with a return on investment (from not having to change support providers) of £1.48 per £1 spent. Moreover, these returns are additive – these three changes resulted in savings of £8.43 for each £1 spent, and the total SROI ratio on this initiative (taking into account all of the changes, both positive and negative, and the proportion that should be attributed to the user-experience audits) averaged £11.40 per £1 spent over the 2½ years following the audits.

Provided with the kind agreement of Hugo Minney, PhD, The Social Return Co.

Example A.4 – SROI and Fair Repairs

Fair Repairs is a social enterprise that aims to address unemployment in social-housing areas by creating opportunities for local people (the long-term unemployed or those experiencing significant barriers to employment) to do local work for real pay. The core component of the Fair Repairs model is the recruitment of long-term unemployed people and the provision of both personal and professional support to enable them to return to work. The business is financially self-sustaining through contract work for repairs and maintenance.

Fair Business received funding for the development of Fair Repairs from Social Ventures Australia (SVA) as part of the Supporting Social Enterprise Project, in partnership with the Australian Government's Department of Education, Employment and Workplace Relations (DEEWR). An SROI assessment was commissioned by SVA to create a baseline analysis of the impact Fair Repairs has had on major stakeholders, including:

- Employees, who experience increased self-confidence, employment, a sense of belonging and improved quality of life, as well as increased dreams and plans for the future.
- Trainees, who experience increased self-confidence and a sense of belonging, as well as increased confidence in obtaining employment.
- Fair Business itself, which gains an increased capacity to replicate Fair Repairs in other locations.
- Housing NSW, which gains: increased experience among housing residents in Claymore that the estate is vibrant, confident and safe; increased income from housing residents, due to them paying some rent; and increased capacity to facilitate the employment of social-housing residents through social-obligations clauses.
- Federal government, which gains increased savings in welfare payments, and increased income taxes.
- Western Sydney TAFE, which is training an increased number of disadvantaged people.
- Campbelltown City Council, which notes increased local business activity.

The analysis found that, based on conservative assumptions, the social value generated per stakeholder group is as shown in Table A.1.

Table A.1 – Social value from Fair Repairs

Stakeholders	Social value
Employees	$361,358
Fair Business	$324,000
Housing NSW	$156,272
Federal government	$75,031
Trainees	$26,115
Western Sydney TAFE	$21,350
Campbelltown City Council	$19,937
Totals	
Social value	$999,901
Present Value	$943,675
Net Present Value	$738,098

Note – the numbers above do not add to the totals shown as there were other (relatively minor) recipients and some of the contributions were pro-bono but have a value associated.

For every $1 invested in the programme, $4.59 of social value is created for stakeholders over a two-year period, with 72% generated in the first year.

Based on a Case Study available at http://www.fairrepairs.org.au and provided with the kind assistance of Kelly McJannett and Mark Bonnell.

A.3 CUSTOMER/CITIZEN BENEFITS – THE 'TIME SAVINGS' METHOD

As far as user time savings are concerned, HM Treasury Green Book guidance is that, when valuing working-time savings for businesses (employers' time), the time saved should be valued at the gross wage rate plus non-wage labour costs (national insurance and pension contributions). In the case of time savings to citizens/non-business users ('own' time, which can be working or non-working time), relevant guidance can be found in research into the value of travel-time savings undertaken by Mackie et al (2003) for the Department for Transport (DfT). This recommends the use of standard values (averaged across income groups) modified where necessary for socio-economic status, rather than specific values for different groups. The research suggests standard rates for working time and non-working time as follows:

- **Time savings in working time** – the DfT research quotes rates of £17.44 per hour for car drivers and £25.17 per hour for rail passengers. HM Treasury e-government guidance (2003) also suggests that, where more accurate estimates are difficult to obtain, a conservative estimate of £20 per hour at 2002 prices be used for working-time savings for customers.

- **Customer time savings in non-working time** – the research quotes a standard valuation of time saved at £3.74 per hour at 1998 prices, averaged across all modes of transport. The research also found that people value walking and waiting time more highly than car travel time, and it is consequently recommended that the former be valued at twice the car-driving rate.

It should be noted that there is some argument about the use of standard rates, which do have theoretical shortcomings – particularly in the assumption of equal marginal utility of time for all groups of users. In practice, 'willingness to pay' analysis could be undertaken for the various user groups, but this can be expensive and there is always the risk of spurious accuracy. The Booz Allen Hamilton study that provided the basis for the US VMM, for example, strongly recommends that, when time savings are monetarized, a single rate for all citizens is used. The authors add that using higher rates for some *risks skewing services and raises questions of equitable treatment*".

Most recently (2009), following extensive work in relation to customer journey mapping and as part of a project to determine the 'total cost to serve', HM Revenue & Customs agreed with HM Treasury that a standard rate of £13.60 per hour (later updated to £14.20) should be used to value user time savings, whether in working time or in non-working time.

Appendix B

Appendix B – Benefits Management Documentation

This appendix contains:

- Table B.1: Typical contents of the main portfolio-level benefits management documentation (developed from the guidance in 'Management of Portfolios': MoP).

- Table B2: Typical contents of the main initiative-level benefits management documentation (from 'Managing Successful Programmes': MSP).
- Table B.3: A Benefit Profile template (from the Office of Government Commerce: OGC, 2005).

Table B.1 – Portfolio-level benefits management documentation

Portfolio Benefits Management Framework – typical contents
■ Outline of the high-level benefits the portfolio is designed to achieve and the metrics to be used to assess their realization.
■ Benefits eligibility guidance – the detailed rules on the identification, categorization, quantification, valuation and validation of benefits.
■ Approaches to benefits mapping to be applied.
■ Treatment of benefits throughout the business change lifecycle – from Business Case, through stage/phase gates, portfolio-level, post-implementation and post-investment reviews, to integration into business as usual (BAU).
■ Definition of roles and responsibilities for benefits forecasting, tracking and reporting.

Portfolio Benefits Realization Plan – typical contents
■ Statement of the main benefits forecast to be realized in the year ahead, analysed by business unit and benefit category, including:
☐ Scale of impact.
☐ Profile throughout the year (when they will be realized – if not monthly, then usually at least quarterly).
☐ Metrics to be used to assess benefits realization.
■ Portfolio-level benefits key performance indicators (KPIs) to be used and any baseline performance.
■ Risks to benefits realization and mitigating actions planned.

Portfolio Dashboard Report – typical benefits-related contents
■ Latest benefits forecast, analysed by business unit and benefit category.
■ Realization to date compared with plan.
■ Scale, source and type of emergent benefits and dis-benefits identified.
■ Status on key risks, issues and dependencies.
■ Portfolio-level benefits KPIs – current performance compared with baseline.

Table B.2 – Initiative-level benefits management documentation

Benefits Management Strategy – typical contents
■ Scope and explanation of which areas of the business will be covered by benefits management and realization activity.
■ Measurement methods and processes that will be used to monitor and assess the realization of the benefits (including the level of granularity to be applied in the Benefits Realization Plan).
■ A description of the functions, roles, accountabilities and responsibilities for benefit planning and realization, aligned with the programme's organizational structure.
■ Priorities for the programme in terms of benefit types to be sought (for example, cashable direct), to inform the filtering and prioritization process.
■ Processes to ensure that benefits are not double-counted and that cumulative benefits are achievable.
■ The relationships between capabilities and the benefits.
■ Clarity, if necessary, as to opportunities to be managed in relationship to risk management.
■ The relationship with other programme information.
■ Categories to be used by the programme or inherited from a portfolio.
■ Any organizational-specific information or headings that should be included in the benefit profiles.
■ Tools, systems and sources of information that will be used to enable measurement.
■ Critical success factors against which the effectiveness of benefits management should be measured.
■ Clarification of benefits-related terminology appropriate to the organization.
■ The review and assessment process for measuring benefits realization, covering who will be involved in the reviews, and how and when the reviews will be carried out.
■ Standards for identifying, mapping, monitoring and reviewing the programme's benefits.
Benefits Realization Plan – typical contents
■ A schedule detailing when each benefit, dis-benefit or group of benefits will be realized (typically as a chart with benefits of the same measure aggregated over time intervals through the life of the programme's Business Case).
■ Appropriate milestones for benefits reviews to take a forward view of the likelihood of ongoing success.
■ Estimated effort and costs associated with the plan.
■ Detail of transition schedules.
■ Benefit reporting schedule, which is submitted to the Programme Board.
■ Relationship between outcomes and benefits in the schedule.
■ Dates when specific outcomes that enable the benefits will be achieved.
■ Dependencies external to the programme.
■ Details of any handover and embedding activities, beyond the mere implementation of a deliverable or output, to enhance the process of benefits realization after the capability has been delivered; this part of the Benefits Realization Plan is also referred to as a transition plan.
■ Reference to how the benefits realization will be maintained after programme closure.
■ Benefits Maps.

Benefit Profile – typical contents
■ Reference number or identifier.
■ Description of the benefit (or dis-benefit).
■ Programme or organizational objectives supported and the related observable outcomes from the programme implementation.
■ Category or categories that are appropriate to the benefits.
■ KPIs in the business operations that will be affected by the benefit, both immediately after realization and for the future.
■ Current or baseline performance levels, and improvement or deterioration trajectory anticipated.
■ Benefits realization and business change costs.
■ Capabilities required for the benefit to be realized: the project(s) within the programme directly related to the realization of the benefit.
■ Outcomes that will need to be in place to enable the benefits realization.
■ Business changes required for realization (to process, culture, people, policy).
■ Related issues and risks to the full realization of the benefit.
■ Any dependencies on contributory events, programmes or projects outside the boundary of this programme.
■ Who is responsible for realizing this benefit (typically the Business Change Manager for this area of the business).
■ Attribution: the benefits owner and the operations area that will receive this benefit.
■ Measurement (financial wherever possible)*.

* Note that this is an area in which this Guide takes a somewhat different line from MSP, which states, *"best practice is to express benefits in financial terms wherever possible"*. Clearly, monetary measures are required where financial benefits are concerned, but in the case of non-financial benefits, non-monetary measures are more appropriate. That's not to say that attributing monetary values to non-financial benefits should not be done – but it should be restricted to the cost-benefit appraisal. For benefits management purposes, monetary values should not be attributed to non-financial benefits. This approach is also advocated by Bradley/TSO (2010).

Guidance on **benefits mapping** is in Section 5.2.2.

Formats for the **Benefits Realization Report** are discussed in Section 8.4.3.1.

Note: as with many standard templates, the following should be adapted to reflect the organization's circumstances.

Table B.3 – Benefit Profile template[1]

SAMPLE BENEFIT PROFILE TEMPLATE			
No.	*Unique number*	Owner	*Named individual*
Profile Agreement Date	*Sign-off date*	Profile Last Reviewed	*Insert date*
Benefit Overview		*High-level description – link to strategic goal*	
Detailed Description:			
Describe the main attributes of the benefit and its relationship with other benefits and the eventual outcomes (e.g. as enabler, intermediate or end benefit). *May also be a description of an unexpected side-effect or dis-benefit that must be managed.*			
Actions taken:			
List the outcomes of Benefit Review with dates and reasons.			
Stakeholders		*Major individuals or groups impacted by the benefit*	
Benefits Valuation		*Whether tangible/financial*	
Key assumptions		*Show assumptions about probability or value of benefit*	
Risks to benefit		*List specific risks or link to risk register*	
Costs		*Costs associated with measurement or realization*	
Performance Measure(s)		*KPIs now – or in the future. If not capable of direct measurement, what trend analysis or other test can be used to track achievement?*	
Target Performance Realization Date(s) *Profile showing any 'lag time', or changes over time*		*Expected performance at each milestone or trajectory intersect and 'end state' performance*	
Measurement Source		*System or information source(s) required for measurement*	
Measurement Frequency		*Milestone or trajectory period (quarterly, annually, 2-yearly etc)*	
Measurement Roles		*Information system owners*	
Dependencies		*Cross-reference to other benefits (number of profile) or list external dependencies (environmental, other projects, technical etc)*	

---

1 From: OGC (2005) *Managing Benefits: An Overview*, v1.0.

Appendix C

Appendix C – Benefits Management Roles and Responsibilities

This appendix contains:

- Table C.1: Portfolio-level benefits management: key roles and responsibilities in a *'Management of Portfolios'* (MoP) environment (based on the guidance contained in MoP).

- Table C.2: Initiative-level benefits management: key roles and responsibilities in a *'Managing Successful Programmes'* (MSP) environment (based on the guidance contained in MSP and in *'Portfolio, Programme and Project Offices'*: P3O).

Table C.1 – *Portfolio-level benefits management: key roles and responsibilities in an MoP environment*

Key roles	Benefits management responsibilities
Portfolio Direction Group (PDG)/Investment Committee (IC) – the governance body where decisions about the inclusion of initiatives in the change portfolio are made.	■ Approves the portfolio Benefits Management Framework and changes to it. ■ Approves the portfolio-level Benefits Realization Plan (usually annually). ■ Undertakes regular portfolio-level reviews to confirm that the portfolio remains on course to deliver the desired strategic benefits and outcomes. ■ Considers investment appraisal and portfolio prioritization reports in deciding on the composition of the portfolio. ■ Ensures that any conflicts between portfolio delivery and business as usual (BAU) that cannot be resolved by the Portfolio Progress Group/Change Delivery Committee are addressed effectively. ■ Receives and approves the conclusions and recommendations of start-gate reviews and post-implementation and post-investment reviews.
Portfolio Progress Group (PPG)/Change Delivery Committee (CDC) – the governance body responsible for monitoring portfolio progress and resolving issues that may compromise delivery and benefits realization.	■ Ensures that all programmes and projects comply with the requirements specified in the Benefits Management Framework. ■ Monitors delivery of the portfolio-level Benefits Realization Plan, via the Portfolio Dashboard Report, and approves in-year changes to the benefits forecast. ■ Ensures that risks and dependencies affecting benefits realization are effectively managed. ■ Approves communications on portfolio progress, including benefits realization. ■ Receives and approves the conclusions and recommendations of 'in-flight' stage/phase gate reviews.

Table continues

Table C.1 continued

Key roles	Benefits management responsibilities
Business Change Director/ Portfolio Director – the Management Board member responsible for the Portfolio Strategy and providing clear leadership through its life.	■ Champions the implementation of portfolio-level benefits management across the organization. ■ Secures any investment required for benefits management. ■ Gains relevant Management Board approval for the portfolio-level Benefits Realization Plan. ■ Ensures that the benefits management practices are documented in a portfolio Benefits Management Framework, are kept up to date, and are amended in the light of lessons learned.
Portfolio Benefits Manager (reporting to the Portfolio Manager/Head of the Portfolio Office) – ensures that a consistent 'fit for purpose' approach to benefits management is applied across the portfolio and that benefits realization is optimized from the organization's investment in change.	■ Develops and maintains the organization's portfolio Benefits Management Framework. ■ Considers and advises the Portfolio Manager and/or Director on changes to the portfolio Benefits Management Framework. ■ Provides training and awareness-building sessions on the application of the portfolio Benefits Management Framework. ■ Participates in investment appraisals, ensuring that Business Case benefits forecasts are consistent with the organization's benefits eligibility rules. ■ Works with the Business Change Managers to promote more effective benefits management practices. ■ Facilitates benefits-mapping workshops. ■ Provides advice and support to project and programme management (PPM) and BAU colleagues on the development of initiative-level benefits forecasts and Benefits Management Strategies. ■ Provides assurance on the effectiveness of benefits management practices at initiative level. ■ Maintains the portfolio-level benefits forecast and ensures that double counting is minimized. Updates the forecast to reflect approved initiative-level changes at stage/phase gates and portfolio-level reviews. ■ Coordinates the production of the annual portfolio Benefits Realization Plan. ■ Consolidates progress reports for the Portfolio Dashboard Report and for periodic portfolio-level reviews. ■ Escalates any benefits-related issues via the Portfolio Manager to either the PDG/IC or PPG/CDC. ■ Monitors effective management of dependencies and risks as they relate to benefits management – and escalates issues where required via the portfolio reporting process. ■ Sets the standards for, and monitors, post-implementation reviews and participates in post-investment reviews to compare the benefits realized with the benefits forecast and identify lessons learned in relation to benefits management for wider dissemination.

Table C.2 – Initiative-level benefits management: key roles and responsibilities in an MSP/P3O environment

Key roles	Benefits management responsibilities
Senior Responsible Owner (SRO) – the single individual with overall responsibility for ensuring that a project or programme meets its objectives and delivers the projected benefits.	■ Reports to the sponsoring group on the delivery of the programme benefits as described in the Benefit Profiles. ■ Ensures that the programme and the business areas affected maintain a focus on benefits delivery. ■ Ensures that the Benefits Management Strategy is created, adjusted, improved and enforced. ■ Maintains a focus on business performance sustainability during transition. ■ Chairs benefits reviews involving relevant stakeholders, business managers and possibly internal audits. ■ Liaises with the sponsoring group on the validation of all benefits claimed by the programme. ■ Authorizes benefits achievements.
Programme Manager – the role responsible for the set-up, management and delivery of a programme. Typically allocated to a single manager.	■ Develops the Benefits Management Strategy on behalf of the SRO with the Business Change Managers and relevant stakeholders from the affected business areas. ■ Develops the Benefits Realization Plan and Business Case in consultation with the Business Change Managers, relevant stakeholders and members of the project teams. ■ Ensures that the delivery of capability is aligned to optimize the realization of benefits. ■ Initiates benefits reviews as part of the Benefits Realization Plan or in response to any other triggers.
Business Change Manager – the role responsible for benefits management, from identification through to realization, and for ensuring that the implementation and embedding of the new capabilities are delivered by the projects. Typically allocated to more than one individual and also known as 'change agent'.	■ Identifies and quantifies the benefits (and dis-benefits) with the support of relevant stakeholders, the Programme Manager and members of the project teams. ■ Delivers particular benefits as profiled; this extends to ensuring that commitments and actions that have been attributed to operational areas are delivered. ■ Provides information to support the creation and delivery of the Benefits Realization Plan. ■ Develops and maintains the Benefit Profiles. ■ Ensures there is no double counting of benefits. ■ Maintains engagement with key individuals responsible for benefits delivery within the operations. ■ Sets business performance deviation levels and early-warning indicators to support benefits realization. ■ Initiates benefits reviews after the programme has closed.

Table continues

Table C.2 continued

Key roles	Benefits management responsibilities
Programme Office – the function providing the information hub and standards custodian for a programme and its delivery objectives. Could provide support for more than one programme. May include a **benefits role (Benefits Manager)** to provide a benefits realization support service to programmes, business managers and Business Change Managers.	**Programme Office** ■ Supports the Programme Manager in preparing and updating the Business Case. ■ Monitors the progress of benefits realization against plan. ■ Gathers information for the benefits reviews. ■ Produces performance reports as defined by the Programme Manager. ■ Maintains benefits information under change control and maintains audit trails of changes. **Benefits role/Benefits Manager** ■ On behalf of the SRO, Programme Manager and Business Change Manager, lead identification activities for benefits and dis-benefits. ■ Develop and maintain the programme Benefits Maps. ■ Facilitate agreement of the Benefits Management Strategy between the SRO, Programme Manager and Business Change Managers. ■ Facilitate agreement of the Benefits Realization Plan between the SRO, Programme Manager and Business Change Managers. ■ Facilitate the agreement of the Benefit Profiles between the Business Change Managers and Benefit Owners. ■ Establish the infrastructure required to implement the Benefits Management Strategy. ■ Track and report on the realization of benefits by the business. ■ Work with the business managers or Business Change Managers to identify additional opportunities for benefits realization. ■ Work with the business managers or Business Change Managers to minimize any dis-benefits. ■ Assess change requests for their potential effect on benefits realization. ■ Assist the SRO in leading benefits reviews. ■ Regularly review and improve the effectiveness of benefits management arrangements. ■ Assess benefits planning and realization across a number of programmes or projects to identify gaps, overlaps and conflicts and eliminate double counting in the benefits plans of individual programmes and projects. ■ Provide scrutiny of a Business Case from a business perspective.
Benefit Owner – the person responsible for the realization of a specific benefit. Note that the role may well extend beyond the life of a programme.	■ Agrees the Benefit Profile prepared by the Business Change Manager. ■ Monitors the successful delivery of enabling and business changes. ■ Collects and reports data to evidence the realization of benefits.

Appendix D

Appendix D – Cognitive Biases Affecting Benefits Management

Table D.1 – Cognitive biases affecting benefits management

Cognitive biases	Impact on benefits management
The illusion of control Confusing activity with results and the misconception that by preparing reports and analysis we are in control of reality. This is nicely summed up by Brian Quinn, who says, *"A good deal of corporate planning ... is like a ritual rain dance. It has no effect on the weather that follows, but those who engage in it think it does. ... Moreover, much of the advice related to corporate planning is directed at improving the dancing, not the weather."*	'Box ticking' approaches where there is a focus on adherence to process rather than realization of benefits.
The status quo bias The tendency to apply processes even when they have failed to deliver in the past. Einstein is commonly reported to have defined insanity as doing the same thing over and over again and expecting different results – yet that is what often happens in practice.	Failure to adopt more effective practices even when it is apparent that what we're doing isn't working, on the assumption that we've just got to try a little harder or that the benefits will be realized next year. This helps explain the 'knowing–doing' gap.
The sunk cost effect Investment decisions should be based on incremental (future) costs and benefits and should ignore what has already gone. But managers find it difficult to ignore spend to date when deciding whether to continue to invest in an initiative. Piattelli-Palmarini (1994) says, *"once we have actually committed a large sum, we are inclined to add to it more than we would ever have accepted to spend at the beginning"*. The causes are, according to psychologists: the over-generalization of the 'don't waste' rule; organizational pressures against admitting mistakes; and managers' over-confidence that they can turn things around.	Continuing to invest when the future benefits don't justify the costs required to realize them. There is consequently a pressure to overstate benefits to help make the case for continued investment. This helps explain what Banfield (2011) calls the *"conspiracy of continuation"*, where initiatives are rarely stopped once they are started.
Confirmation bias and being slow to change our minds Confirmation or expectation bias means that we tend to recognize evidence that supports our beliefs and ignore evidence that counters them. Linked to this, we are slow to change our minds when the evidence suggests we should.	Failing and low-value initiatives are not stopped as early as they should be. Ayres (2007), for example, says, *"humans not only are prone to make biased predictions, we're also damnably overconfident about our predictions and slow to change them in the face of new evidence."*

Table continues

Table D.1 continued

Cognitive biases	Impact on benefits management
Framing – the way options are presented affects the choice made Choice should be independent of irrelevant alternatives, but Simonson (1989) gives the example of two cars: car A is superior on attribute 1 (for example, petrol consumption) and car B on attribute 2 (for example, safety). How do we choose between them? If our preferred choice is car A but our partner is unsure, we can steer the investment decision our way by including a third option (termed a 'decoy option'): car C, which is inferior to A on both attributes. The result is that more people choose car A when A, B and C are offered than when just A and B are offered. Another example concerns our asymmetric attitude to risk: we tend to be risk averse when a problem is stated in terms of gains, but risk seeking when it is stated in terms of avoiding losses.	Sub-optimal decisions are made about which options to invest in and consequently lower benefits are realized than would otherwise have been possible from the available funds.
Mental accounting The tendency to allocate funds into 'buckets' – which leads to statements such as *"it's time to invest in one part of the business because they haven't had as much as others in the past"*.	This bias fails to recognize that investment funds are fungible, i.e. each unit of currency is the same as all others. Because of mental accounting, it seems only fair that we spread the money around, irrespective of the cost-benefit case for doing so. The result is that sub-optimal investment decisions are made and consequently lower benefits are realized than would otherwise have been possible from the available funds.
Ignoring regression to the mean Expecting extreme results to be followed by extreme results, whereas regression to the mean suggests that, over time, extreme results will tend to be followed by events closer to the mean/average.	This helps explain the belief that the 'stick' is more powerful than the 'carrot' and the assumption that if we can hold people accountable with appropriate 'consequences' then benefits will automatically be realized. When performance exceeds target, this is rewarded and is then often followed by performance closer to the average. Thus we instinctively 'learn' that rewards are unreliable. In contrast, the use of punishment when performance is below average is seen to work when performance subsequently improves. But in both cases the cause may be less about the use of 'incentives' and 'consequences' and more about regression to the mean. As Gilovich (1991) says, *"Regression effects teach us specious lessons about the relative effectiveness of reward and punishment."*

Cognitive biases	Impact on benefits management
The affect heuristic When appraising something we like, we tend to minimize the risks and costs and exaggerate the benefits (see also the consideration of optimism bias in Chapter 5) – and when it's something we don't like, we do the opposite. For example, the assumptions held by those with strong views either for or against nuclear power tend to colour their appraisal of the case.	Inadequate appraisal prior to investment – and the failure to identify optimistic assumptions underpinning benefits forecasts. This is then compounded by confirmation bias (see above) and the endowment effect – see below.
The endowment effect The tendency to value something we possess at a higher value than we would be willing to pay to obtain it.	Once an initiative is started and funds committed, there is a tendency to overvalue the benefits forecast.

Table D.2 – Cognitive biases affecting benefits forecasting

Cognitive biases	Impact on benefits forecasting
Expectation or confirmation bias	The tendency for forecasters to select evidence that confirms existing beliefs and assumptions, and to discount or ignore evidence that conflicts with these beliefs. An example is what Kahneman (2011) calls the *"illusion of validity"*, i.e. the tendency to ignore even statistical evidence when it conflicts with our pre-conceived beliefs.
The planning fallacy	The belief that our current initiative will realize the forecast benefits, despite an awareness that many similar change initiatives have failed to do so in the past. Or what the World Bank refers to as the *"EGAP"* principle: the assumption that *"Everything Goes According to Plan"* (which it rarely does).
Availability bias	The information that is most easily available is thought to be the most relevant and we don't consider the implications of information that may be harder to obtain. The benefits forecasts can consequently be based on unreliable data.
Groupthink	The tendency to confuse truth with assumptions – and this tendency is reinforced when the majority of those involved share the same set of beliefs and values. Thus we become overly confident in our forecasts and ignore information to the contrary.
The framing effect and loss aversion	The tendency to place a higher value on losses avoided than on equivalent gains. For example, Cialdini (2007) provides the following example: *"... homeowners told how much money they could lose from inadequate insulation are more likely to insulate their homes than those told how much money they could save."* Hastie and Dawes (2001) report that *"most empirical estimates conclude that losses are about twice as painful as gains are pleasurable"*. Thus a Business Case that is framed in terms of what might go wrong if the initiative were not to proceed (for example, lives lost) appears more compelling than a Business Case prepared on the basis of the same initiative's positive outcomes (for example, lives saved).

Table continues

Table D.2 continued

Cognitive biases	Impact on benefits forecasting
Anchoring and adjustment	In preparing forecasts we 'anchor' on, and give disproportionate weight to, the first estimate (no matter how reliable or relevant) and then make insufficient adjustment to reflect the specific circumstances. As a result, in many cases, 10% provision for contingency is unlikely to be sufficient. For example, Collins and Bicknell (1998) argue: *"Not all computing projects fail – only most of them. Now and again serendipity sees a company or government department buying and implementing a system that does as much as half of what was originally intended."*
Biases affecting our ability to handle probability	These biases have an impact on assessments of risk and assessment of the probability that benefits will be realized. They include drawing overconfident conclusions from small samples and ignoring base-rate probabilities – an example of what Kahneman (2011) refers to as *"WYSIATI"* (*"What You See Is All There Is"*), i.e. the tendency to evaluate what is before us without asking what other information might be available.
Confusing correlation and causation, and assuming the 'arrow of causation'	Thus if factor A is seen to be correlated with factor B, we are too keen to attribute causation rather than asking whether there might be another factor that causes the change in both A and B. Similarly, we assume that B is caused by A, although it is possible that the 'arrow of causation' is the reverse of that assumed, i.e. B may well lead to A. The consequence is *"blindness to the extent of our ignorance and a derogation of the role of chance in life"* (Hastie and Dawes, 2001). As Taleb (2004) says, people are fooled by randomness: *"The brain sees the world as less, far less, random than it actually is"*. We are consequently overly confident in our appraisals and fail to make sufficient provision for ongoing learning.

Appendix E

Appendix E – Benefits Management Skills and Competencies Log

In the following log, skills/competencies are rated as *General Awareness (GA)*, *Medium-level Knowledge (MLK)* or *Practical Expertise (PE)*. The individual's current skills/competency level and the target level of the specific role should be identified – along with development strategies to close any identified gaps. Note: the ideal skill/ competency level will depend on the individual's role and career aspirations, i.e. *PE* is not necessary in all areas or for all participants engaged in benefits management. If benefits management represents a substantial part of someone's duties, that person will require at least *GA* in most, if not all, areas and should aim to acquire *MLK* within a relatively short period. *PE* is likely to take longer, as it will depend on extensive practical experience across the areas identified. The assessment should be updated on at least an annual basis – to assess the impact of experience and training on the development of skills and competencies, and to inform the training and development plan of team members.

The Team Leader may also use these assessments to:

a. Ensure an appropriate spread and depth of skills across the team and across all areas.

b. Develop target profiles for each role to assist in job planning, recruitment and career development.

Areas of skill and competency	Current skill/competency level (GA/MLK/PE*)	Target skill/competency level (GA/MLK/PE*)	Strategies to close skills gaps		
			Formal training	Practical/work-based experience	Other – reading, CoI membership etc.
Benefits management context					
Driver-based analysis to articulate strategic objectives in measurable terms.					
Designing benefits-management governance arrangements and the respective roles of: Portfolio Direction Group; Portfolio Director; Portfolio Progress Group; Portfolio Benefits Manager; Senior Responsible Owner (SRO); Programme Manager; Benefits Managers; Business Change Manager; and Benefit Owners.					
Designing a strategy to implement more effective benefits management, including effective, ongoing participative stakeholder engagement.					
Undertaking benefits-management maturity and health-check assessments.					
Undertaking assessment of benefits management impact.					
Benefits management practice 1 – Identify & Quantify					
Facilitating benefits workshops.					
Benefits mapping.					
Customer insight.					
Baselining current performance.					
Preparing accurate and reliable benefits forecasts utilizing both 'inside'- and 'outside'-view approaches.					

Areas of skill and competency	Current skill/competency level (GA/MLK/PE*)	Target skill/competency level (GA/MLK/PE*)	Strategies to close skills gaps		
			Formal training	Practical/work-based experience	Other – reading, CoI membership etc.
Benefits management practice 2 – Value & Appraise					
Valuing cashable efficiency benefits.					
Valuing non-cashable efficiency benefits.					
Valuing non-financial benefits.					
Application of cost-benefit analysis.					
Application of cost-effectiveness analysis.					
Application of real options analysis.					
Application of multi-criteria analysis.					
Application of value management techniques.					
Benefits management practice 3 – Plan					
Benefits validation.					
Benefits prioritization.					
Managing pre-transition activity.					
Selecting appropriate benefits measures.					
Designing and applying a framework for benefits risk management.					
Designing and applying a framework for benefits opportunity management.					
Planning stakeholder engagement strategies.					
Preparing a Benefits Management Strategy.					
Preparing a Benefits Realization Plan.					
Preparing Benefit Profiles.					

Table continues

Areas of skill and competency	Current skill/competency level (GA/MLK/PE*)	Target skill/competency level (GA/MLK/PE*)	Strategies to close skills gaps		
			Formal training	Practical/work-based experience	Other – reading, CoI membership etc.
Benefits management practice 4 – Realize					
Transition management.					
Tracking and reporting benefits realization, including applying the techniques of 'management by exception', 'one version of the truth' and 'clear line of sight' reporting.					
Designing and conducting staff, customer and management surveys.					
Designing and applying strategies to identify emergent benefits.					
Designing and applying strategies to mitigate dis-benefits.					
Designing and applying strategies to engage stakeholders in benefits realization by winning hearts and minds. This includes: designing measures that engage, and narrative leadership.					
Benefits management practice 5 – Review					
Participating in benefits reviews at start gate.					
Participating in a pre-mortem.					
Participating in benefits reviews for 'in flight' initiatives.					
Participating in post-implementation reviews.					
Developing reference class data.					

Areas of skill and competency	Current skill/competency level (GA/MLK/PE*)	Target skill/competency level (GA/MLK/PE*)	Strategies to close skills gaps		
			Formal training	Practical/work-based experience	Other – reading, CoI membership etc.
Portfolio-based benefits management					
Preparation of, and testing for adherence to, benefits eligibility rules.					
Preparation of a portfolio-level Benefits Realization Plan.					
Review of benefits at stage/phase gates and applying the technique of 'staged release of funding'.					
Managing benefits post-initiative closure.					
Monitoring benefits realization, including via a Portfolio Dashboard Report.					
Participating in post-investment reviews.					
Preparation of a Benefits Management Framework.					

Appendix F

Appendix F – Benefits Logic Map for Benefits Management

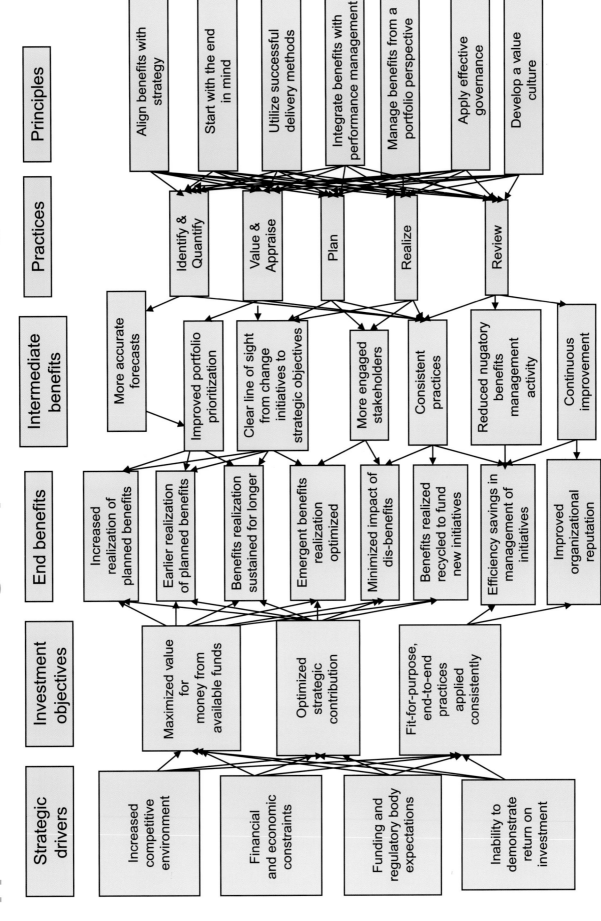

Principles
- Align benefits with strategy
- Start with the end in mind
- Utilize successful delivery methods
- Integrate benefits with performance management
- Manage benefits from a portfolio perspective
- Apply effective governance
- Develop a value culture

Practices
- Identify & Quantify
- Value & Appraise
- Plan
- Realize
- Review

Intermediate benefits
- More accurate forecasts
- Improved portfolio prioritization
- Clear line of sight from change initiatives to strategic objectives
- More engaged stakeholders
- Consistent practices
- Reduced nugatory benefits management activity
- Continuous improvement

End benefits
- Increased realization of planned benefits
- Earlier realization of planned benefits
- Benefits realization sustained for longer
- Emergent benefits realization optimized
- Minimized impact of dis-benefits
- Benefits realized recycled to fund new initiatives
- Efficiency savings in management of initiatives
- Improved organizational reputation

Investment objectives
- Maximized value for money from available funds
- Optimized strategic contribution
- Fit-for-purpose, end-to-end practices applied consistently

Strategic drivers
- Increased competitive environment
- Financial and economic constraints
- Funding and regulatory body expectations
- Inability to demonstrate return on investment

Appendix G

Appendix G – OGC Gateway Reviews – Coverage of Benefits and Benefits Management

Review	Focus and purpose	Documentation	Areas to probe including	Evidence expected including
Gateway 0: Strategic assessment	This review focuses on the programme or project business justification. Purposes include – ensure that the project or programme is supported by users and stakeholders and contributes to the organization's business strategy.	Project or Programme Brief including a high-level description of the benefits, the key drivers for the project/programme and how it will contribute to the business strategy.	Are the required skills and capabilities for this programme/project available?	Evidence that the organization has access to the skills and capabilities it needs to achieve the desired outcomes from business change.
			Is there an understanding of the business needs?	An outline of the required outputs/outcomes.
Gateway 1: Business justification	This review focuses on the project's business justification. Purposes include – confirm that the Business Case is robust: that is, in principle it meets the business need and is likely to achieve value for money; establish that the project is likely to deliver its business goals and that it supports wider business change, where applicable.	The Strategic Outline Case.	Is there a clear and agreed understanding of the business goals and how the project will achieve these?	A strategy for achieving business benefits defined and agreed with the stakeholders.
			Is the high-level business case (Strategic Outline Case) complete?	The preferred option is likely to offer value for money.
			Have the risks for the preferred option been fully assessed?	Assessment of risks, costs and benefits to demonstrate appropriate balance of risk and reward in the preferred option.

Table continues

Review	Focus and purpose	Documentation	Areas to probe including	Evidence expected including
Gateway 2: Procurement strategy	This review assesses the project's viability, its potential for success and whether the project is ready to invite proposals or tenders from the market. Purposes include – confirm the Outline Business Case now the project is fully defined.	Outline Business Case – does it demonstrate contribution to business strategy? An initial plan for realizing the benefits.	Are the benefits to be delivered by the project understood and agreed with stakeholders? Is there an initial plan for realizing benefits?	Plan for realizing benefits, showing costs offset by improved quality of service and/or savings over the project's expected life.
		Specification of the project's expected outputs and outcomes	Strategic fit: Does the Business Case continue to demonstrate business need and contribution to the business strategy?	Continued confirmation that the project will meet business need (including confirmation that priorities remain unchanged where any external factors might have an effect).
			Value for money	Updated Business Case on the basis of the full project definition, market assessment and initial benefits plan. Projects that are not designed to achieve a financial return should include comparisons with similar successful projects to assess the potential to achieve value for money and to set targets.

Review	Focus and purpose	Documentation	Areas to probe including	Evidence expected including
Gateway 3: Investment decision	This review confirms that the recommended investment decision is appropriate before the contract is placed. Purposes include – confirm the Full Business Case and benefits plan now that the bid information has been confirmed.	Full Business Case, Benefits Management Strategy, benefits management plans and responsibilities for delivery.	Has the proposed solution affected the expectations of business benefits?	Updated plan for benefit realization and Benefit Profiles.
			Has the most appropriate option been selected?	Cost/benefit/risk analysis against final bid information and results of evaluation, including sensitivity analysis.
			Is there an agreed Benefits Realization Plan?	Benefits Management Strategy and plans, including: ▪ Critical success factors. ▪ Individuals responsible for delivering and harvesting benefits identified. ▪ Agreed process for measuring benefit. Post-implementation review plan identifies review points and benefits to be assessed; payment mechanisms linked to benefits realization, where appropriate.
			Are the long-term contract, administration plan and benefit measurement process complete?	Key measures of benefit agreed.

Table continues

Review	Focus and purpose	Documentation	Areas to probe including	Evidence expected including
Gateway 4: Readiness for service.	This review focuses on: whether the solution is robust before delivery; how ready the organization is to implement the business changes that occur before and after delivery; and whether there is a basis for evaluating ongoing performance.	Updated Business Case and plans for benefits realization which reflect the effect of any requirements changes.	Does the project still meet the needs and objectives of the business, users, government and department?	Project Board endorsement of updated Business Case and benefits plans.
			Are there any changes between award of contract and completing of transition/testing that affect the business change programme?	Updated Business Case and benefit plan for the business change.
	Purposes include – check that the Business Case is still valid; that the original projected business benefit is likely to be achieved; and that lessons for future projects are identified and recorded.	Lessons learned during the project (if the project ends at implementation). Benefits Management Plan.	Is the organization ready for business change?	Agreed plans for business preparation, transition and operational phases.
			Is the Business Case still valid?	Likely to deliver value for money.
			Is the client ready to adopt new ways of working, where applicable?	New business processes have been thoroughly worked out, tested and are ready to go 'live'.
				Information and support is available.
				Where applicable, members of the public as end-users are aware of the new service and can find out more if they want.
			Is there a process to measure benefits?	Performance-enhancement process agreed with service provider and documented in contract before award.
				Means of measuring performance agreed with service provider.
			Are there procedures for long-term success?	Detailed plans, roles, responsibilities and organization in place for benefits management.
			Is there a process for post-implementation reviews?	Plan for post-implementation reviews endorsed by supplier and internal and external parties.

Review	Focus and purpose	Documentation	Areas to probe including	Evidence expected including
Gateway 5: Operations review and benefits realization	This review focuses on ensuring that the project delivers the benefits and value for money identified in the Business Case and benefits plans. Purposes include – assess whether the Business Case justification for the project at Gateway Review 3 was realistic; assess whether the anticipated benefits at this stage are actually being delivered.	An assessment of the benefits delivered to date and expectations for the future.	Have the business benefits been realized as set out in the Business Case? Did the organization achieve more? What is the scope for improved value for money? Has the department benchmarked its contract-related processes by comparing with other equivalent organizations? Does the organization have a well-defined, implemented and effective process for embedding improvements based on the lessons learned from the project?	Findings from post-implementation review/post-project review, including whole-life value targets achieved. Updated business and benefits capture plans compared with Gateway Reviews 3 and 4. Assessment of benefits in current operating regime using the benefits-measurement basis defined at Gateway 4. Anticipated future benefits. Details of efficiency gains expected and achieved. Benchmarking assessments of processes such as: investment decisions/project justification; and benefits management. A mechanism for capturing and recording the initial data; internal evaluation of lessons learned; mechanisms and policy for making information available within and outside the organization; a process for feeding back to departmental project teams; feedback into knowledge network; direct feedback to Gateway team; participation in knowledge-sharing forums sponsored by OGC and others.

Appendix H

Appendix H – P3M3 Benefits Management Assessment

Portfolio Level

PfM3 – benefits management – level 1	PfM3 – benefits management – level 2	PfM3 – benefits management – level 3	PfM3 – benefits management – level 4	PfM3 – benefits management – level 5
Description	**Description**	**Description**	**Description**	**Description**
There is some recognition that initiatives may exist within the organizational and divisional portfolio to enable the achievement of benefits for the organization. However, there is no defined benefits realization process.	The development of the investment cycle will increase the awareness of the importance of identifying benefits and subsequently tracking whether they have been realized. However, the realization of benefits is still likely to be patchy, inconsistent and unmonitored.	There is a centrally managed framework used for defining and tracking the realization of portfolio-level benefits across the business operations.	The benefits realization and management process is well established, measurable and is integrated into how the organization manages itself.	Benefits realization is integral to the development of business strategy decision-making. There is evidence of continual improvement.

Table continues

Table continued

PfM3 – benefits management – level 1	PfM3 – benefits management – level 2	PfM3 – benefits management – level 3	PfM3 – benefits management – level 4	PfM3 – benefits management – level 5
Specific attributes	**Specific attributes**	**Specific attributes**	**Specific attributes**	**Specific attributes**
1. Initiatives may identify some business benefit generally.	1. Evidence of individuals or local functions using a process for defining business benefits, but little formal benefits tracking, management or ownership.	1. Explicit statements on how benefits enabled by initiatives actually contribute to business value and strategic objectives.	1. Benefits realization and management process well established across all initiatives, with outputs and benefits actively measured, managed and owned, and an identified link between outcomes and the organizational performance framework.	1. Benefits realization and management process exists and is embedded across the organization, with benefits realization explicitly aligned to organizational performance framework and outcomes.
2. Any benefits identified tend to be subjective rather than objective.	2. Some initiatives will be expected to identify benefits and how to achieve them, but this is deployed inconsistently.	2. Clear organizational policies relating to benefits management deployed through initiatives (e.g. programme benefits management strategies).	2. Clear accountability for benefits realization is defined within portfolio roles.	2. Measurement of benefits realized informs the organization's strategic objectives and priorities, enabling adjustments to strategy where necessary.
3. May be some statements on the purpose of some initiatives but not providing a clear view of what success will look like.	3. Likely to be overlap and double counting of benefits between initiatives, with a poorly defined process to identify these.	3. Business or service areas actively engaged in defining and realizing benefits.	3. There is a portfolio of strategic benefits that the portfolio manages through prioritization of initiatives.	3. Benefits realization and management process is continually improved based on lessons learned and process metrics.
	4. Some alignment of identified benefits to the organizational objectives, but likely to be unquantified and patchy.	4. May be an organizational design authority with responsibility for benefits across portfolio.	4. Dependencies between benefits identified and managed.	4. Externally imposed organizational delivery targets integrated into benefits realization and management process.
		5. Benefits are owned and the performance management process ensures their realization; ownership may be cascaded but with a clear trail of accountability for benefits realization.	5. Business areas performance-managed to deliver benefits.	
		6. Strategic benefits fully documented with clear links between initiatives and business change activities.	6. Performance metrics tracked across the business to measure improvements against baselines and targets.	
		7. Changes to individual initiatives are assessed for impact on benefits realization.	7. Lessons from benefits realization performance embedded into expectations from initiatives.	
		8. Defined process for identifying and realizing opportunities.	8. Benefits realization integrated into organizational performance management framework.	
		9. Process in place for validating the realization of benefits and refining targets.	9. Benefits measurement tracks positive and negative effects on the business against a range of operational measures.	
		10. Benefits realization objectives linked to operational business plans.		

Generic attributes

1. Training provision is uncoordinated, with little or no knowledge sharing.

2. Key individuals lack experience.

3. No standard roles, and responsibilities are not defined or are generic.

4. Some information available but is outdated, unstructured and dispersed.

5. Limited, if any, formal checking or review.

6. Plans, if any, are conceptual or merely sequences of events with rough timescales.

7. Planning, if any, likely to be an initial activity with little maintenance of ownership or tracking.

Generic attributes

1. Localized information structures, with some information sharing between teams.

2. Focus on documentation during start-up and definition, but not maintained over initiative's life cycle.

3. Limited localized information controls, with no formal release management arrangements.

4. Local reviews, with some corrective actions undertaken within the group.

5. Generic training may be provided in key concepts, and there may be individuals undertaking qualification training.

6. Local sharing of knowledge may exist but mostly ad hoc.

7. Key individuals may have practical delivery experience and track record.

8. Roles, responsibilities and competencies defined in some areas but not consistently across the organization.

9. Plans exist but are not underpinned by consistent development methodology, yet may still be effective locally.

10. Planning seen as activity tracking rather than proactive/forecasting.

11. Estimation is more 'guesstimation' and does not use standard techniques.

Generic attributes

1. Information has a refresh cycle or is regularly accessed.

2. Organization-wide information standards on confidentiality, availability and integrity.

3. Formal information release management procedures.

4. Independent reviews take place.

5. Scrutiny largely for compliance reasons, identifying failures rather than opportunities for improvement.

6. Plans developed to a central and consistent standard that is output- or goal-based.

7. Plan development takes into account a range of relevant factors.

8. Evidence of effective estimating techniques.

9. Dependencies are identified, tracked and managed effectively.

10. Training is focused on the organization's approaches and raising competence of individuals in specific roles.

11. Forums exist for sharing organizational experience to improve individual and organizational performance.

12. Centrally managed role definitions and sets of competencies defined and used to support appointments.

Generic attributes

1. Information is current and extensively referenced for better decision-making.

2. Trend analysis and measurement undertaken on performance information to identify improvement opportunities.

3. Knowledge management is a central function and is used to help improve performance and planning.

4. Reviews focus on opportunities to improve as well as compliance.

5. Plans kept up to date, with the application of sophisticated planning techniques and recognition of interdependencies.

6. Extensive training is provided, focusing on personal development and performance improvement.

7. Evidence of interventions to avoid conflicts and take advantage of opportunities.

8. Mentoring and individual development is used to improve organizational performance.

9. Succession plans exist for key roles.

Generic attributes

1. Information is valued, with continual maintenance and reference.

2. Evidence of extensive intelligence-gathering processes, with information disseminated through a variety of channels.

3. Review and improvement is continual and proactive, with lessons being shared openly.

4. Planning inherent in decision-making process, with adjustments and implications managed and deployed.

5. Active management of interdependencies between initiative plans and other business plans.

6. Estimations are accurate and used effectively to ensure delivery.

7. High levels of competence embedded in all roles and seen as part of career paths.

8. Knowledge transfer is an inherent behaviour within the organization.

9. Skills embedded into organizational leadership and management development programmes.

Programme Level

PgM3 – benefits management – level 1	PgM3 – benefits management – level 2	PgM3 – benefits management – level 3	PgM3 – benefits management – level 4	PgM3 – benefits management – level 5
Description There is some recognition that the concept of benefits can be differentiated from programme outcomes.	**Description** Benefits are recognized as an element within programme business cases. There may be some documentation regarding who is responsible for particular benefits and their realization, but this is unlikely to be followed through or consistent.	**Description** There is a centrally managed and consistent framework for defining and tracking the realization of benefits arising from programme outcomes.	**Description** Benefits management is embedded within the programme management approach and there is a focus on delivery of business performance from programme outcomes. Programme performance metrics are collected and analysed.	**Description** Benefits management is embedded within the organizational approach to strategic change and is assessed as part of the development of organizational strategies. Business performance metrics are linked to, and underpin, the recognition of benefits realization. There is evidence of continual improvement.
Specific attributes 1. No consolidation of project benefits. 2. Benefits defined in terms of outputs and results rather than measurable performance improvement. 3. Benefits management has no common understanding or definitions, but may be elements of a common vocabulary. 4. Descriptions of benefits are brief and may be simply bullet point lists. 5. No evidence of specific ownership of actions associated with benefits realization.	**Specific attributes** 1. Benefits described and defined but not consistently across the organization's programmes or within individual programmes. 2. Benefits, where they exist, largely regarded as project orientated and will vary in different areas. 3. Evidence of recognition of need to track benefits beyond 'go live' activities in some areas. 4. Some localized ownership of benefits. 5. Measurement criteria for benefits may exist locally, but not consistently applied. 6. Different areas manage and account for benefits in different ways. 7. Communities of practitioners may exist and occasionally collaborate.	**Specific attributes** 1. Centrally defined benefits measurement and assessment mechanisms in place and used by all programmes. 2. Centrally managed set of processes, tools and templates used for benefits management activities. 3. Programme life cycle includes realization of benefits beyond the delivery of capability by individual projects. 4. Allocation of ownership for business activities required to release the benefits (broader than ownership of benefits profiles). 5. Full description of each benefit and detailed explanations of how they will be achieved in structured documentation with sign-offs. 6. Benefit reviews scheduled for all programmes.	**Specific attributes** 1. Processes in place to identify and resolve double counting of benefits. 2. Executive Board receives regular information on benefits realization progress. 3. Use of industry techniques to assess and measure progress (e.g. Balanced Scorecard). 4. Business performance measured against historic trends, and impact of programmes and projects on business performance fully understood. 5. Benefits defined at programme level, cascaded down to projects and tracked. 6. Benefits categorized, with a mix of long and short-term benefits being pursued by programmes; recognition of differences between strategic benefits applicable to all programmes and those specific to individual programmes or projects.	**Specific attributes** 1. Clear links between strategic decision-making processes and benefits realization, with management of these links embedded. 2. Strategic objectives have defined beneficial impacts that are clear and aligned with programme priorities. 3. Development and use of innovative techniques based on experience. 4. Management of opportunities to enhance benefits realization potential embedded within the organization. 5. Strategic priorities seen to affect benefit realization measures and priorities.

7. Benefits reviewed by all Programme Boards as a standard activity. 8. Evidence of common approach to defining relationship between project deliverables, achievement of outcomes and realization of benefits. 9. Reporting of key performance indicators relating directly to benefits. 10. Benefits identified at outset of programmes and underpinning information development.	7. Benefit reviews undertaken regularly and action taken to leverage opportunities. 8. 'Dis-benefits' identified and actively managed as part of benefits management processes. 9. Various benefit measures designed and applied, depending on circumstances. 10. Ownership of benefits management processes, with evidence of active improvement and alignment. 11. Flexibility in deployment of benefits management processes. 12. Benefits management well established, with proven track record in managing and realizing benefits across the organization. 13. Knowledge has been gained and is stored and utilized to manage benefits across the organization.

Table continues

Table continued

PgM3 – benefits management – level 1	PgM3 – benefits management – level 2	PgM3 – benefits management – level 3	PgM3 – benefits management – level 4	PgM3 – benefits management – level 5
Generic attributes	**Generic attributes**	**Generic attributes**	**Generic attributes**	**Generic attributes**
1. Training provision is uncoordinated, with little or no knowledge sharing.	1. Localized information structures, with some information sharing between teams.	1. Information has a refresh cycle or is regularly accessed.	1. Information is current and extensively referenced for better decision-making.	1. Information is valued, with continual maintenance and reference.
2. Key individuals lack experience.	2. Focus on documentation during start-up and definition, but not maintained over initiative's life cycle.	2. Organization-wide information standards on confidentiality, availability and integrity.	2. Trend analysis and measurement undertaken on performance information to identify improvement opportunities.	2. Evidence of extensive intelligence-gathering processes, with information disseminated through a variety of channels.
3. No standard roles, and responsibilities are not defined or are generic.	3. Limited localized information controls, with no formal release management arrangements.	3. Formal information release management procedures.	3. Knowledge management is a central function and is used to help improve performance and planning.	3. Review and improvement is continual and proactive, with lessons being shared openly.
4. Some information available but is outdated, unstructured and dispersed.	4. Local reviews, with some corrective actions undertaken within the group.	4. Independent reviews take place.	4. Reviews focus on opportunities to improve as well as compliance.	4. Planning inherent in decision-making process, with adjustments and implications managed and deployed.
5. Limited, if any, formal checking or review.	5. Generic training may be provided in key concepts, and there may be individuals undertaking qualification training.	5. Scrutiny largely for compliance reasons, identifying failures rather than opportunities for improvement.	5. Plans kept up to date, with the application of sophisticated planning techniques and recognition of interdependencies.	5. Active management of interdependencies between initiative plans and other business plans.
6. Plans, if any, are conceptual or merely sequences of events with rough timescales.	6. Local sharing of knowledge may exist but mostly ad hoc.	6. Plans developed to a central and consistent standard that is output- or goal-based.	6. Extensive training is provided, focusing on personal development and performance improvement.	6. Estimations are accurate and used effectively to ensure delivery.
7. Planning, if any, likely to be an initial activity with little maintenance of ownership or tracking.	7. Key individuals may have practical delivery experience and track record.	7. Plan development takes into account a range of relevant factors.	7. Evidence of interventions to avoid conflicts and take advantage of opportunities.	7. High levels of competence embedded in all roles and seen as part of career paths.
	8. Roles, responsibilities and competencies defined in some areas but not consistently across the organization.	8. Evidence of effective estimating techniques.	8. Mentoring and individual development is used to improve organizational performance.	8. Knowledge transfer is an inherent behaviour within the organization.
	9. Plans exist but are not underpinned by consistent development methodology, yet may still be effective locally.	9. Dependencies are identified, tracked and managed effectively.	9. Succession plans exist for key roles.	9. Skills embedded into organizational leadership and management development programmes.
	10. Planning seen as activity tracking rather than proactive/forecasting.	10. Training is focused on the organization's approaches and raising competence of individuals in specific roles.		
	11. Estimation is more 'guesstimation' and does not use standard techniques.	11. Forums exist for sharing organizational experience to improve individual and organizational performance.		
		12. Centrally managed role definitions and sets of competencies defined and used to support appointments.		

Project Level

PjM3 – benefits management – level 1	PjM3 – benefits management – level 2	PjM3 – benefits management – level 3	PjM3 – benefits management – level 4	PjM3 – benefits management – level 5
Description	**Description**	**Description**	**Description**	**Description**
There is some recognition that the concept of benefits can be differentiated from project outputs.	Benefits are recognized as an element within project business cases. There may be some documentation regarding who is responsible for particular benefits and their realization, but this is unlikely to be followed through or consistent.	There is a centrally managed and consistent framework for defining and tracking the realization of benefits from project outputs.	Benefits management is embedded within the project management approach and there is a focus on delivery of business performance from project outputs. Project performance metrics are collected and analysed.	Benefits management is embedded within the organizational approach to change and is assessed as part of the development of organizational strategy. Business performance metrics are linked to, and underpin, the recognition of benefits realization. There is evidence of continual improvement.

Table continues

PjM3 – benefits management – level 1	PjM3 – benefits management – level 2	PjM3 – benefits management – level 3	PjM3 – benefits management – level 4	PjM3 – benefits management – level 5
Specific attributes	**Specific attributes**	**Specific attributes**	**Specific attributes**	**Specific attributes**
1. Requirements defined in terms of features and results rather than measurable performance improvement.	1. Evidence in some projects of understanding of differences between product features, outputs and outcomes.	1. Measures of project success are becoming defined and explicit.	1. Processes in place to identify and resolve double counting of benefits.	1. Clear links between strategic decision-making and benefits realization.
2. Benefits seen as justification rather than core element of project's delivery.	2. Responsibility for benefits may be assigned within some project business cases but outside project team.	2. Common approach and processes that ensure consistency across all projects in relation to benefits measurement and realization.	2. Benefits defined at programme level and may be cascaded down to projects.	2. Evidence of development and innovation of techniques based on experience of realizing a variety of benefits in several different environments.
3. Little or no recognition of how benefits are to be managed and realized.	3. Role of sponsor or project executive in benefits management and realization may be articulated in some projects.	3. Benefits management process described within project business case.	3. Benefit reviews undertaken regularly and action taken to leverage opportunities.	3. Active management of opportunities to enhance benefits realization.
	4. May be some benefit measurement criteria.	4. Changes to project considered against impact on benefits.	4. Complex variety of benefits measures designed and applied according to circumstances (e.g. Balanced Scorecard).	4. Decisions taken to balance benefits and 'dis-benefits' based on statistical measures.
	5. Different areas manage and account for benefits in different ways.	5. Common set of tools and templates used for benefits management activities, including their detailed description.	5. Common, performance-based benefits measurement and assessment mechanisms in place.	5. Strategic priorities affect benefit measures (e.g. changes to strategic key performance indicators are filtered down into projects).
	6. Post-project reviews focused on project activities and deliverables rather than achievement of benefits.	6. Benefits documents stored centrally and subject to change control.	6. Clear and active ownership of plans to improve performance from project outputs.	6. Post-project benefit reviews studied, trends established, and lessons learned fed back into benefits realization planning and other management activities.
		7. Detailed statements explaining how benefits will be achieved from project deliverables.	7. Processes for management of benefits realization owned, reviewed and being improved.	
		8. Benefits calculated in financial terms against centrally managed assessment criteria.	8. The organization ensures that claimed benefits are realistic and endorsed by the sponsor or project executive.	
		9. Clear responsibilities for benefits realization cited in business cases.		
		10. Post-project benefit reviews used to report formally on outcomes and benefit realization.		

Generic attributes	Generic attributes	Generic attributes	Generic attributes	Generic attributes
1. Training provision is uncoordinated, with little or no knowledge sharing.	1. Localized information structures, with some information sharing between teams.	1. Information has a refresh cycle or is regularly accessed.	1. Information is current and extensively referenced for better decision-making.	1. Information is valued, with continual maintenance and reference.
2. Key individuals lack experience.	2. Focus on documentation during start-up and definition, but not maintained over initiative's life cycle.	2. Organization-wide information standards on confidentiality, availability and integrity.	2. Trend analysis and measurement undertaken on performance information to identify improvement opportunities.	2. Evidence of extensive intelligence-gathering processes, with information disseminated through a variety of channels.
3. No standard roles, and responsibilities are not defined or are generic.	3. Limited localized information controls, with no formal release management arrangements.	3. Formal information release management procedures.	3. Knowledge management is a central function and is used to help improve performance and planning.	3. Review and improvement is continual and proactive, with lessons being shared openly.
4. Some information available but is outdated, unstructured and dispersed.	4. Local reviews, with some corrective actions undertaken within the group.	4. Independent reviews take place.	4. Reviews focus on opportunities to improve as well as compliance.	4. Planning inherent in decision-making process, with adjustments and implications managed and deployed.
5. Limited, if any, formal checking or review.	5. Generic training may be provided in key concepts, and there may be individuals undertaking qualification training.	5. Scrutiny largely for compliance reasons, identifying failures rather than opportunities.	5. Plans kept up to date, with the application of sophisticated planning techniques and recognition of interdependencies.	5. Active management of interdependencies between initiative plans and other business plans.
6. Plans, if any, are conceptual or merely sequences of events with rough timescales.	6. Local sharing of knowledge may exist but mostly ad hoc.	6. Plans developed to a central and consistent standard that is output- or goal-based.	6. Extensive training is provided, focusing on personal development and performance improvement.	6. Estimations are accurate and used effectively to ensure delivery.
7. Planning, if any, likely to be an initial activity with little maintenance of ownership or tracking.	7. Key individuals may have practical delivery experience and track record.	7. Plan development takes into account a range of relevant factors.	7. Evidence of interventions to avoid conflicts and take advantage of opportunities.	7. High levels of competence embedded in all roles and seen as part of career paths.
	8. Roles, responsibilities and competencies defined in some areas but not consistently across the organization.	8. Evidence of effective estimating techniques.	8. Mentoring and individual development is used to improve organizational performance.	8. Knowledge transfer is an inherent behaviour within the organization.
	9. Plans exist but are not underpinned by consistent development methodology, yet may still be effective locally.	9. Dependencies are identified, tracked and managed effectively.	9. Succession plans exist for key roles.	9. Skills embedded into organizational leadership and management development programmes.
	10. Planning seen as activity tracking rather than proactive/forecasting.	10. Training is focused on the organization's approaches and raising competence of individuals in specific roles.		
	11. Estimation is more 'guesstimation' and does not use standard techniques.	11. Forums exist for sharing organizational experience to improve individual and organizational performance.		
		12. Centrally managed role definitions and sets of competencies defined and used to support appointments.		

Appendix I

Appendix I – Managing Benefits Health-check Assessment

Complete the following 10 assessments for your portfolio or change initiative. Be honest and be aware of the cognitive biases discussed in Chapters 4, 5 and 9. Consider asking a range of stakeholders to complete the assessment and compare the answers, including calculating: the average score for each statement (by giving scores as follows: Always = 3, Usually = 2, Occasionally = 1, Never = 0); the total score out of 30; and the variation in assessment by different stakeholders (for example, by calculating the standard deviation for each statement and in total).

Then, if you score less than 25 – consider what actions are required (suggested potential actions are shown in the final column). If you score 25 or more – congratulations, but check: are you really optimizing benefits realization (in terms of realizing planned benefits, leveraging emergent benefits, and mitigating dis-benefits) and do you have the evidence to demonstrate this? If you really are at 25 or above, not only will you be optimizing benefits realization, but you will also have the evidence to demonstrate this.

Key benefits management statements	Always	Usually	Occasionally	Never	Suggested potential actions
1. The benefits from our change initiative(s) are clearly identified in measurable terms that demonstrate strategic contribution.					Benefits-led change ('Start with the end in mind'); driver-based analysis; benefits mapping; customer insight; start gate.
2. Benefits forecasts are robust and realizable.					Reference class forecasting; stochastic forecasting; Delphi technique; conversion ratios; sensitivity and scenario analysis; booking the benefits; pre-mortems.
3. Benefits are expressed and quantified consistently by all change initiatives so enabling reliable portfolio prioritization.					Portfolio Benefits Management Framework including benefits eligibility rules; decision conferencing.
4. Responsibilities are clearly defined for realizing each benefit and for delivering the business and enabling changes on which benefits realization is dependent.					Benefit Profile and Benefits Realization Plan; booking the benefits.
5. We don't stop at the hurdle rate of return, but instead look for all potential benefits.					The 'dog that didn't bark' test; benefits categorization framework; benefits opportunity management.
6. The investment rationale and value-for-money position is tested on a regular basis with formal recommitment to benefits realization so that there are no 'orphan' initiatives.					Stage/phase gates with 'staged release of funding'; benefits contracts.
7. Measures used provide a 'rich picture' on benefits realization and rather than encouraging perverse incentives they engage the user in exceeding forecast.					Suite of leading and lagging measures, proxy indicators, evidence events, case studies, surveys and stories.
8. Benefits realization is monitored on an active basis with prompt corrective action being taken to address emerging shortfalls and to mitigate known and emergent dis-benefits.					Benefits Dashboard reporting; 'management by exception'; 'one version of the truth'; 'clear line of sight' reporting.
9. Effective action is taken to identify and leverage emergent benefits.					Ongoing participative stakeholder engagement; benefits opportunity management.
10. Checks are undertaken to assess whether the performance matched the promise and identify and apply lessons learned.					Formal post-implementation and post-investment reviews; deep dive reviews.

Glossary

Glossary[2]

Accountable

Personally answerable for an activity. Accountability cannot be delegated, unlike responsibility.

Accounting rate of return

The average annual accounting profit divided by the average investment cost.

Additionality

The benefits from an initiative that would not have been realized if the initiative had not been undertaken.

Aggregated risk

The overall level of risk to the portfolio when all the risks are viewed as a totality rather than individually. This could include the outputs of particular scenarios or risk combinations.

APMG-International

The accreditation body and examination institute for all 'Best Management Practice' qualifications.

Appraisal

Evaluation of options or an initiative prior to investment.

As-is state

The current operating structure and performance of the parts of the business which will be impacted by a programme.

Assumption

A statement that is taken as being true for the purposes of planning, but which could change later. An assumption is made where some facts are not yet known. There is a risk that assumptions are not correct.

Assurance

All the systematic actions necessary to provide confidence that the target (system, process, organization, programme, project, outcome, benefit, capability, product output, deliverable) is appropriate. Appropriateness might be defined subjectively or objectively in different circumstances. The implication is that assurance will have a level of independence from that which is being assured.

ATO

An Accredited Training Organization, assessed and accredited by APMG-International to provide training courses and examinations.

Baseline

A reference level against which an entity is monitored and controlled.

Behavioural economics/finance

The study of the effects of psychology on investment decision-making and financial management.

Benefit

The measurable improvement resulting from an outcome perceived as an advantage by one or more stakeholders, which contributes towards one or more organizational objective(s).

Benefit Owner

A person responsible for the realization of a benefit.

Benefit Profile

Used to define each benefit (and dis-benefit) and provide a detailed understanding of what will be involved and how the benefit will be realized.

Benefits eligibility rules

The set of rules about what benefits can and can't be claimed, and how they should be categorized, quantified and valued.

---

2 Definitions in italics are sourced from existing Cabinet Office *'Best Management Practice'* or other 'OGC Portfolio Product' publications. Where other definitions are sourced from another official text, the source is stated. Definitions not in italics and with no source identified are specific to this Guide.

Benefits management

The identification, definition, tracking, realization and optimization of benefits at initiative and portfolio level.

Benefits Management Cycle

The cycle that encompasses the following five practices: Identify & Quantify; Value & Appraise; Plan; Realize; and Review.

Benefits Management Framework (portfolio)

The document that provides all stakeholders with a single, authoritative and up-to-date source of advice on the portfolio management practices adopted by the organization, and its governance arrangements.

Benefits Management Strategy

Defines the approach to realizing benefits and the framework within which benefits realization will be achieved.

Benefits Map

A network of benefits, usually linked to one or more of the bounding investment objectives, which maps all the cause and effect relationships.

Benefits realization management

The process of organizing and managing, so that potential benefits, arising from investment in change, are actually achieved. It is a continuous process running through the whole change lifecycle and should be the central theme of any change initiative, whether applied to the whole portfolio, a programme or a project.

Benefits Realization Plan (portfolio)

The document that summarizes the benefits forecast to be realized in the year ahead and so provides a clear view of the planned returns from the organization's accumulated investment in change. It also provides the baseline against which to assess the benefits actually realized.

Benefits Realization Plan (programme)

The document used to track realization of benefits across the programme and set review controls.

Benefits Register

Summary document that contains key information from the benefit profiles.

Best Management Practice

A defined and proven method of managing events effectively.

Bounding objectives

The set of end objectives (usually three or four) defining the boundary of a programme or project.

Business as usual (BAU)

The way the business normally achieves its objectives.

Business Case

The justification for an organizational activity (strategic, programme, project, operational) which typically contains costs, benefits, risks and timescales and against which continuing viability is tested.

Business change authority

An individual who represents a group of Business Change Managers, similar to a senior BCM or Business Change Sponsor.

Business change lifecycle

A generic name used to represent any organizational process or framework which helps to guide the delivery of programmes and projects using a collection of repeatable processes and decision points.

Business Change Manager (BCM)

The role responsible for benefits management, from identification through to realization, and for ensuring that the implementation and embedding of the new capabilities are delivered by the projects. Typically allocated to more than one individual and also known as 'Change Agent'.

Business change team

A group of specialists appointed to support a Business Change Manager in the business change management aspects of benefits realization.

Business model

A cause and effect model which describes the assumptions about how the organization creates and delivers value to customers or citizens.

Capability

The completed set of project outputs required to deliver an outcome; this exists prior to transition. It is a service, function or operation that enables the organization to exploit opportunities.

Capital Asset Pricing Model (CAPM)

A model that estimates the required return on an investment as the risk-free rate of return plus a premium reflecting the extent to which that investment's return varies in relation to the market as a whole.

Centre of excellence (CoE)

A coordinating function ensuring that change initiatives are delivered consistently and well, through standard processes and competent staff. It may provide standards, consistency of methods and processes, knowledge management, assurance and training. It may also provide strategic oversight, scrutiny and challenge across an organization's portfolio of programmes and projects. It may be a function within the wider scope of a Portfolio Office. This function provides a focal point for driving the implementation of improvements to increase the organization's capability and capacity in programme and project delivery.

Champion-challenger model

A technique whereby everyone is expected to comply with the defined portfolio processes (the current 'champion') but anyone can recommend a change (a 'challenger'). Once adopted, the 'challenger' becomes the new 'champion' process. Such challengers should be encouraged as a way of ensuring engagement across the organization, and the number of submissions received should be monitored on a regular basis.

Change Manager

Reports to the Business Change Manager (BCM) and may operate at a project level to support benefits realization, namely focus on realization of a particular benefit.

Clear line of sight

A technique that seeks to ensure a transparent chain from strategic intent through to benefits realization.

Coefficient of variation

The standard deviation of an initiative's returns divided by its expected value – a relative measure of risk.

Contingent valuation

Values determined by asking people how much they would be willing to pay for a good or service ('willingness to pay'), or how much they would be willing to accept to give it up ('willingness to accept').

Cost-benefit analysis

Analysis which quantifies in monetary terms as many of the costs and benefits of a proposal as feasible, including items for which the market does not provide a satisfactory measure of economic value. Source: HM Treasury *Green Book.*

Cost-effectiveness analysis

Analysis that compares the cost of alternative ways of producing the same or similar outputs. Source: HM Treasury *Green Book.*

Cross-organizational programme

A programme requiring the committed involvement of more than one organization to achieve the desired outcomes. Also referred to as a 'cross-cutting' programme.

Customer insight

Defined by the Government Communication Network's Engage Programme as: *"A deep 'truth' about the customer based on their behaviour, experiences, beliefs, needs or desires, that is relevant to the task or issue and 'rings bells' with target people."*

Deadweight

Benefits that would have been realized in any case, even if the initiative had not been undertaken.

Decision-conferencing

A technique whereby managers consider and debate in a facilitated workshop the relative weightings to attach to the organization's strategic objectives; the criteria to be used to assess strategic contribution in each case; and the scores to allocate to individual initiatives. In this way the portfolio governance body comes to a collective decision on the composition of the portfolio. This has been found to be very effective in terms of optimizing portfolio returns, and also results in enhanced commitment to the portfolio and to the portfolio management processes.

Delphi technique

Where forecasts are derived from a panel of subject-matter experts who provide their estimates anonymously and then revise them in the light of the estimates of their peers.

Development pipeline

The initiatives under development, concept and feasibility testing, prior to formal inclusion in the portfolio as 'live' programmes and projects.

Dis-benefit

A measurable decline resulting from an outcome perceived as negative by one or more stakeholders, which reduces one or more organizational objective(s).

Discounted cash flow (DCF)

Discounting forecast cash flows to determine the present value of an initiative. Undertaken by applying a discount factor to the cash flows reflecting the organization's cost of capital (adjusted for any initiative-specific risks).

Discounting

Converting future costs or benefits to present values using a discount rate.

Dog that didn't bark test

Assessing not only the identified benefits, but also asking whether there are any additional benefits that haven't been included. From the Sherlock Holmes story 'Silver Blaze' where the crucial evidence was that the dog didn't bark. This is referred to by Kahneman (2011a) as 'WYSIATI' ('What You See Is All There Is'). The risk is that we only consider the benefits included in the Business Case rather than also asking what other benefits may be possible.

Double counting

Where the same benefits are claimed by, and used to justify, more than one initiative.

Economic benefits/value

Benefits that have a monetary value attributed to them, but where the underlying benefit relates to time savings or some performance improvement

– where there may be some financial impact but the benefit is itself non-financial. Also see 'financial/benefits value'.

Emergent benefits

Benefits that emerge during the design, development, deployment and application of the new ways of working, rather than being identified at the start of the initiative.

Enabler

Something that can be developed/built/acquired, normally from outside the environment in which it will be embedded and where the benefits will be realized.

End benefit

One of a set of benefits which collectively are equivalent to a bounding objective.

Evaluation

Assessment undertaken after implementation to assess whether the anticipated outcomes and benefits were realized and what lessons and insights can be applied to future change initiatives.

Expected value

Expected value is calculated by multiplying the average impact by the probability percentage.

Financial benefits/value

Benefits where there is a direct (cashable) impact on cash inflows (revenue generated) or outflows (costs saved). Also see 'Economic/benefits value'.

Formative evaluation

An ex-post evaluation in which the focus is on learning to improve performance. It is essentially forward-looking as opposed to summative evaluation which compares actual performance against what was originally planned.

Generic risk

Risks that apply to benefits management across the portfolio, such as those arising from inaccurate forecasting, including non-realization of anticipated benefits.

Governance (business change)

Encompasses the structures, accountabilities and policies, standards and process for decision-making within an organization for business

change to answer the key strategic questions of
'Are we doing the right things?', 'Are we doing
them the right way?', 'Are we getting them done
well?' and 'Are we getting the benefits?'

Health check

A health check is a quality tool that provides a
snapshot of the status of a project, programme or
portfolio. The purpose of a health check is to gain
an objective assessment of how well the project,
programme or portfolio is performing relative to
its objectives and any relevant processes or
standards. A health check differs from a gated
review in that it is a tool used for assurance
purposes by the portfolio office to inform specific
actions or capability maturity development plans,
whereas a gated review is part of formal
governance arrangements.

Hurdle rate of return

The target rate of return set by an organization,
which potential investments need to achieve in
order to be considered for funding. Also used as
the discount rate to convert future cash flows into
the Net Present Value.

Initiative (change initiative)

A programme or project.

Intangible benefits

Benefits that are difficult to quantify and measure
reliably, such as improved staff morale and
decision-making. In such cases proxy indicators of
such benefits can be developed.

Intermediate or enabling benefit

Benefits which will occur between the
implementation of early changes and the
realization of the end benefits.

Internal Rate of Return (IRR)

The annual percentage return (forecast or actual)
from an initiative, at which the present value of
the total cash inflows equals the present value of
the total cash outflows.

Investment decision

The decision to proceed with a programme or
project. Also describes the entire lifecycle of a
programme or project from inception (pre-start-
up) to use (closure).

Key performance indicator

A metric (either financial or non-financial) that is
used to set and measure progress towards an
organizational objective or BAU operations.

Leadership

The ability to direct, influence and motivate
others towards a better outcome.

Management Board

Generic term used to describe either a Project
Management Board, Programme Management
Board or Portfolio Management Board, or any
combination based on the P3O context.

Management by exception

A technique by which variances from plan that
exceed a pre-set control limit are escalated for
action, for example where spends exceed budget
by 10%.

Management of value

A systematic method to define what value means
for organizations, and to communicate it clearly
to maximize value across portfolios, programmes,
projects and operations.

Managing Successful Programmes (MSP)

An OGC publication/method representing proven
programme management good practice in
successfully delivering transformational change,
drawn from the experiences of both public and
private sector organizations.

Market price or value

The price at which a good or service can be
bought or sold, which is determined by the forces
of demand and supply in a market.

Maturity level

A well-defined evolutionary plateau towards
achieving a mature process (five levels are often
cited: initial, repeatable, defined, managed and
optimizing).

Maturity model

A method of assessing organizational capability in
a given area of skill.

Measure

A quantity, derived from a set of metrics, whose
change in the desired direction would help to
confirm that the related benefit is being realized.

Modular initiatives

An initiative that is broken down into modules, each of which delivers some benefits and where the decision to cease investment does not effectively mean that all prior investment is wasted.

Monte Carlo Simulation

A technique to calculate the probability distribution of possible outcomes. Commonly applied using relevant software.

Multi-criteria analysis

A technique applied to the appraisal of options (option appraisal), an initiative (investment appraisal), or to rank initiatives (portfolio prioritization). Designed in part to address the issue of unreliable financial forecasts. It is based on assigning weights to relevant financial and non-financial criteria, and then scoring options or initiatives in terms of how well they perform against these criteria. Weighted scores are then summed, and can be used to rank options/initiatives including by means of a Portfolio Map or by dividing the total score by the cost of the option/initiative to calculate a score per £/$/€ invested.

Net Present Value (NPV)

The value of future net cash flows (inflows less outflows) discounted at the relevant cost of capital. Where the cash outflows exceed the inflows the result is the Net Present Cost or NPC.

Objective

The intended outcome or goal of a programme, project or organization.

Office of Government Commerce

OGC (former owner of '*Best Management Practice*'). Now part of the Efficiency and Reform Group in Cabinet Office, HM Government.

OGC Gateway review

A review of a delivery programme or procurement project carried out at a key decision point by a team of experienced people, independent of the project team.

One version of the truth

A technique whereby each element of portfolio progress reporting (costs, benefits, progress etc.) is derived from an agreed source managed by the Portfolio Office. Individual initiatives and other organizational functions will provide data inputs in relation to cost, benefit, delivery progress, resource requirements, dependency and risk status – and to an agreed schedule. The resulting consolidated data will be recognized as the authoritative source of information on portfolio progress used for monitoring, reporting and management decision-making.

Operations

Business as usual in an organization.

Opportunity

An uncertain event that could have a favourable impact on objectives or benefits.

Opportunity cost

The value of the next best alternative foregone.

Opportunity value benefits

The value of staff time saved where there is no immediate saving in budgets, unit costs or costs avoided. Rather the staff time saved can be redeployed to activities that would otherwise not have been undertaken. The result may be an improvement in quality, outputs and outcomes.

Optimism bias

Defined by the HM Treasury *Green Book* as '*the demonstrated systematic tendency for appraisers to be over-optimistic about key project parameters, including capital costs, operating costs, works duration and benefits delivery. To address this, adjustments should be made to the estimates of programme and project costs, benefits and works duration based on empirical data.*' Standard adjustments are included in the HM Treasury *Green Book* and on the HMT website.

Outcome

The result of change, normally affecting real-world behaviour or circumstances. Outcomes are desired when a change is conceived. Outcomes are achieved as a result of the activities undertaken to effect the change; they are the manifestation of part or all of the new state conceived in the blueprint.

Output

The tangible or intangible artefact produced, constructed or created as a result of a planned activity.

P3M3

The Portfolio, Programme and Project Management Maturity Model, which provides a framework with which organizations can assess their current performance and put in place improvement plans.

P3RM

The abbreviation for project, programme and portfolio management and risk management.

Pareto rule

Also known as the 80:20 rule, which states that 80% of gains will come from 20% of study activity.

Payback

The period of time before the cash inflows from an investment exceed the accumulated cash outflows. Can use discounted or undiscounted cash flows.

PESTLE

Acronym for 'political, economic, social, technological, legal and environmental'. A technique used generally in organizational change management to undertake an environmental scan at a strategic level.

Plan

A detailed proposal for doing or achieving something, detailing what, when, how and by whom.

Portfolio

The totality of an organization's investment (or segment thereof) in the changes required to achieve its strategic objectives.

Portfolio dashboard

A technique to represent decision support information at an amalgamated level using tabular and graphical representation such as graphs and traffic lights.

Portfolio Definition Cycle (from MoP)

One of the two continuous cycles within the portfolio management model containing portfolio management practices related to defining a portfolio, i.e. understand, categorize, prioritize, balance, and plan.

Portfolio Delivery Cycle (from MoP)

One of the two continuous cycles within the portfolio management model containing portfolio management practices related to delivering a portfolio, i.e. management control, benefits management, financial management, risk management, organizational governance, stakeholder engagement, and resource management.

Portfolio Delivery Plan

A collection of tactical information regarding the planned delivery of the portfolio based on the overarching Portfolio Strategy. The Portfolio Delivery Plan usually focuses on the forthcoming year in detail in terms of schedule, resource plans, costs, risks and benefits to be realized.

Portfolio Direction Group/ Investment Committee

The governance body where decisions about inclusion of initiatives in the portfolio are made.

Portfolio management

Portfolio management is a coordinated collection of strategic processes and decisions that together enable the most effective balance of organizational change and business as usual.

Portfolio Office

An office which is established centrally to manage the investment process, strategic alignment, prioritization and selection, progress tracking and monitoring, optimization and benefits achieved by an organization's projects and programmes on behalf of its senior management.

Portfolio, Programme and Project Offices (P3O)

The decision-enabling and support business model for all business change within an organization. This will include single or multiple physical or virtual structures, i.e. offices (permanent and/or temporary), providing a mix of central and localized functions and services, and integration with governance arrangements and the wider business such as other corporate support functions.

Portfolio Progress Group/ Change Delivery Committee

The governance body responsible for monitoring portfolio progress and resolving issues that may compromise delivery and benefits realization.

Post-implementation review

The process of determining the nature and value of benefits achieved and lessons learned from the project.

Post-investment review

An in-depth, independent review undertaken after initiative closure on behalf of the governance body that authorized the original investment.

PPM

The abbreviation for project and programme management.

PRINCE2

A method that supports some selected aspects of project management. The acronym stands for PRojects IN Controlled Environments.

Programme

A temporary, flexible organization created to coordinate, direct and oversee the implementation of a set of related projects and activities in order to deliver outcomes and benefits related to the organization's strategic objectives. A programme is likely to have a life that span s several years.

Programme management

The coordinated organization, direction and implementation of a dossier of projects and transformation activities (i.e. the programme) to achieve outcomes and realize benefits of strategic importance to the business.

Programme Manager

The role responsible for the set-up, management and delivery of a programme; typically allocated to a single individual.

Project

A temporary organization that is created for the purpose of delivering one or more business outputs according to a specified Business Case.

Project management

The planning, delegating, monitoring and control of all aspects of the project, and the motivation of all those involved, to achieve the project objectives within the expected performance targets for time, cost, quality, scope, benefits and risks.

Qualitative benefits

Benefits of a subjective or intangible nature.

Quantitative benefits

Benefits expressed in terms of a quantifiable improvement (in financial, percentage or other numerical terms) for example, costs (£/$/€) or time saved (hours/minutes).

Real option

An option based on the right to buy/sell a tangible, rather than a financial, asset. Can be used to incorporate the value of flexibility and uncertainty into investment appraisal.

Real price

Cash flows adjusted for general inflation.

Reference class forecasting

A technique where forecasts of an initiative's duration, costs and benefits are derived from what actually occurred in a reference class of similar projects.

Responsible

Used to describe the individual who has the authority and is expected to deliver a task or activity; responsibility can be delegated.

Revealed preference

Determining 'willingness to pay' or 'willingness to accept' from observed behaviour. For example, the average house price next to an airport runway, compared with a similar house elsewhere.

Risk

An uncertain event or set of events that, should it occur, will have an effect on the achievement of objectives. A risk is measured by a combination of the probability of a perceived threat or opportunity occurring and the magnitude of its impact on objectives.

Risk management

The systematic application of principles, approach and processes to the tasks of identifying and assessing risks, and then planning and implementing risk responses.

Senior Responsible Owner (SRO)

The single individual with overall responsibility for ensuring that a project or programme meets its objectives and delivers the projected benefits.

Sensitivity analysis

A technique for testing the robustness of a calculation or model by assessing the impact of varying the input, to reflect the risk that the calculation or model might not be accurate.

Sponsor

The main driving force behind a programme or project. Some organizations use the term Sponsor instead of SRO.

Stage/phase gate review

Structured reviews of a project, programme or portfolio as part of formal governance arrangements carried out at key decision points in the lifecycle to ensure that the decision to invest as per agreed Business Cases and plans remains valid.

Stakeholder

Any individual, group or organization that can affect, be affected by, or perceives itself to be affected by, an initiative (programme, project, activity, risk).

Standard deviation

A measure of the distribution of values around the mean/average.

Start gate

A stage/phase gate review which applies at the early stages of the policy-to-delivery lifecycle. It offers departments the opportunity to gain independent assurance on how well practical delivery issues are being addressed in preparing for implementation.

Strategic misrepresentation

A term coined by Professor Bent Flyvbjerg to refer to the planned, systematic distortion or misstatement of costs and benefits to justify an investment.

Strategic objectives

The measurable outcomes that demonstrate progress in relation to the organization's mission and to which the portfolio should contribute. According to Peter Drucker they fall into eight types:

- *Market standing: desired share of the present and new markets.*
- *Innovation: development of new goods and services, and of skills and methods required to supply them.*
- *Human resources: selection and development of employees.*
- *Financial resources: identification of the sources of capital and their use.*
- *Physical resources: equipment and facilities and their use.*
- *Productivity: efficient use of the resources relative to the output.*
- *Social responsibility: awareness and responsiveness to the effects on the wider community of the stakeholders.*
- *Profit requirements: achievement of measurable financial well-being and growth.*

Strategy

The approach or line to take, designed to achieve a long-term aim. Strategies can exist at different levels in an organization – in 'Managing Successful Programmes' there are corporate strategies for achieving objectives that will give rise to programmes. Programmes then develop strategies aligned with these corporate objectives against particular delivery areas.

Switching point or value

The value of a variable at which point the decision to invest or not invest changes.

SWOT analysis

Acronym for 'Strengths, Weaknesses, Opportunities and Threats'. A technique to determine favourable and unfavourable factors in relation to business change or current state.

Three-point estimating

A technique whereby project estimates are prepared on three bases: best case scenario; worst case; and most likely.

To-be state

The future planned state of an organization as described by the blueprint.

Tranche

A programme management term describing a group of projects structured around distinct step changes in capability and benefit delivery.

Transformation

A distinct change to the way an organization conducts all or part of its business.

Transition Plan

The schedule of activities to cover the 'transition' phase of the Benefits Realization Plan.

Value

The benefits delivered in proportion to the resources put into acquiring them.

Value for Money (VfM)

HM Treasury (2004) defines value for money as *"the optimum combination of whole-of-life costs and quality".*

Value Management Office

A unit or function established to ensure that the organization optimizes the return from its accumulated investment in change.

Value Profile

A representation of the relative importance of the primary value drivers to the client body and end users.

Weighted Average Cost of Capital (WACC)

The average cost of capital (from equity and debt capital), weighted to reflect the proportion of each form of financing used. Used in determining the discount rate to apply to initiative cash flows.

Willingness to accept

The amount that someone is willing to accept to give up a good or service. Estimated via revealed or stated preferences.

Willingness to pay

The amount that someone is willing to pay to acquire a good or service without a market value. Estimated via revealed or stated preferences.

References

References

Altschuler, A. & Luberoff, D. (2003) *Mega-Projects – The Changing Politics of Urban Investment*, The Brookings Institution.

Andrew, J.P. & Sirkin, H.L. (2006) *Payback,* Harvard Business School Press, Boston, MA.

APM (2006) *Body of Knowledge*, 5th edition.

APM (2009) *Benefits Management – A Strategic Business Skill for All Seasons.* Available at: http://www.apm.org.uk/sites/default/files/APM_BenefitsManagement.pdf. [Last accessed 13 July 2012].

APM (2010) *Benefits Realisation – What Are Your Chances of Success? Understanding How the Right Behaviours Drive Success.* Available at: http://www.apm.org.uk/sites/default/files/APM%20Chances%20of%20SuccessBroA4.pdf [Last accessed: 9 Feb 2012].

APM (March, 2011) *Delivering Benefits from Investments in Change: Winning Hearts and Minds.* Available at: http://www.apm.org.uk/news/delivering-benefits-investments-change.

APM (June, 2011) *Delivering Benefits from Investments in Change: Creating Organisational Capability.* Available at: http://www.apm.org.uk/news/delivering-benefits-investment-change-creating-organisational-capability.

APM (May, 2012a) *Delivering Benefits from Investment in Change – An Essential Part of Everyday Business.*

APM (May, 2012b), *Delivering Benefits from Investment in Change – Beyond 'Business as Usual' to 'Value as Usual'.*

APM & CIMA (May, 2012). *Delivering the Prize – A Joint All-Ireland Study on Change Leadership and Benefits Realisation.* Available at: http://www.apm.org.uk.

Ariely, D. (2009) *Predictably Irrational,* Harper.

Asch, S. Conformity experiments. See http://en.wikipedia.org/wiki/Asch_conformity_experiments

Aspire Europe Newsletter (July, 2010). Available at: http://www.aspireeurope.com.

Ayres, I. (2007) *Supercrunchers: Why Thinking-by-Numbers Is the New Way to be Smart,* Bantam, New York.

Ballhaus (2005) quoted in Virine, L. & Trumper, M. (2008) *Project Decisions – The Art and Science,* Management Concepts, p. 267.

Banfield, T. (2011) Director of NAO. Reasons to be Cheerful, *Project Magazine* May, 2011.

Beer, M. & Nohria, N. (May, 2000) Cracking the Code of Change, *Harvard Business Review.* Abstract: http://hbr.org/2000/05/cracking-the-code-of-change/ar/1.

Beer, M., Eisenstat, R.A. & Spector, B. (November-December, 1990) Why Change Programs Don't Produce Change, *Harvard Business Review*, p. 158.

Benko, C. & McFarlan, F.W. (2003) *Connecting the Dots,* Harvard Business School Press, Boston, MA.

Bennis, W. (1996) Leader as Storyteller, *Harvard Business Review.*

Bradley, G. (2006) *Benefits Realisation Management*, Gower.

Bradley, G. (2010) *Fundamentals of Benefits Realization*, TSO.

Cabinet Office (2007) *How to Measure Customer Satisfaction: A Toolkit for Improving the Customer Experience in Public Services.*

Cabinet Office (2008) *Promoting Customer Satisfaction: Guidance on Improving the Customer Experience in Public Services.* Available at: http://webarchive.nationalarchives.gov.uk/+/http://www.cabinetoffice.gov.uk/media/cabinetoffice/corp/assets/publications/delivery_council/pdf/cust_sat_guidance1.pdf [Last accessed: 2 Apr 2012].

Cabinet Office (2010) *Customer Journey Mapping Guide for Practitioners.*

Cabinet Office (2010) *Customer Journey Mapping Guide for Managers.*

Cabinet Office (March, 2009) *Civil Service Reform Working Paper.* Available at: http://webarchive. nationalarchives.gov.uk/+/http://www. cabinetoffice.gov.uk/media/124376/civilservice_ reform_paper.pdf [Last Accessed: 6 Feb 2012].

Cabinet Office (2011) *Managing Successful Programmes*, TSO, London.

Cabinet Office, Office of the Third Sector (2009) *A Guide to Social Return on Investment.* Available at: http://www.socialevaluator.eu/ip/uploads/ tblDownload/SROI%20Guide.pdf [Last accessed: 23 Jan 12].

Cameron, E. & Green, M. (2009) *Making Sense of Change Management: A Complete Guide to the Models Tools and Techniques of Organizational Change,* p. 332, Kogan Page.

Capability Management (2006) *Research into the Management of Project Benefits, Findings Report 2004-06.*

Cialdini (2007) *Influence – The Psychology of Persuasion,* Collins Business Essentials.

CIO Council (2002) *Value Measuring Methodology – How-To-Guide.* Available at: http://www.cio. gov/documents/ValueMeasuring_Methodology_ HowToGuide_Oct_2002.pdf [Last accessed: 9 March 2012].

Collins T. & Bicknell, D. (1998) *Crash – Learning From The World's Worst Computer Disasters,* Simon & Schuster.

Collins J.C. & Porras, J. (2002) *Built to Last: Successful Habits of Visionary Companies,* Harper Business Essentials.

Common Glossary. Available at: http://www. best-management-practice.com/officialsite. asp?DI=575004

Communities and Local Government (2007) *Optimism Bias in the Appraisal of Regeneration Projects: Research Report.* Available at: http:// www.communities.gov.uk/publications/corporate/ optimismbias [Last Accessed: 9 Feb 2012].

Cooper, R. & Edgett S. (June, 2006) Ten Ways to Make Better Portfolio and Project Selection Decisions, PDMA *Visions Magazine.*

Cooper, R.G. & Edgett, S.J. (2007) *Generating Breakthrough New Product Ideas,* Product Development Institute Inc., Canada.

Cross, M. (2002) Why Government IT Projects Go Wrong, *Computing,* 11 September 2002: pp. 37–40.

Curley, M. (2004*) Managing Information Technology for Business Value*, Intel Press, Hillsboro.

Davidson Frame, J. (1994) Selecting Projects That Will Lead to Success, in Dye, L.D. & Pennypacker, J.S. (Eds.) (1999) *Project Portfolio Management,* CBP.

Davies, H.D. & Davies, A.J. (2011) *Value Management – Translating Aspirations into Performance,* Gower.

Dearing, A., Dilts, R. & Russell, J. (2002) *Alpha Leadership,* Wiley.

Deci – Quoted in Pink, D. (2010) *Drive – The Surprising Truth About What Motivates Us,* Canongate Books Ltd.

Defra 4 Es model – For more information see: http://archive.defra.gov.uk/environment/economy/ documents/sustainable-life-framework.pdf.

Denning, S. See: http://www.stevedenning.com/ slides/HarvardMgtCommunicationTellingStories May06.pdf [Last accessed: 04.04.12] and Denning, S. (2001) *The Springboard,* Butterworth Heinemann.

D&VAM – The D&VAM has since been replaced by the '*ICT Business Case Guide and Tools*'. Nevertheless, as with the US VMM, the D&VAM provides a useful insight into ways in which assessments of social value can be combined with more traditional CBA.

DVLA Case Study (2005) – See: http://www.cwiep.org.uk/trim/files/BenefitsManagementCaseStudy.pdf [Last accessed: 24 Apr 2012].

eGovernment Economics Project – Measurement Framework Final Version (2006). Available at: http://www.umic.pt/images/stories/publicacoes200709/D.2.4_Measurement_Framework_final_version.pdf [Last accessed: 5 Mar 2012].

Farbey, B., Land, F. & Targett, D. (1999) The Moving Staircase – Problems of Appraisal and Evaluation in a Turbulent Environment, *Information Technology & People*, Vol. 12, No. 3, pp. 238–52.

Flanagan, J. & Nicholls, P. *Public Sector Business Cases using the Five Case Model: A Toolkit.* Available at: http://www.hmtreasury.gov.uk/d/greenbook_toolkitguide170707.pdf [Last accessed: 10 May 2012].

Fleming, D – See: http://www.makingstories.net/narrative_leadership_by_David_Fleming.pdf [Last accessed: 04.04.12]

Flyvbjerg, B. (2006) From Nobel Prize to Project Management: Getting Risks Right. *Project Management Journal,* August 2006, pp. 5–15.

Flyvbjerg, B., Bruzelius, N. & Rothengatter, W. (2003) *Megaprojects and Risk – An Anatomy of Ambition*, Cambridge University Press.

Flyvbjerg, B., Mette, K., Skamris, H. & Søren, L.B. (2005) How (In)accurate are Demand Forecasts in Public Works Projects, *Journal of the American Planning Association*, Vol. 71, No. 2, Spring 2005.

Ford, J.D. & Ford, L.W. (2002) Conversations and the Authoring of Change, in Holman, D. & Thorpe, R. (Eds.) *Management and Language,* Sage.

Fowler, A. & Lock, D. (2006) *Accelerating Business and IT Change Transforming Project Delivery*, Gower.

Gauld, R. & Goldfinch, S. (2006) *Dangerous Enthusiasms,* Otago University Press.

Giddens, A. See http://en.wikipedia.org/wiki/Ontological_security.

Gilovich, T. (1991) *How We Know What Isn't So,* Free Press.

Glynne, P. From APM & CIMA (May, 2012). *Delivering the Prize – A Joint All-Ireland Study on Change Leadership and Benefits Realisation.*

Government Communication Network Engage Programme definition of customer insight. Available at http://www.idea.gov.uk/idk/core/page.do?pageId=9531286 [Last accessed 24 July 2012].

Gulliver, F.R. (1987) Post-Project Appraisals Pay, *Harvard Business Review,* March-April, 1987.

Hall, S., Lovallo, D. & Musters, R. (March, 2012) How to Put Your Money Where Your Strategy Is, *McKinsey Quarterly.* Quoted in Simms (2012).

Hammond, S.H., Keeney, R.L. & Raiffa, H. (1998) The Hidden Traps in Decision Making, *Harvard Business Review,* Sept–Oct 1998. Available at https://blog.itu.dk/SPFL2-F2010/files/2010/04/the20hidden20traps20in20decision20making.pdf [Last accessed 6 Mar 2012].

Harford, T. (2006) *The Undercover Economist,* Abacus, London.

Hastie, R. & Dawes, R.M. (2001) *Rational Choice in an Uncertain World,* Sage.

Hawkins, J. & Matheson, A. (2010) *BC Stats Business Indicators – Public Sector Engagement and Service Satisfaction: What Do They Both Have in Common?* Available at: http://www.bcstats.gov.bc.ca.

Hawthorne experiments undertaken by Elton Mayo. See http://en.wikipedia.org/wiki/Hawthorne_effect.

Heintzman, R. & Marson, B. (2005) People, Service and Trust: Is There a Public Sector Service Value Chain? *International Review of Administrative Sciences, 71.*

Herzberg, F. (2003) One More Time: How Do You Motivate Employees? *Harvard Business Review,* January 2003.

Heskett, J.L., Sasser, E.W. Jr. & Schlesinger, L.A. (1997) *The Service Profit Chain: How Leading Companies Link Profit and Growth to Loyalty, Satisfaction, and Value.* New York: The Free Press. See also, Heskett, J.L., Jones, T.O., Loveman, G.W., Sasser, E.W. Jr. & Schlesinger, L. A. (1994) Putting the Service-Profit Chain to Work, *Harvard Business Review.* Available at http://pagesetup.com/images/content/hbr-article.pdf [Last accessed: 26 Jan 2012]. See also: http://hbr.org/2008/07/putting-the-service-profit-chain-to-work/ar/pr [Last accessed: 26 Jan 2012].

HMRC *Costing Customer Time*, Research Paper. Available at: http://www.hmrc.gov.uk/research/cost-of-time.pdf.

HM Treasury, *Assessing Business Cases – 'A Short Plain English Guide'.* Available at: http://www.hm-treasury.gov.uk/d/greenbook_businesscase_shortguide.pdf [Last accessed: 9 Mar 2012].

HM Treasury (2003a) *The Green Book – Appraisal and Evaluation in Central Government*, http://www.hm-treasury.gov.uk/data_greenbook_index.htm.

HM Treasury (2003b) *Measuring the Expected Benefits of e-Government.* Available at: http://ctpr.org/wp-content/uploads/2011/03/HMTGuidelinesVersion1_4.pdf [Last accessed: 7 Mar 2012].

HM Treasury (2004), *Regularity, Propriety and Value for Money.* Available at: http://www.hmtreasury.gov.uk/d/Reg_Prop_and_VfM-November04.pdf.

Hobbs, B. The Multi-Project PMO: A Global Analysis of the Current State of Analysis. A White Paper prepared for the PMI by Dr Brian Hobbs, University of Quebec at Montreal, Canada. Available at: http://www.telefonica.net/web2/tenstep/documentos/Hobbs.pdf [Last accessed: 28 Feb 2012].

Hoffman, E.J. (2011) *Knowledge Management in NASA. Complex Project Management Global Perspectives and the Strategic Agenda to 2025.* Compendium of Working Papers, ICCPM. Available at: http://www.iccpm.com.

ICCPM (2011) *Complex Project Management Global Perspectives and the Strategic Agenda to 2025 – The Task Force Report and Compendium of Working Papers.* Available at: http://www.iccpm.com.

Jenner, S. (2010) *Transforming Government and Public Services – Realising Benefits through Project Portfolio Management*, Gower. Extracts reproduced with the kind agreement of the publisher.

Jenner, S. (2011) *Realising Benefits from Government ICT Investment – A Fool's Errand?* Academic Publishing. Extracts reproduced with the kind agreement of the publisher.

Jenner, S. & Byatt, G. (2012) Coming of Age – Research Into Portfolio Management Maturity Reveals Its Success Factors in Practice, *Project Manager,* Dec 11–Jan 12, pp.14–16.

Kahneman, D. (2011a) *Thinking, Fast and Slow*, Allen Lane.

Kahneman, D. (2011b) – See: http://skepticalblog.wordpress.com/2011/06/20/adversarialcollaboration/.

Kaplan, J. (2005) *Strategic IT Portfolio Management*, PRTM, Inc., USA.

Kaplan, R.S. & Norton, D.P. (1996) *The Balanced Scorecard*, Harvard Business School Press.

Kearns, I. (2004) *Public Value and E-Government*, Institute for Public Policy Research, Available at: http://www.ippr.org/publicationsandreports/publication.asp?id=478 [Last accessed: 9 Mar 2012].

Kelly, G., Mulgan, G. and Muers, S. (2002) *Creating Public Value: An analytical framework for public service reform*, Strategy Unit, Cabinet Office.

Klein, G. (1998) *Sources of Power*, MIT Press.

Kohlrieser, G., Goldsworthy, S. & Coombe, D. (2012) *Care to Dare: Unleashing Astonishing Potential Through Secure Base Leadership*, John Wiley & Sons.

Kotter, J.P. (1995) Leading Change: Why Transformation Efforts Fail, *Harvard Business Review*, March–April 1995.

Kotter, J.P. (1996) *Leading Change,* Harvard Business School Press. ISBN 978-0875847474.

KPMG (2005) *Global IT Project Management Survey.* Available at: *http://www.kpmg.com/cn/en/issuesandinsights/articlespublications/pages/global-it-project-management-survey-200508.aspx* [Last accessed: 28 July 2012].

Lengyel, D. (2011) NASA – Exploration Systems Mission Directorate (ESMD) Integrated Risk and Knowledge Management System, *Complex Project Management Global Perspectives and the Strategic Agenda to 2025. Compendium of Working Papers,* ICCPM. Available at: http://www.iccpm.com.

Lin, C., Pervan, G. & McDermid, D. (2005) IS/IT Investment Evaluation and Benefits Realization Issues in Australia, *Journal of Research and Practice in Information Technology,* Vol. 37, No. 3, August 2005.

Lovallo, D. & Kahneman, D. (2003) Delusions of Success – How Optimism Undermines Executives' Decisions, *Harvard Business Review,* July 2003.

MacGregor Burns, J. (1978) *Leadership*, Harper and Row.

Marchand, D.A. (2004) Extracting the Business Value of IT: It is Usage, Not Just Deployment that Counts!, *Capco Institute Journal of Financial Transformation,* Issue 11, August 2004, p. 127. Quoted in Jenner (2010).

Marchand, D.A. & Peppard, J. (2008) Designed to Fail: Why IT Projects Underachieve and What to Do about It. IMD Working Paper, *IMD 2008-11,* IMD International, Lausanne, Switzerland. Available at: http://www.som.cranfield.ac.uk/som/dinamiccontent/media/ISRC/Designed%20to%20Fail%20Working%20Paper.pdf [Last accessed: 15 Mar 2012].

McConnell, S. (1996) *Rapid Development.* Redmond, WA: Microsoft Press. Quoted in Virine, L. & Trumper, M. (2008) *Project Decisions – The Art and Science.* Management Concepts, p. 91.

McKee, R. *Storytelling That Moves People.* Available at: http://hbr.org/web/special-collections/insight/communication/storytelling-that-moves-people [Last accessed: 04.04.12].

Meadows, D.H. (2008) *Thinking in Systems – A Primer,* Earthscan.

Moore, M.H. (1995) *Creating Public Value: Strategic Management in Government,* Harvard University Press, Cambridge, MA.

Moorhouse. *Benchmarking SROs' Attitudes – The Quandary of the SRO.* Available at: http://www.moorhouseconsulting.com/news-and-views/publications-and-articles/benchmarking-sros-attitudes-the-quandary-of-the-sro.

Moorhouse (2009) *The Benefits of Organisational Change.* Copies of this and other reports referenced can be requested at: http://www.moorhouseconsulting.com/news-and-views/publications-and-articles.

Moorhouse (2012) *Barometer on Change.* Available at: http://www.moorhouseconsulting.com/news-and-views/publications-and-articles/barometer-on-change-2012.

Mott MacDonald (2002) *Review of Large Procurement in the UK.* Available at: http://www.hm-treasury.gov.uk/d/7(3).pdf [Last accessed: 6 Mar 2012].

NAO/OGC *List of Common Causes of Project Failure.* Available at http://www.parliament.uk/documents/post/pr200.pdf, Page 8 [Last accessed: 27 July 2012].

NAO (2006) *Delivering Successful IT-Enabled Business Change.* Available at: http://www.nao.org.uk/publications/0607/delivering_successful_it-enabl.aspx [Last accessed: 16 Mar 2012]. Also see: http://www.publications.parliament.uk/pa/cm200607/cmselect/cmpubacc/113/11305.htm.

NAO (2009) *Helping Government Learn.* Available at: http://www.nao.org.uk/publications/0809/helping_government_learn.aspx [Last accessed: 9 Mar 2012].

NAO (2011) *Initiating successful projects*. Available at: http://www.nao.org.uk/idoc.ashx?docId=BB01ED1563624CFBA4944F01D4178A41&version=-1.

NECCC IT Governance Work Group (2005) *Technology Investment Selection and Protection: The Governance Challenge*. Available at: http://www.contentlcc.com/images/IT_governance.pdf [Last accessed: 12 Feb 2012].

OGC (2003) *Gateway News*, December 2003.

OGC (2005a) *Successful Delivery Toolkit*.

OGC (2005b) *Managing Benefits: An Overview*, v1.0.

OGC (2008) *Portfolio, Programme and Project Offices*, TSO, London.

OGC (2009) *Managing Successful Projects with PRINCE2*, TSO, London.

OGC (2010a) *Management of Risk: Guidance for Practitioners*, TSO, London.

OGC (2010b) *Management of Value*, TSO, London.

OGC (2011) *Management of Portfolios*, TSO, London.

OGC (2011) *Common Glossary of Terms and Conditions*, Version 8.

Payne, M. (2007) Benefits Management – Releasing Project Value Into the Business, *Project Manager Today*.

Peppard, J., Ward, J. & Daniel, E. (2007) Managing the Realization of Business Benefits from IT Investments, *MIS Quarterly Executive, 6* (1).

Pfeffer, J. & Sutton, R.I. (2000) *The Knowing–Doing Gap*, Harvard Business School Press.

Phillips, L.D. & Bana e Costa, C.A. Transparent Prioritization, Budgeting and Resource Allocation with Multi-Criteria Decision Analysis and Decision-Conferencing. *Ann Oper Res* (2007) 154:54–68 Published online: 17 May, 2007 Springer Science+Business Media, LLC 2007.

Piattelli-Palmarini, M. (1994) *Inevitable Illusions*, John Wiley & Sons, Inc., New York.

Public Sector Programme Management Approach (PSPMA) used by the London Councils includes information and guidance on benefits realization management. The material is available at http://pspmawiki.londoncouncils.gov.uk/index.php/Main_Page (provided with the kind agreement of Lorna Gill).

Quinn, B. – See: http://www.hpmd.com/hpmd/wquotes.nsf/8525625300698704852556 2f001195f6/2573bfd50105108a8525625400 158694!OpenDocument.

Retna, S – See: http://www.computerworld.com/s/article/98169/Maximizing_Return_on_IT_Investments_With_Enterprise_Portfolio_Management_Part_1?taxonomyId=73&pageNumber=1 [Last accessed: 5 Feb 2012].

Rock, D. & Schwartz, J. (2006) *The Neuroscience of Leadership*. Available at: http://www.freepatentsonline.com/article/Training-Media-Review/159183325.html [Last accessed: 23 Feb 2012].

Russo, J.E. & Schoemaker, P.H. (1990) *Decision Traps Decisions – How to Make the Right Decision First Time*, Simon & Schuster.

Sanwal, A. (2007) *Optimizing Corporate Portfolio Management*, John Wiley, Hoboken, NJ.

Satir, V. – For example, see: http://www.intuition.org/txt/satir2.htm.

Schaffer R.H. & Thomson H.A. (1992) Successful Change Programs Begin with Results, *Harvard Business Review*, January–February, pp. 80–9. Available at: http://www.business.unr.edu/faculty/kuechler/788/successfulChangeProgramsBeginWithResults.pdf [Last accessed: 6 Jan 2012].

Schwab, C, M. (1917), *Succeeding with What You Have*. Available at: http://www.rodneyohebsion.com/charles-m-schwab.htm (Last accessed: 3 Jan 2012].

Seddon, J. (2008) *Systems Thinking in the Public Sector*, Triarchy Press, Axminster.

Seldon & Colvin (2003) quoted in Cameron, E. & Green, M. (2009), p. 228, Kogan Page.

Senge, P. (1999) *The Fifth Discipline, Random House.*

Simms, J. (2008) *Solving the Benefits Puzzle.* Available at: http://www.totallyoptimizedprojects.com. Kindle edition: http://www.amazon.co.uk/Solving-the-Benefits-Puzzle-ebook/dp/B006I1IUCK/ref=sr_1_1?ie=UTF8&qid=1341845537&sr=8-1.

Simms, J. (2012) *The 'Capital Crime'.* Available as a Kindle edition via Amazon.

Simonson, I. (1989) Choice Based on Reasons: The Case of Attraction and Compromise Effects. *Journal of Consumer Research, 16,* 158–74.

Snowden, D. – From Cooke-Davies, T. (2011) Executive Reflections as a Leader, in ICCPM (2011).

Surowiecki, J. (2004) *The Wisdom of Crowds,* Abacus, London.

Taleb, N.N. (2004) *Fooled by Randomness,* Penguin, London.

Taleb, N.N. (2007) *The Black Swan,* Allen Lane, England.

Thorp, J. & Fujitsu Consulting Center for Strategic Leadership (2003) *The Information Paradox – Realizing the Business Benefits of Information Technology,* McGraw-Hill.

Value Measuring Methodology – More information is available at http://search.usa.gov/search?affiliate=CIOMain&locale=en&query=VMM. Note: It is unclear whether this frameworks is still in widespread use – for example, the named contact on the VMM FAQ document is no longer available. Nevertheless, it is considered that the VMM provides a useful insight into ways in which assessments of social value can be combined with more traditional CBA.

Veltech, M. (2009) New Peaks for youth justice, *CIO UK,* October 2009, pp. 26–9.

Ward J. (August, 2006) *Delivering Value from Information Systems and Technology Investments: Learning from Success. A report of the results of an international survey of Benefits Management Practices in 2006.* Available at: http://www.som.cranfield.ac.uk/som/dinamic-content/research/documents/deliveringvaluereport.pdf [Last accessed: 22 Mar 2012].

Ward, J. & Daniel, E. (2006) *Benefits Management – Delivering Value from IS & IT Investments,* Wiley.

Ward, J. & Daniel, E. (2012) *Benefits Management: How to Increase the Business Value of Your IT Projects,* 2nd edition, Wiley.

Ward J., Daniel, E. & Peppard, J. (2008) Building Better Business Cases for IT Investments, *MIS Quarterly Executive, 7 (1).*

Ward, J., de Hertog, S. & Viaene, S. (2007) Managing Benefits from IS/IT Investments: An Empirical Investigation into Current Practice. *Proceedings of the 40th Hawaii International Conference on Systems Science,* Hawaii, 2007.

Wilford, A. (2011) from 'Complex Project Management Global Perspectives and the Strategic Agenda to 2025 Compendium of Working Papers'. International Centre for Complex Project Management. Available at: http://www.iccpm.com.

Index

Index